Bittersweet Memories

*LIFE, LOVE, HEALING, AND
DISCOVERING MY TRUE SELF*

Janet Smith

To my husband, Leo, I thank you for the love, encouragement, and support you gave me in making this book possible.
To Kristy Phillips, my editor, I thank you for giving me the opportunity to speak my voice.

My journey has been one of trauma and abuse experienced during my life's earlier years.

My journey has taken me on a winding path in search of and discovery of my true self.

My journey has been a search for understanding, acceptance, and belonging.

My journey has been difficult, heartbreaking, and very painful at times.

-AND-

My journey has been filled with an enormous amount of love, joy, and happiness.

My journey has been one of slowly discovering how to heal my heart, body, and soul.

My journey will continually be one of reaffirming and accepting who I was meant to be.

Contents

Introduction   xi

Chapter 1   1
MY INHERENT TRAITS

Chapter 2   8
TRAUMA AND ABUSE

Chapter 3   10
*MY FAMILY – FROM THE OUTSIDE
LOOKING IN*

Chapter 4   13
MY FAMILY – LOOKING THROUGH MY EYES

Chapter 5   16
A TRAUMATIC AND ABUSIVE CHILDHOOD

Chapter 6   38
MY FIRST LOVE

Chapter 7   57
NAVIGATING LIFE ON MY OWN

Chapter 8   59
A NEW LOVE INTEREST

Chapter 9   68
*RELEASING A REBELLIOUS CHILD FROM
WITHIN*

Chapter 10   85
FALLING IN LOVE WITH THE GUITAR MAN

Chapter 11   134
MY GUARDIAN ANGEL

Chapter 12   147
LIFE WITH LEO

Chapter 13   163
MARRIAGE INTO A READY-MADE FAMILY

Chapter 14   183
PHYSICAL HELL INVADES MY BODY

Chapter 15   190
LIFE'S EVENTS MOVE FORWARD AROUND
MY SURGERIES

Chapter 16   199
THE REVOLVING DOOR OF FAMILY

Chapter 17   207
MEANWHILE, A NEW JOB IN THE SCHOOL
DISTRICT

Chapter 18   209
OUR TIME FINALLY CAME

Chapter 19   213
SHARING A LAST DAY WITH MY LOVING
GRANDPA

Chapter 20   215
BROTHER BOB RETURNS

Chapter 21   219
THE EFFECT OF THE NARCISSIST'S ACTIONS
IN MY LATE YEARS

Chapter 22   224
THE VOLCANO WITHIN ERUPTS

Chapter 23   228
A LEAP OF FAITH: STARTING ALL OVER
AGAIN

Chapter 24   237
THE DEATH OF THE GUITAR MAN

Chapter 25   240
SAYING GOODBYE TO MY LOVING
GRANDMA

Chapter 26   242
THE DEATH OF THE AUTOCRATIC
NARCISSIST

Chapter 27   245
MOM RETURNS HOME

Chapter 28   247
MOM'S TRAGIC DEATH

Chapter 29   251
AN EXHAUSTING DOUBLE MOVE

Chapter 30   253
FIBROMYALGIA HITS WITH A VENGEANCE

Chapter 31 257
LEO'S CANCER DIAGNOSIS

Chapter 32 259
MY RHEUMATOLOGIST AND I PART WAYS

Chapter 33 261
*BALANCING WORK, PLAY, AND OUR
HEALTH*

Chapter 34 264
*NO PARENT SHOULD HAVE TO BURY THEIR
CHILD*

Chapter 35 278
LEO'S OPEN-HEART SURGERY

Chapter 36 280
A FRIGHTENING EMOTIONAL BREAKDOWN

Chapter 37 282
RETIREMENT BECKONS

Chapter 38 285
MY HEART GRIEVES FOR MY FIRST LOVE

Chapter 39 292
MAKING SENSE OF IT ALL

Chapter 40 301
MOVING FORWARD AS THE TRUE ME

Introduction

Writing my story has been a wonderful gift to myself, a reminder of all I've experienced and how much I've gone through in my life's journey to date. A large part of my healing and discovering the true me came in the process of writing the story, including the most powerful, intense, and significant events that have become deeply ingrained and embedded into my memory banks throughout my entire life.

I found that the more I wrote, the more certain memories I'd forgotten or consciously didn't want to remember were triggered by dreams, nightmares, and events beyond my control. That, in turn, helped me learn more about how I perceived myself. As my writing progressed, I was able to see the full display of my inherent traits plus the unresolved effects of the trauma and abuse as they played out in my life. It was amazing and eye-opening to see my life unravel and unfold in ways I never realized had happened.

The process of writing my story has been a very long and difficult, yet extremely rewarding, endeavor. It has been much-needed work to get me to where I am at last—looking forward to living out the remainder of my life with resolve and acceptance of my inherent traits, as well as the trauma and abuse I've experienced, while using all of it to be the best person I can be: my true self.

Chapter One

MY INHERENT TRAITS

There are certain feelings and reactions within myself that I've been vaguely aware of since as far back as I can remember. For years, there were no words I knew or understood that I could use to describe what was happening within and to me. It wasn't even until later in life that I learned that these feelings and reactions were traits that existed. I wasn't imagining them, and they had names attached to them. Plus, it turns out these traits were part of the hardwiring in my brain. That is, they weren't learned but were inherent to who I am. These traits are introverted and highly sensitive.

Yet, finally being aware of these traits versus understanding them are two different things. I experienced trauma and abuse during the earlier years of my life, and it took a lot of research and learning about these things and the relationships between them before I could finally make sense of everything—including why I always felt the way I did about things and why I was so deeply and intensely affected by what I experienced, the decisions I made, and the actions I took. I felt different from most everyone else, and the worst part was not being able to explain to anyone what I was feeling for fear of feeling even more different than I already was. Consequently, I ended up keeping things bottled inside for way too many years, and I fought hard not to feel like an outsider.

It wasn't until my late thirties that I was told that part of those feelings I'd had all my life were traits of being an introvert. It wasn't until my late fifties that I was told those other feelings were traits of being highly sensitive. I was forty-two when I spoke up for the first time to a therapist about my childhood trauma and abuse. I was sixty-one when I first told a therapist about my rebellious side and the abuse I'd experienced at the hands of my first husband.

But there was also much love, happiness, and joy throughout my life's journey that I appreciated greatly, even when I didn't clearly understand what the other feelings meant or how to deal with them despite them gnawing at me under the surface of my being. There was much hope that I would someday gain enough insight, strength, and courage to rip off the layers of who I felt I'd always been told I was or who I'd been molded into, to become the person I always inherently felt was the real me.

The Traits

To visualize what I was wrestling with, usually daily, it helps to have some kind of reference for what consumed my inner being all this time. Although this list doesn't cover everything, it is by far the closest I've found to what I experienced.

Introverts

There are basically four types/traits of introverts. Each type exhibits certain traits, and it's possible to have one, two, three, or all four of these types/traits at different times or simultaneously:

- Social: likes to be alone; prefers not to socialize or socializes only in small groups
- Thinking: likes to think about anything and everything; self-reflective; self-conscious
- Anxious: is self-conscious and/or gets anxious in social situations
- Restrained: reserved; enjoys being social in small groups

Traits that an introvert may exhibit:

- Has limited social energy
- Is easily overstimulated and overwhelmed in a very busy place
- Reenergizes and recovers when quietly by themself
- Spends a lot of time alone
- Is often mistaken for being shy
- Takes a while to warm up to new people
- Likes deep and meaningful conversations
- Hates being the center of attention

Highly Sensitive Personality (HSP)

Most people, to some degree or other, exhibit traits that are considered sensitive. However, if you are indeed a true highly sensitive personality, then the brain, the nervous system, and certain genes are wired differently than those of most people.

- The dopamine is used differently to help with overstimulation.
- The mirror neurons are more active, creating more emotional responsiveness and empathy.
- The ventromedial prefrontal cortex enhances emotions and sensory stimuli; consequently, things are processed more deeply.
- The cingulate and insula areas show increased activity, making a person more sensitive to subtleties in and around themselves.

Traits that an HSP may exhibit:

- Has a rich and complex inner life
- Generally tends to be rather deep
- Needs close relationships
- Gets easily overwhelmed
- Has difficulty performing a task when being observed
- Easily startles; body releases adrenaline very quickly and metabolizes it very slowly
- Is sensitive to pain, caffeine, and hunger
- Readily notices sensory changes and inner bodily sensations
- Is often negatively affected by loud noises, strong scents and smells, or bright lights
- Seems to be a very good listener with a tendency toward compassion and empathy

- Can be predisposed or gravitate to help those with broken wings
- Falls in love faster, deeper, and more intensely than others
- Is prone to low self-esteem and doubt about their self-worth

Highly Sensitive Introvert

There's much overlap between the traits of an introvert and a highly sensitive personality. A great article that captures this is "13 Problems Only Highly Sensitive Introverts Will Understand," written by Jenn Granneman. It offers excellent insight into what she describes as problems, which I think of more as challenges, for those of us who are highly sensitive introverts:

- Noise can feel like a full-on assault on their senses.
- Little sleep equals hell; every little irritation from lack of sleep is ratcheted up exponentially.
- They're frequently emotionally exhausted. Rather than just sensing the emotions of others, they absorb the emotions of others and start feeling those emotions themselves.
- They often have very strong positive and emotional reactions to things that are thoughtful or inspiring, such as movies, books, music, or art; most absolutely abhor violence.
- They tend to overanalyze every little word and gesture that other people say or do, as they often pick up on things other people miss.

- They socialize differently than a lot of people; spending a prolonged amount of time in a noisy, crowded environment making small talk can be too much or too overwhelming.
- Injustice and cruelty are serious subjects that they do not take lightly.
- Vacations can be anything but relaxing because sleeping in a different bed in an unfamiliar environment with different sounds disturbs their senses.
- They tend to be more sensitive than others to dips and spikes in blood sugar levels; they can get irritable and be unable to concentrate, going from hungry to hangry instantly.
- Having to do something quickly or simply running late to an appointment can leave them anxious and flustered.
- They're highly empathetic and aware of the feelings of others, so they often say yes in order to not let others down, even though they would prefer to say no.
- Change is hard, as they tend to find comfort in routine because it's far less stimulating or overwhelming than changing to something new.

Statistics indicate that only 16 percent to 21 percent of the population are both highly sensitive and introverted (yes, there are highly sensitive extroverts). As an HSP introvert, it has often been difficult for me to understand the other 79 percent to 84 percent of the population who don't relate to the way I feel because these feelings are such an integral part of my being. It's not a matter of being right or wrong about what or how one feels. I just have no concept of what it feels like not to have the sensitivities I do when it comes to sound, smell, taste, touch, and emotions, as I've had them since birth. And for me, they are such deep and intense sensitivities, whether they be emotional, mental, or physical—especially when it comes to areas of love and pain.

Chapter Two

TRAUMA AND ABUSE

In addition to those feelings and reactions I've experienced ever since I can remember (from being a highly sensitive introvert), I experienced trauma in the form of emotional, mental, and psychological abuse during my childhood and teen years, which left intensely unhappy memories surrounding my family of origin. Additionally, with my first husband, I suffered years of emotional, mental, psychological, and physical abuse that left deep scars in my psyche.

Just as with the traits of highly sensitive introverts, there are often traits or feelings that become ingrained in and are exhibited by people who experience and fail to address the long-term effects that abuse of any kind may have. Many times, these traits are also the same ones seen in highly sensitive personalities, except one is due to inherent brain wiring and the other to environment.

Someone who has experienced trauma and abuse may exhibit:

- High anxieties (fear, worry, uneasiness)

- Stress (frustration or nervousness)
- Fear
- Depression
- Low self-esteem (lack of confidence in oneself)
- Low self-worth (lack of value in oneself)
- Low self-confidence (lack of trust in oneself)
- Self-blame (feeling at fault for things that go wrong)
- Hyperanalysis (of one's own actions and decisions)
- Constant approval seeking
- Trust issues
- Hypervigilance (highly alert to potential danger or threat, whether real or imagined)
- Sleep disturbances
- Exaggerated startle response
- Post-traumatic stress disorder
- Chronic pain
- Frequent headaches/migraines
- Frequent indigestion
- Substance abuse

Chapter Three

MY FAMILY – FROM THE OUTSIDE LOOKING IN

D ad was born in Grinnell, Iowa, in 1924, a farm boy and the oldest of the two brothers in his family. He was raised, from a very early age, mainly by two spinster schoolteacher aunts and his own devices when his strict and religious parents were no longer able to maintain control over him. He had an extremely high IQ, an insatiable thirst for knowledge, the gift of gab, and a never-ending desire to travel. From an early age, he was always scheming for ways to make enough money so he could leave his Iowa roots behind and make something more of himself than a poor farm boy.

Mom was born in Mount Vernon, Washington, in 1929 during the Depression. My grandparents were married in late 1928, when my grandmother dropped out of school to become a housewife and, soon after, a mother while my grandfather found work to support them. They were lucky in that they always had food on their table, clothes on their backs, and an extended family that helped each other out. It wasn't an easy life, and my grandparents always tried to steer Mom toward a post-graduate education or job they hoped would allow her more life and work choices than they felt those of their generation had.

In May 1941, after Dad graduated from high school, he attended community college for a couple of years and traveled for a few years. Then he and his best friend came across the country from Iowa, eventually ending up in Mount Vernon. There, he picked up odd jobs, one of which was working maintenance at the church my mother attended in Mount Vernon. That was where my parents met at a church function in 1946. Not long after, Dad joined the army and was stationed in Seattle, Washington. Shortly after Mom graduated from high school in 1947, she ran off to Seattle to be closer to him, and they were married two months later.

My sister was born in 1948 in Seattle, where Dad was still stationed. When Dad was discharged in 1949, he received a monthly allotment from the army in return for moving back to Iowa to work on and help run his parents' family farm for two years. Consequently, he moved the family to Iowa for two years. Then, in early spring 1952, when the monthly allotments ended, they returned to Mount Vernon, where I was born later that summer.

Over the next four years, Dad was a cannery supervisor and a reserve police patrolman in Mount Vernon. In 1956, the family moved to California, where Dad went to work for an old friend as an insurance salesman for two years. Then, in 1958, he moved the family to Sedro-Woolley, Washington, where Mom's parents lived. Eventually, he went to work for the Washington State Employment Office, working his way up through the ranks, first as a case worker in Bellingham, then in Mount Vernon as an assistant manager, and finally in Anacortes as a manager.

Mom went to work processing medical claims at the

Skagit County Medical Bureau in Mount Vernon. Later, when we moved to Anacortes, she became a receptionist at a local doctor's office. In 1967, my parents opened a small part-time retail business on the side in Anacortes, dealing mainly in Native American handicrafts and beads as a build-up to their eventual retirement from their full-time jobs.

Chapter Four

MY FAMILY – LOOKING THROUGH MY EYES

Publicly, Dad was seen as a nice, friendly, outgoing man. He was a good man who did a lot of good things for our community. As for family, we were well provided for. We always had a roof over our heads, food on the table, and clothes to wear. From a distance, I could see that man.

Yet, from as far back as I can remember, I felt like he was a control freak, an autocratic narcissist with inappropriate boundaries and some irrational rules that we, as a family, were required to follow. There was never any of what people then would have considered physical abuse on his part, as spanking and the belt across the backs of the calves were considered appropriate discipline in those days. His style lent more to emotional, mental, and psychological trauma, with a healthy dose of sarcasm and intimidation thrown in. It was the kind of thing that produces fear, anxiety, self-doubt, low self-esteem, and pain, leaving deep scars that are invisible to the outside world.

Publicly, Mom was seen as a kind, helpful person. I always thought of her as a quiet, private, yet emotionally unavailable person. She tended to follow Dad's lead, though she often seemed frustrated, even angry, at having to deal with the high levels of maintenance he required. Mainly, I just saw the pain Mom carried—always trying to live up to my dad's demands and unrealistically high expectations, and attempting her entire adult life to regain her parents' approval after she ran off at eighteen and married Dad against their wishes. In fact, their marriage initially caused a very painful rift in the family. Her father refused to even see or speak to Mom once she married Dad, putting her mother awkwardly in the middle of their feud. It wasn't until Mom gave birth to my older sister that her father finally relented, and Mom, along with my sister—but not so much Dad—were welcomed back into the family.

Mom oversaw the household—cooking, cleaning, shopping, and taking care of us kids. Since Dad didn't do physical work (he mowed the lawn occasionally), Mom also took care of the garden and yard. When I started first grade, she began working full-time outside the home because Dad was temporarily out of work at the time. Even after he started working though, Mom continued working to help support the family while Dad dabbled on the weekends in his many get-rich-quick schemes and hobbies, which always made the subject of money, or the lack thereof, a source of contention. "What's yours is mine, and what's mine is mine" came into play, as Dad controlled the income and household finances, doling out only the amount of money he felt Mom needed to buy groceries, clothes, and other essentials for the family. However, she was a bargain shopper, so most of the time, she had extra money left over after expenses. She hid that money from Dad so she could buy a few things for herself. Most of all, though, Mom was a truly creative soul, always doing some kind of craft, sewing our clothes, and gardening

—not just because she was helping make ends meet but because she enjoyed doing those things.

I was born in 1952, a little over four years after my sister. From the very beginning, I was as opposite from her in temperament and personality as night is from day. I've always loved my sister, but we were never very close. I thought it was because she was more reserved than I was, and she interpreted the world much differently than I did. She was the one who avoided the drama in the house, while I always seemed to be the source of it or, at the very least, somewhere close to the middle of it. She was the quiet, intellectual bookworm who retreated a lot to her room to read and study while I was more interested in getting work done so I could play outside with a few friends. She seemed to always follow the rules, but I always felt the need to question them when, in my mind, I didn't think they made sense. Essentially, it felt like my parents thought she was the good girl and I was the bad girl.

My loving grandparents on my mom's side were my one true saving grace, my salvation from all the tensions at home. I know my parents, in their own way, loved me. Yet, truthfully, I never really felt loved by them. However, I KNEW my grandparents loved me unconditionally, and I saw that they enjoyed being with me as much as I enjoyed being with them. With them, I could be and act like a child, not a little adult. I loved spending as much time as possible with them. But most of all, I loved the feeling I had when I was with them—one of truly feeling wanted and loved.

When my grandmother told me that my parents didn't like kids or like being around kids, I already knew it was true.

Chapter Five

A TRAUMATIC AND ABUSIVE CHILDHOOD

Birth through Grade School

I was told that as a baby, I was colicky and cried a great deal of the time. I was told that at four years old, I contracted the German measles, which I almost died from. My tonsils were removed when I was five because of numerous sore throats and ear infections. The impression I always got from my parents was that I was basically a sickly young child and a somewhat difficult one to deal with at that.

As children, from a very young age, my sister and I were taught to be obedient little adults, rarely ever allowed to just be kids. No matter what we did, Dad set high and often unrealistic expectations that we were expected to achieve and excel at regardless of whether we were age-capable of it or not. His most famously used clichés were "Kids are to be seen, not heard"; "When I say jump, you ask how high"; "There's only two ways to do things, my way and the right way, and they're both the same"; and "What's yours is mine, and what's mine is mine."

16

The only thing I know or even remember about kindergarten is I attended it while we still lived in California. I remember turning six and starting first grade in Sedro-Woolley because of circumstances. I suffered quite a bit from stomachaches in the morning before school and often couldn't eat the breakfast I was served without getting sick. That, in turn, made it very tense at the breakfast table, as we were always required to clean our plates regardless. My mother was usually frustrated by the whole scenario, as Dad had already left for work by that time of the morning, and she needed everything to go smoothly, since she was on a tight schedule to get to work herself. Ultimately, that meant any ramifications of my not eating breakfast before school were going to be dealt with later that evening when Dad got home, something I always had the entire day to look forward to.

I was told that earlier in life, I was a picky eater and would often throw the food I didn't like across the room. I'm sure there was a punishment of some kind to deter that behavior. However, it wasn't until I was six and starting school that my earliest memories surrounding the issue of food were first imprinted in my brain. My parents, plus the doctor who did home visits, said the stomachaches I was having in the mornings while trying to eat were all in my head to gain attention. (Little was known about separation anxiety then.)

Consequently, my parents started a new tactic to get me to eat: if I didn't eat my breakfast in the morning, they would serve it to me cold at dinnertime, and I would have to eat it before I could eat any of the hot dinner. After a period during which that didn't work, they decided to set me in the empty bathtub in the bathroom with my cold breakfast and hot meal, then leave me to eat by myself as an isolation punishment, since we always sat down together as a family at the dinner table. I don't remember exactly how many times that happened, but the one meal I tossed in the garbage instead of flushing it down the toilet was discovered the next morning, putting an end to that type of punishment.

Instead, they turned eating breakfast into a game, mostly on the weekends, when Dad was around for breakfast. For example, there were pancake-eating contests, with the winner being the one who ate the most pancakes. Food became a reward and a sense of comfort rather than a punishment. I don't remember exactly when it happened, but eating without any incentives from my parents finally kicked in before the end of first grade—and it wasn't just at breakfast but all the time. Even then, there were still some irrational rules when it came to eating. The one I remember the most was that I wasn't allowed to eat bacon inside a piece of folded-over toast. Period. Because Dad said so. Bacon had to be eaten along with toast but always separately. I never understood what difference it made, but I knew it meant trouble for me with Dad if I questioned his decisions. All of this combined was the beginning of my lifelong body image problems and yo-yo weight gains/losses.

Grade school itself was a nightmare. Because of my now ingrained eating habits, I went from being a beanpole to a fatty in a fairly short period of time. I was taunted, bullied, and made fun of by the other kids for being heavy and different. It didn't help that my parents gave me the nicknames "Chatty Cathy" and "Calamity Jane" because, at school and home alike, I often got in trouble for talking more than I was allowed and getting hurt because I apparently didn't pay attention to what I was doing or where I was going. Other nicknames they gave me were "Snuffles," because of my allergies, and "Stinkpot" for who knows why. Inwardly, though, I was an extremely anxious child whose physical awkwardness and lack of social skills made it difficult to fit in or make lasting friends. I joined the Brownies and later the Girl Scouts, which was fun even though it eventually became just another activity I was expected to excel at.

Since both my parents worked, my sister and I became latchkey kids—the only ones in our neighborhood block in the late 1950s who didn't have at least one parent who stayed at home with the kids. In the mornings, we were expected to do morning dishes, then leave in time to walk the half mile to school without being tardy. Every afternoon, when we got home from school, we'd find the detailed list of things Mom wanted us to do before she got home from work, including instructions on what needed to be done to get dinner started. We were supposed to stay inside until either she or Dad got home, unless the list included yard work. And there were to be no friends over except for a select few whose parents my parents knew and trusted.

Starting when I finished first grade, my sister spent summers picking strawberries in the fields. I passed my days at my aunt's house, which was just a few blocks away from our house. Once the berry bus picked up my sister, I'd ride my bike over to our aunt's and stay until my sister got home from working in the fields. I didn't mind that, as I got to be a kid for a while. But then I'd have to ride my bike back home, and we'd start down the list of things Mom had left us to do. The year I turned nine, I went to work picking strawberries with my sister. This whole work experience, which for me eventually expanded into working in the raspberries and cucumbers, went on every summer until my sister graduated from high school. That, along with Mom's endless work lists, was how we spent summer "vacations."

One of the worst surprises of my grade school years came during the summer after sixth grade, when I was almost twelve. I went to the bathroom and, along with horrible abdominal cramps, discovered I was bleeding heavily into my underwear. It was a day my sister and I were home alone, not working out in the fields. I started screaming at the top of my lungs, as I had no idea what was going on. I went into a panic attack, scared I was bleeding to death. My sister called my grandmother, who immediately came to the house to help and explain what was going on. I think afterward, she even took my sister and me out for ice cream to lift the mood and lessen the shock. Mom had never said anything to me or prepared me in any way for what was happening. I was so angry and disappointed that she never took the time to do that beforehand, which would have saved me from a horrible experience.

Middle and High School

Around my twelfth birthday, Dad was promoted to manager of the Anacortes office. One of the stipulations of his promotion was that we had to live within the Anacortes city limits. For that to happen, my parents had to sell the house in Sedro-Woolley before they could buy a house in Anacortes, which didn't happen before school started. So, instead of changing schools during the school year, my parents enrolled us in Anacortes. My sister had only two years left of high school and was curious about what life would be like in another town. But it was a difficult move for me, as I was just starting middle school.

To make it work, we had to get up with Dad, real early in the mornings, so he could drop us off at school, where we'd have to wait a while before they even unlocked the doors. After school was out, we'd have to walk to his downtown office and wait there until he got off work around five. Then we'd head home to Sedro-Woolley. It made for a long day and was hard to get used to. But within a month or so, my parents were able to sell the house in Sedro-Woolley and buy a house in Anacortes. It was off the left-hand hillside before you turned left into Anacortes, and it was Mom's dream home—a newer home with lots of space.

One of the most upsetting parts of living in Anacortes for me was that we'd moved about thirty miles, which was a long-distance phone call from where my grandparents lived. From the time we'd moved back to Sedro-Woolley from California, they'd been my saving grace from the tensions of our household, providing a place where I could feel the love I never felt at home. Now, I wasn't able to spend as much time with them as I could or call them to talk. So I mainly saw them only on the holidays. Their love for me was no less than it had ever been before. But losing access to the peace of their house and the love they showered me with was painful.

Middle school was an especially emotional and stressful time. It was a new school for me, and because we hadn't lived in Anacortes before I started school, I knew absolutely no one. It was terrifying for the socially awkward, anxious person who lived inside what was now a quickly maturing physical body that made me feel overweight compared to the other girls. It was very damaging to my already low self-esteem. I had a hard time making friends, and a lot of times, I simply felt alone and misunderstood by those around me. Everything—what I wore, the activities I participated in, and who I hung out with—was pretty much dictated to me by my parents. Negotiations and objections weren't allowed.

I was often compared to my older sister and how she excelled or handled things. I was then either allowed or not allowed to do those same things as I got older based on how well she had dealt with them or felt about having done them. It felt like my parents always thought she was the good, quiet, compliant, obedient one, and I was the bad, noisy, needy one—the one who questioned everything and constantly needed to be disciplined. It was as if they wanted me to be just like her, not who I was.

In the fall of 1966, after my sister graduated, she moved to Seattle to attend the University of Washington. I was just starting my last year of middle school, and even though we were not that close, I really missed her. She came home the following summer to live and work until fall quarter started, and the tension in our household became even more intense as Dad and Mom expected her to live under their rules once again. She also returned the next two summers after that to live and work, and each summer, it was the same thing. The worst part was that every time she left, I dreaded being the lone child in the house once again, feeling like I was at the mercy of whatever was going on in our family at the time.

By high school, my stress level remained high, and my emotions were all over the place. Though I now had a few girlfriends to hang out, go places, and have sleepovers with, I was always self-conscious when we were in a group. Would I fit in? Was I behaving like I was expected to? Was I appropriate? One time, a girlfriend told me I always looked down my nose at everyone else, and I was absolutely devastated. I had no idea what made her think that. Afterward, I became even more self-conscious about how I acted and what I said, which made me even more anxious as time went on.

As for boys, since I wasn't allowed to date until I was sixteen, I became the one they talked about their girlfriends to, not the one they were interested in dating. The very few dates I went on after I was sixteen were mainly one-time events and far apart, though not necessarily due to a lack of interest. Few guys asked me out for a second date, and I never made it to a third. Disappointingly, I never understood why. If I were to guess, I would say it was due to my awkward social skills and the fact that I was self-conscious about my weight, along with the clothes I wore and my anxiety over not knowing how to act. There were also times I experienced panic attacks during a date.

Beginning at age twelve and going all through high school, I suffered tremendously from intense menstrual cramping, heavy flows, erratic periods, and excruciating headaches. My moods and weight fluctuated greatly, which made me extremely self-conscious on top of everything else. Mom took me to the doctor she worked for, and he diagnosed me as having cluster headaches due to my extreme periods. I was told to take Midol. He said that should take care of things, but it never did. At times, I'd be in so much pain that the doctor eventually gave me samples of Darvon to see if that would help. However, my parents thought I couldn't possibly be in that much pain and said I didn't need to be taking it. Dad was always telling me to "suck it up" and "quit whining." He also told me that "it's merely mind over matter." As things never did get better, though, the doctor finally convinced Mom midway through my senior year to let me go on birth control pills, which helped tremendously with the headaches and periods. Although that often leads to vaginal yeast infections, those were so much easier to deal with than the alternative I'd been dealing with since I was twelve.

Just like they didn't inform me about my period, neither of my parents ever mentioned or discussed the topic of sex. They did take my sister and me to a drive-in theater to see a family-oriented sex education movie that was made to give parents a way to start a discussion with their teenagers. But after they watched it with us, nothing was ever discussed about it. The only thing I got out of the movie was don't lie down in the back seat of a car with a boy, or you'll get pregnant. Additionally, sex education class in high school was a total joke. Ninety-eight percent of it was related to personal hygiene, 1 percent to learning the names of the reproductive organs, and 1 percent to the physical aspects of having sex. The 2 percent not related to hygiene was mainly taught by making us watch a film, with the girls separated from the boys and each group watching a different film. In essence, my sister and I were both left to figure it out on our own, as we were with most other aspects of life.

My school schedule was heavy—often mentally and physically draining—with my parents' expectations that I had to excel at everything (academics, music, singing lessons, playing guitar, after-school activities, etc.). If I got a B+, Dad wanted to know why I didn't get an A-. If I got an A-, it was why didn't I get an A? And if it was an A, why wasn't it an A+? Regardless of all my efforts, by the time I graduated high school, I felt like I was a disappointment to my parents because my sister graduated number two in her class, while I graduated in a nine/ten tie in mine.

Work

Dad always drilled a work ethic into us since, according to him, you were lazy if you weren't working. Starting at age nine, I worked in the fields every summer, focused on earning money for college. In fact, my parents felt that most things I did should revolve around making money for college, with no consideration given to whether I even wanted to go (which I didn't). By middle school, I was babysitting on Friday and Saturday evenings for a few families in our neighborhood. The summer after I started high school, Dad sold our house and bought a piece of property on Commercial Avenue so he could start a Native American handicraft store in the large building (previously a mortuary/church) adjacent to the older house on the lot. Dad spent the first year buying out several stores that were going out of business to get supplies and initial merchandise. I had to help clean out and pack up the stores, move the merchandise home, unpack and clean it, and set it up in the store on my evenings and weekends. When it was all ready, the store was open Monday through Saturday during the summer months and only Saturdays the rest of the year. Dad and Mom were still several years away from retirement, and Dad technically wasn't allowed to have a second job. Starting when I was fifteen, he had me working full-time in the store during the summer (no more working in the fields!) and helping on weekends if they needed it. He kept track of my wages and the balance due to me, keeping it in their personal bank account as my college fund. I also kept track of it on my own, so I always knew what I was due. My personal spending money came in the form of a small monthly allowance plus earnings from a part-time weekend job I got cleaning the doctor's office where Mom worked and babysitting most weekend nights.

The Impact of Dad's Religious Searchings

Dad was also on a mission during this period to find a religion that suited him (i.e., in which he could be God), and he made it mandatory that we accompany him.

In earlier years, my sister and I were sent to Bible classes at the Methodist church in Sedro-Woolley. At that time, Dad and Mom would only occasionally attend services. When we moved to Anacortes, however, Dad had us attend the Presbyterian church for a time (my sister also attended the Methodist church). Then he switched us to the Unitarian church.

Later, still restless in his search, he got involved in Native American religious ceremonies (which at the time were illegal) through close connections he had with the local tribe. For reasons I never knew, it had made him an honorary member. By that time, my sister had moved out, but Mom and I were still expected to go with him. Although Mom knew several of the women in the tribe, I didn't know anyone and felt extremely uncomfortable, as I knew Mom and I weren't exactly welcome. We were allowed to attend only because of Dad's honorary status. I went with him and Mom several times. But I experienced terrifying screaming nightmares afterward. So Dad decided I didn't have to go with them anymore.

Just as I was graduating from high school, they once again moved on, this time becoming Bahai. However, this time, it was without me in tow, which was fine with me. I'd seen enough hypocrisy and sanctimoniousness through all of Dad's religious searchings to last me a lifetime.

Especially during my last year of high school, I found my beliefs toward organized religion and church being replaced by my views and belief in spirituality. I'd always believed in God, a loving entity, whose focus was on love, kindness, empathy, compassion, grace, and forgiveness. And I believed in the equality of all humanity, regardless of race, color, ethnicity, economic and social status, gender identification, or sexual orientation. I suppose you could say I was idealistic.

My Reprieve: Music

Music and singing offered me one reprieve from all the twisted pieces of growing up. I'd always loved music and, from a very young age, could remember the words to all the songs that played on the radio. I thought I had a good singing voice and was in choir all through middle and high school, as well as a musical chorale in high school. Unfortunately, the choir teacher chided me for auditioning with outdated music for the chorale tryout, and something was mentioned about my voice being too wispy for solos. After that, my parents insisted on singing lessons with current music with the intention that I would excel at that too, which took some of the enjoyment out of it.

When I was in middle school, my great-grandmother gave me one of her old guitars, and I taught myself how to play it. I would eventually get a newer guitar, then an electric guitar, and I mainly played for my own enjoyment. At one point, I played guitar in a small band in high school, although I think we practiced more than anything else since I remember playing at only one party venue the whole time. I even entered a talent show contest, singing and playing a guitar. Yet with both the band and the talent show, I was stricken with stage fright and was terrified of singing and playing in front of a large group of people. It turned out okay, but I was extremely uncomfortable with both experiences.

Around that same time, there was a couple (Gun and Cookie) living behind us who had a small child I babysat most weekend nights. Gun was stationed at NAS Whidbey, as was Keith, a friend who lived with them. Keith had played in a rock 'n' roll band back in his hometown of Chicago and would often practice his electric guitar in their open garage during his downtime. I loved listening to and watching him practice from my bedroom window, which was right above their house, where I could see into the open garage. Keith would wave when he'd see me hanging out my bedroom window watching, then play a concert for his captive audience of one. When I was babysitting, I could hear the music coming inside their house, as the open garage was straight out back. Eventually, as we got to know each other and he found out I had an electric guitar, he offered to give me tips on how to play it better and taught me more songs to play. It was music heaven for me, a place to escape to when things got too overwhelming for me both at home and school.

My Dad's Family

It wasn't until I was in high school that I finally spent time with my dad's parents. They sold their house in Grinnell, Iowa, and moved to Anacortes to be closer to Dad in their later years. I vaguely remembered them from a few trips they'd made to visit us when we still lived in Sedro-Woolley and from a trip Dad took my sister and me on to visit them in Iowa. But I never got to really know them very well, even after they moved to Anacortes. Other than an occasional Friday lunch, Sunday afternoon family dinner at their house, or times when I'd play Scrabble with my grandfather after school, I didn't spend much time with them. They were nice enough, but it was hard to relate to their strict routines, reserved personalities, and undemonstrative mannerisms. Plus, they were deeply religious, which dictated what was appropriate or inappropriate behavior regardless of circumstances. It was easy to see why Dad was so difficult for them to handle as a child and how he grew into the autocratic narcissist he was. A lot of it was due to being raised by his two spinster aunts, who'd spoiled him and catered to his every want, whim, and desire.

Uncomfortable Situations

While I was growing up, there were often times I felt Dad's remarks and actions made people uncomfortable (possibly were even offensive or inappropriate), but I wasn't sure. I had no one to compare them to or anyone I could talk to about them. I never said anything and just kept my feelings to myself. But I often wondered about them.

When we went places in my younger years, Dad would see a particular type of woman and say out loud, "Now, that's MY kind of woman—built like a brick outhouse." I would look at Mom and then at the woman, and it was apparent they didn't look anything alike. I'd wonder how Mom felt about it, but she never said anything to him at the time, so I guess she didn't mind. But for some reason, I always felt sorry for her.

As I got older, Dad often remarked, "You stink," to me.

Mom never said anything, and I was already very self-conscious, so that just made it worse. I didn't find out until decades later that it was his way of criticizing me for wearing any kind of perfume. Also, when it came to makeup, Mom only wore lipstick. When I started wearing a little makeup besides lipstick (a touch of blush, lightly applied mascara, and an occasional light shade of eye shadow), he would tell me I looked like a "painted lady."

I was also instructed not to tell anyone about all the vacations or places we went to. His reasoning was he didn't want anyone to come rob the house while we were gone. But that meant I never got to share my excitement with anyone, as it always had to be a secret. Even when we returned, Dad didn't want people to know where we'd been or what we'd done.

When I was thirteen, we took a family trip to Mexico. Dad "innocently" set up my sister and me to attract young men to our table as potential tour guides for the day. Mom thought it was "cute." I was well-developed at age thirteen and a bit confused about the mixed emotions I felt when a young man who'd taken a liking to me was more than happy to give the whole family a tour of Veracruz and join us for dinner that night. The next day, we attracted two other young men who offered to take the whole family to a grand ball at a fancy hotel that night. We were supposed to leave by train that evening, but Dad wanted to go to the dance (although Mom claimed it was my sister and I who wanted to go). So he rescheduled our tickets to the following morning. Although our parents were right there with us enjoying themselves, local custom required my sister and me to be escorted by and dance with these young men the entire evening in return for the invitation. If someone else wanted to dance with us, the men had to give their permission, which they refused to do. After the party ended around three in the morning, we took a taxi to the train station, where we slept on benches the rest of the night, using our luggage as pillows.

On that same trip, we took a bus from Mexico City to the small village of Amecameca, a small agricultural area about an hour and a half outside the city. We wandered around the outdoor market, checked out one of the churches, and got a pop with cookies for breakfast. Then Dad took off with a man he'd met who worked for the railroad company, saying he'd be back in an hour, leaving Mom, my sister, and me sitting on a bench. None of us spoke Spanish, so we just sat there watching people go by for the longest time, waiting for Dad to come back. There was a church behind us, so to pass the time, the three of us finally walked up to check it out, then went back and sat on the bench again. After we waited a few hours with no food or drink, Dad and the man came back, both obviously quite drunk. Then we (including the drunk railroad company man) caught the last train returning to Mexico City, and Dad threw up out the open train window all the way back. After we arrived, the man helped us get Dad back to the hotel, and Mom, my sister, and I finally went to get something to eat and drink. When we returned to the room, Dad and the man were supposed to be sleeping it off. Turns out, the man had taken Dad's bed, and Dad had taken Mom's bed, so Mom ended up sleeping with me. Unfortunately, the man was up and down all night, lightly slapping Dad to wake him up to talk to him. It was a bit unnerving and scary, as I could hear the commotion going on all night. I don't think anyone got much sleep. The next morning, Dad escorted the man to the railroad station and put him on the train back to Amecameca. Dad was grumpy with a hangover, Mom was disgusted with Dad, and no one was happy that day.

Once, when I was sixteen, Dad had me accompany him on a two-day business trip to a men's prison on Vancouver Island, since Mom was unavailable that weekend. It was my job to talk to and entertain the various inmates waiting to see Dad about selling their crafts in our store. We were all in one big room, my table wasn't far from where he was talking to the men one-on-one, and there were plenty of guards in the room, so I wasn't afraid. I was, however, a bit anxious and unnerved knowing these men were the highest-level offenders—murderers, rapists, and armed robbers.

On weekends during my high school years, Dad had this thing about meeting new people and inviting them over to the house for dinner, expecting Mom to be the hostess and cook for everyone. If I was home, he'd also want me to play guitar and entertain these new friends. It often made me feel uncomfortable—like being on display. I was also uneasy, as there was, at times, quite a bit of drinking going on. In that case, he would invite these friends to spend the night. The thing is, the only empty bedroom was upstairs next to mine, and I didn't always feel safe not knowing who these people were. The upstairs bathroom was across from my bedroom door, and I was aware of people going in and out of it all night, which made me anxious, hoping no one would mistake my bedroom for the guest room in their drunken state. In the morning, I would wake up to Mom cooking breakfast for everyone, something Dad always expected her to do. At least everyone was mostly sober by then.

Plus, who could forget the night Dad (and Mom) wanted to teach me about drinking even though I'd never had a desire to? He bought several bottles of different wines, including merlot, Chablis, chardonnay, MD 20/20, and Boone's Farm. We started playing cards with two friends of theirs. Then Dad had me keep slowly drinking. He refilled my glass and mixed all the various wines together until my cards were falling out of my hands onto the floor more often than I could keep holding on to them. At that point, Mom and her friend helped me upstairs to my bedroom, where everything started rapidly swirling until I finally passed out on my bed.

I woke up with a terrible headache the next morning, and I threw up the first few times I dragged myself to the bathroom. It was a good thing I started to feel a bit better after I went back to bed and slept a few more hours, since I still had to go clean the doctor's office that afternoon.

Senior Year

In my senior year, we had to write an autobiography in English class. I was unaware when I wrote it how much it honestly reflected how I felt about everything, from my first memories to age seventeen. It shocked me that I wrote the words *controlling* and *being unhappy* at least eight times throughout it and included comments about not really wanting to go to college. There were so many descriptions of my inner feelings that I'd thought about but never put on paper before. That was when I started writing personal journals about all my feelings and the things that happened in what felt, at times, to be a painful and unfair life. It also turned out, though, that my journals became a way for me to express my newly forming views on things I was personally interested in. I was moving toward spirituality, civil rights, equal rights, pacifism, the anti-Vietnam War movement, and efforts to save the environment. After all, I'd seen the assassinations of the Kennedy brothers and Martin Luther King, the rise of the Beatles and the English invasion, the Summer of Love in Haight-Ashbury, Kent State, the anti-war movement, and mandatory draft plastered all over the radio and TV. Who wasn't affected in some way or another?

In January of my senior year, I met Buzz through an old neighbor friend in Sedro-Woolley, and he became my first serious boyfriend. He'd graduated high school the year before and was working temp jobs while deciding what he wanted to do with his life. I should have seen the handwriting on the wall when he completely forgot our first date and stood me up. He did call a few days later to apologize, and we finally connected and saw each other for quite a while. He eventually brought up the subject of having sex, but I kept refusing because I wasn't ready to take that step. And even though we talked about love and marriage after I graduated, we were still at the puppy-love stage at best. A few months later, he told me he'd joined the navy. A few weeks after that, he was gone. We initially wrote back and forth a lot. Then our letters became fewer and farther in between. I became so depressed during that time that I ended up writing him a goodbye letter. While I received one last letter from him, I never heard from or saw him again.

The last month of my senior year, I developed a kidney infection and was treated with heavy antibiotics, which made me nauseous most of the time. I dropped twenty pounds in those four weeks before the night of graduation. That in and of itself was revealing because guys at school who'd never talked to me before or even known I existed started hitting on me once I apparently fit into the category of what was defined outwardly as being thin and cute. The irony was that nothing inside me had changed. Plus, at the time, I was too sick to care about their attention.

Since I felt a bit better the day of graduation and made it through the Class of 1970 graduation ceremony, I left afterward with a small group of friends for an overnight campout at Bowman Bay Park. It wasn't raining, so we were all in our own sleeping bags, lying under the trees and stars. Partway through the night, however, I started feeling nauseous with painful cramps. But I couldn't leave, as the gates had us locked in until morning. Thankfully, a friend let me sleep in his car, lying next to me the rest of the night until the gates opened at dawn. Then he drove me home. Topping things off, when I got home that morning, I got a lecture on how I should never have gone if I was, indeed, that sick. It was another indication from Dad and Mom that they never believed I could possibly be that sick or in that much pain. To them, I was simply a hypochondriac. I spent the next two days continuing to recoup from the kidney infection until Dad felt I'd lain around long enough. He wanted me to start working regardless of how I was still feeling and open the shop up for business.

After Graduation

As my eighteenth birthday was quickly approaching in August, my parents gave me a heads-up that once I turned eighteen, I would no longer be their responsibility and could do whatever I wanted. Of course, there would be a few stipulations and strings attached to that statement.

I would have to start attending Skagit Valley College in the fall. I would have use of a vehicle for driving to and from college plus occasional personal use if I paid for the gas. Lastly, Dad would keep control of my college fund, which

I'd been banking with them since I was nine. He'd dole it out to me for college-related expenses as I needed it. Aside from those things, though, it was going to be "You're on your own, kiddo!"

For someone who'd been raised in an emotionally distant and mentally abusive household with a lot of strict, unreasonable, and what I often felt were irrational rules and expectations, this stage came with a great sense of anticipation and elation. I knew I was more than willing to handle the few strings and stipulations they threw at me in exchange for even a little sense of freedom. On the other hand, I knew I was ill-prepared for the world outside of what always felt to me like a controlling and unhealthy environment, one where the focus on who I should be and what I should do had always been strictly defined and dictated to me by my parents. But I'd been raised to be very dependent rather than independent, so this news also came with a great sense of worry and uneasiness.

The next thing I knew, I was starting to feel like a kid in a candy store for the first time. I alternated between exhilaration over what was going to be my newfound freedom and immense anxiety, a lack of self-confidence, and low self-esteem, as I felt I'd be blindly attempting to find my way with no help or outside guidance.

As I'd continue living at home, I knew my life would become a delicate balance. On the one hand, there was my irrational but never-ending desire for my parents' love and approval along with my need to adhere to their rules over the years. On the other was my need to navigate the turbulent social times and find out what all those feelings and reactions I'd had all those years meant. l wanted to discover who the real me was, not who I felt I was constantly being molded to be. I was idealistic, ready to conquer the world, and extremely naive.

It was during this time that I also found myself totally mesmerized by my first love, which played into the euphoria of soon being cut loose from my parents even though I would be living under their roof, with their rules and expectations always right under the surface of my mind.

Chapter Six

MY FIRST LOVE

The Beginning

I met Brad when I was seventeen, not long after graduation, while I was working in my parents' store. He came in one afternoon to browse around, and since he was the only customer at the time, we struck up a casual conversation as he asked me questions about the Native American items, jewelry, and rings we had in stock. At one point, I showed him a ring out of the display case that he'd asked to see. I used to wear this unique silver ring on my left ring finger, which he'd obviously noticed, as he mentioned how different it was. Then, without skipping a beat, he nonchalantly asked if it was a wedding ring, which made me laugh to myself because of my age. I answered no. I wore it occasionally because I liked it and that was the only finger it fit on. We talked a few minutes more as he continued to browse around, then he thanked me, waved goodbye, and left. Afterward, I didn't give any more thought to it, since we always had people who came in, browsed for a bit, and struck up conversations to pass their time on their way through town to catch the ferry.

To my surprise, Brad stopped by again a week later. This time, we struck up a much longer, more personal conversation. I learned he was stationed at NAS Whidbey and, at twenty-three, was a bit older than other guys I'd met. He was polite, kind, and funny, and he came across as being so full of life that I was immediately drawn to him. It also didn't hurt that he was a tall, lanky, sandy-haired hunk.

Before he left, he asked me out on a date.

And I accepted. At first, I was hesitant to tell my parents anything except that someone I'd met in the store had asked me out, especially because he was older and in the navy. The following Saturday, when he came to pick me up, though, they didn't make a scene, which was a great relief for me.

That one date led to several more, and we were soon seeing each other more often than not. I knew it was happening very quickly, but it was SO exciting to be with a person who knew none of my friends or family before meeting me and had no preconceived notions about who I was or should be. Finally, I started trying to be the person I felt I'd always wanted to be deep inside, and his acceptance of that version of me inspired confidence in myself for the first time ever.

I don't remember what kind of car he had when we first started dating, but soon after, he bought an old blue hearse and turned it into a camper. He bought the material, and I sewed curtains for it, making it an unusual-looking but reliable mode of transportation for us as we happily cruised through that summer together.

From the beginning, I sensed Brad had a deep soul and a spiritual connection with nature. He simply glowed when we spent time outdoors, especially near any kind of water or anywhere in the mountains. We went on all kinds of picnics, walks, and hikes whenever we could. We also took time to explore the Seattle Center, wander through all the local county fairs, take the Ross Dam tour, and scream our lungs out at a Three Dog Night concert in Vancouver, British Columbia. Brad also had a good friend in his squadron who was married, and we double-dated with him and his wife quite a bit, which added to the fun.

No matter where we went or what we did, being with Brad awakened my senses in so many new and different ways that it was completely overwhelming at times. Yet there was no way I wanted to slow things down or change anything, as he made me smile and laugh more than anyone I'd ever known. It was an absolute whirlwind of innocent, exciting, carefree, and fun times—all things I'd never gotten to experience before. It was so incredible!

A Change in Our Relationship

I invited Brad to my eighteenth birthday party in late August, which my parents hosted at their house as an opportunity for extended family to come to celebrate my coming of age. Although Brad couldn't come until later in the day, it worked out great, since we both felt it was the perfect time for him to briefly meet the rest of my family, including my grandparents, aunt, uncle, and three cousins (he'd already met my sister) without being totally over-whelmed. As I imagined would happen, he charmed every-one, and it was such an incredible feeling to have him by my side to celebrate a turning point in my life.

After I turned eighteen, things started to get more serious between us, and it felt like our relationship was at a turning point. I'd known for a while that Brad was more than ready for a physical relationship, but he never pressured me because he knew I wasn't ready yet to go that far. Now that I was eighteen and (already) on birth control pills, the time felt right for me. And to be truthfully honest, the sexual tension that had ignited between us was becoming almost unbearable.

The first time we were intimate was on a soft blanket on a secluded sandy riverbank situated off the beaten path. I don't know whether I was more nervous, scared, or excited to begin with, as I had no idea what to expect. But I soon found myself melting into Brad's arms, following his lead. He knew I was a virgin, and, while we were both obviously hungry with desire, he tried to be as gentle and sensitive as possible as he made love to me. Although it hurt, the entire experience took my breath away, tingling my senses physically and emotionally to a level I hadn't even known existed. It didn't feel dirty, wrong, or in the least bit shameful. It felt like something completely natural between the two of us, considering how we felt about each other then. As time went on, we continued to make love when the mood struck, although it wasn't the most important part of our relationship. It was just a great bonus when it happened.

Over the next several months, Brad continued to sweep this girl completely off her feet! My young, impressionable mind was constantly spinning with the feeling of being truly happy and deeply in love, especially as I knew he felt the same way.

I started attending Skagit Valley College in fall quarter 1970, and we saw each other as much as possible, celebrating the seasonal turn into autumn and spending Thanksgiving together. We also went on as many outdoor adventures as fall weather permitted between his duties and my schoolwork. Brad was the one person I could truly depend on—someone to be close by, to share my time with, to do things with, to hug and hold, to feel loved by, to give my love to, and to make love with. Whether he realized it or not, he was the one person who helped build up my self-confidence and self-esteem to the point that my anxieties and insecurities virtually disappeared.

Popping the Question

It was what I thought was going to be just another late after-noon/evening in early December. I was doing homework at the kitchen table and heard someone pull in the driveway. Brad was in the comfortable habit of spending time with me at the house several times during the week, but I thought it was way too early for him to be there. I looked out and saw that it WAS him. Remembering the time he'd showed up on crutches after spraining his ankle, I thought something was wrong again. When I ran to the door, though, he came rushing in, gave me a big kiss, then grabbed me by the hand with a huge grin on his face. I wasn't sure what was going on, but there was definitely something happening I wasn't yet privy to.

With that huge grin still on his face, he pulled me toward the stairs that led up to my bedroom, which quickly got my attention. We had two unwritten rules that we'd always stuck to when it came to my parents' house: One, Brad was never allowed upstairs in my bedroom. And two, we never made love in my parents' house. But by the time he'd gotten me up to my room that afternoon, I realized what was on his mind. I wish I could say that my refusal to have sex in my parents' house was out of respect for them, but it was more because Dad had been randomly popping in and out the house several times a day since his office had been moved to only a block away from the house.

On this day, however, Brad was obviously throwing caution to the wind, and I found myself blindly following his lead. I couldn't believe he wanted to take this risk—in my bedroom in the midafternoon, in my parents' house, with the extremely high probability we'd get caught! What the hell was he thinking? Then again, at that point, neither one of us even cared anymore.

Afterward, we lay there for only a few minutes, not wanting to push our luck, before we got dressed. As Brad slipped his jeans on, however, he reached into his front pocket and pulled out a small jewelry box. Before I even knew what was happening, he got down on one knee, opened the box so I could see a beautiful diamond ring inside, and asked, "Will you marry me?" I was SO overwhelmed and excited with emotions. It all felt so romantic that without a second thought, I found myself screaming, "Yes! Yes! Yes!"

As fate would have it, at that EXACT moment, we both heard Dad's car turn into the parking area out front, and my panic button started buzzing off the charts! Brad quickly stuck the jewelry box with the ring still in it back into his front pocket, grabbed the rest of his clothes and shoes, triple-hopped down the stairs, somehow managed to get dressed along the way, and was casually sitting at the table by the time Dad made it into the kitchen. I came down a few minutes later, after I'd finally managed to calm myself down. I had some books and papers in my hands like I'd been retrieving something for my studies. Thankfully, a major disaster was avoided, but we never broke those two unwritten rules again.

Since Brad didn't get the opportunity to place the

engagement ring on my finger when he proposed to me that afternoon, he took me out to a romantic dinner to celebrate that evening and finally got to place it on my finger. It was a stunning diamond ring, and it fit perfectly. When we got home, we told my parents that he proposed to me at dinner, and I proudly showed my beautiful ring off to them. What a crazy and exciting way to start out our engagement!

For me, there was just one slight hiccup to the whole thing. After placing the ring on my finger during dinner, Brad slipped it into our conversation that he'd talked to my parents several days before and asked Dad for my hand in marriage. He'd also asked Mom if she'd be able to find the unique silver ring I'd been wearing when we first met so he could make sure the engagement ring was the right size. When he told me all this, in my own mind, I briefly became upset over the fact that my parents knew before I did that he was going to ask me to marry him. My thoughts went right to the notion that it was just another way for Dad to still have some control over me, especially if he'd told Brad no and in spite of his "you're on your own, kiddo" mantra. As for Mom, I was appalled to think she'd been in my room, gone through my things, and invaded my privacy. However, I took a long, deep breath and reminded myself that Brad had talked to my parents only out of respect for traditional values and his desire to make everything perfect. Plus, given that I'd yet to share with him anything about my family issues and dynamics, any upsetting thoughts that had briefly flashed through my mind quickly dissipated. After all, we were both so ecstatic, and all I wanted was for our engagement to start off on a happy note.

Meeting His Parents

Brad was on duty both Christmas Eve and Christmas Day, so I spent Christmas Eve at my grandparents' house, as I had most every year of my life. This time, however, I was showing off my engagement ring to the family. Then I spent Christmas Day impatiently waiting around at home until Brad came over that night so we could have our Christmas together. It was a fun but short night, as the best part of that Christmas season was yet to come!

Early the next morning, Brad picked me up so we could fly to Great Falls, Montana, for a six-day vacation where we would be staying with his parents and sister. I was more than anxious to meet them all for the first time during the holidays. Yet they greeted me with arms wide open as soon as they met me, so I felt totally accepted by his family from the very start. Also, to make sure things went smoothly, Brad told me ahead of time about his parents' house rules regarding unmarried couples: hugging, kissing, and holding hands were the limit. I shared a bedroom with his sister, who was only a few years older than me, and we had a great time bonding as I heard all the stories about Brad's childhood and teenage years. It was a magical week during which Brad gave me a grand guided tour around the town and surrounding area he'd grown up in.

It had snowed about six inches on Christmas Day and more during the week, so we made lots of snowmen and snow angels, went to see The Great Falls, took in an evening at the Christmas lights at the Grotto, and basically just spent a lot of time relaxing and visiting with his parents. It felt like what I always imagined Christmastime was supposed to be like. On New Year's Eve, we enjoyed a fun evening at home, informally celebrating our engagement with his family, playing cards, and eventually ringing in the new year together. The time went by way too fast, and I was sad as we flew back late on New Year's Day. We'd stayed as long as we possibly could, but Brad had to report for duty early the following morning, and he still had to take me home before he could go back to base. I was exhausted by the time he finally dropped me off at home, yet I had a hard time going to sleep. It had been such a perfectly memorable week!

Living a Dream

At that time, Brad was only eleven months away from getting out of the navy. Since we'd already decided to wait until after he was discharged to get married, we hadn't yet settled on details, like exactly when or where we'd get married, what he'd do after he got out of the navy, where we'd live, or how I would continue my schooling. Instead, we put those kinds of plans off until his discharge got closer. That gave us more time to get to know each other even better and for me to finally fill him in on my family issues, which to date he'd thankfully (at least in my mind) never witnessed, known about, or picked up on. Nothing could stop me, however, from immediately starting to daydream about the wedding itself, my wedding dress, our first dance song, the wedding cake, or where we might go on our honeymoon. I was so much in love with this wonderful man, and I couldn't believe how lucky I was to have found someone who was so much in love with me. It was a purely magical time, and everything felt so right! I was the happiest, most confident I'd ever been in my very short life.

Unwelcome News

Two days after I got home, Brad came to see me for the first time since we'd gotten back from Montana, and my world was shattered. That's when he told me that as soon as he'd returned to duty, his squadron received orders to deploy on January 30 for nine months of training and sea duty aboard the USS *Midway* in an undisclosed destination.

My heart collapsed that night when he broke the news to me. In all the excitement of the past six months of falling in love and getting engaged, I'd naively never considered this might happen even though, after all, he WAS in the navy. I was absolutely devastated, and nothing he could say consoled me. I felt terrible because I knew Brad already felt bad enough as it was. But I couldn't help myself and went into total meltdown mode—something he'd never seen me do before. We ended up spending that evening at the house with Brad holding me tight as I sobbed my eyes out until I was too emotionally drained to shed any more tears.

After that night, I always put on a happy face when we were together so as not to upset him, even though I began feeling more sad, anxious, and sick inside as the time of his departure got closer. During the remaining time before his deployment, we spent every possible non-class, non-working waking moment together. Since it was winter and not the warmest out, that meant we mainly hung around the house, took short hikes close by in the area, and simply enjoyed each other's company to the fullest.

The week before he shipped out, he gave up his living quarters on base. My parents let him stay in the extra bedroom downstairs for the remaining time before he left. They also agreed to store his few belongings until he returned. The last evening before he left, Brad told my parents he was taking me out for dinner and a late evening, so he said his goodbyes to them and promised he would see them when he came back on leave in two months.

Saying Goodbye for a While

After Brad said his goodbyes to my parents, we left for dinner, then went to a low-key motel the next town over, where he rented a room for the night so we could have some privacy. We both wanted one last special night together before he shipped out, so I put all my anxieties and worries out of my mind and focused entirely on us. We had a wonderful time talking about our future together, laughing, making love, and lying in the warmth of each other's arms.

Around midnight, he said he needed to get a few hours of shut-eye, so he set the alarm for two o'clock and immediately fell asleep. I was too wound up to sleep, as the realization had finally set in that I had only a few hours left to be with this man I was so in love with. All I wanted to do was lie by his side, feel the warmth of his body, and rest my head on his shoulder as I watched his chest move up and down with each breath.

When the alarm went off, it was really hard to motivate ourselves to move. We finally managed to get up and leave around two thirty in the morning. We barely made it back to my parents' house in time for him to drop off me and the camper he'd sold, then get back to base to report for duty.

Later that morning, I met him on base for the send-off ceremony. I was beside myself watching him leave. Afterward, I had crying jags for days as I tried to deal with the immense loneliness and loss of seeing him daily. After a while, there was even this tiny feeling of abandonment that slowly started to creep into my psyche, which made me feel guilty because it wasn't as if Brad had a choice over whether he left or not.

Lonely and Lost

There I was at the young age of eighteen, still living at home with my parents, attending college, and preparing myself as a soon-to-be wife. I loved and missed Brad SO much. He'd come to be the entire center of my universe, the one person I really depended on. Now, according to my parents, I was once again "on your own, kiddo!" College became my focus, but with Brad gone, my confidence level began dropping almost immediately, and my anxieties, insecurities, and low self-esteem were all resurfacing. I was totally lost on my own.

Right after classes started in the fall, I'd gotten in on an informal "whoever wants to play" card group that played hearts between classes. Through the people I met there, I was also invited to other card games or activities that took place in the evenings. Before Brad left, I would always turn them down because I wanted to spend all my free time with him. After Brad left, though, the card group was a nice distraction from the loneliness I felt and the depression I soon found myself battling. It also helped break up the monotony of my school-homework-home cycle I was experiencing without the love Brad had showered me with daily.

While everyone knew I was engaged and Brad was gone on sea duty, I kept getting invitations to various evening and weekend activities. However, living at home under my parents' rules made attending anything pretty much impossible. Apparently, "occasional personal use of the car if I paid for the gas" didn't include activities that, according to

Mom, weren't proper for an engaged woman to attend (i.e., if there were any males in attendance I might be seen with).

A few weeks after Brad shipped out, some people from our card group came up with a cool idea for a Saturday-night party. It would start at the college with a two-person-per-car scavenger hunt (one driver, one clue reader). Each team would get written directions to the next clue, which was posted somewhere else in the valley. If we followed all the clues correctly (for example, "drive straight ahead for a mile, take a right, then take the third left, go for half a mile, and you'll find the next clue"), the last clue would let us know the address where the party was being held.

I inquired about it, and the only driver still without a partner was Bob, a casual acquaintance from the card group. It sounded like a lot of innocent fun. Plus, I really needed a distraction from my tedious routine and wanted to get out of the house for a while, so I agreed to be Bob's clue reader. That Saturday, Bob picked me up at the house, and we were at the starting line with all the other people and cars when the hunt began.

It was fairly easy to follow the clues, yet at some point, I read something wrong and got us lost. We tried back-tracking to reread the clues, but we finally gave up. Since we'd been planning on eating at the party and were starving, we stopped for a burger and coffee, then Bob dropped me off at home. I have to admit it was a fun, silly night in spite of never having made it to the party. It was mainly a huge reminder to me of how much I missed being with Brad and doing things with him, which in turn made me feel even sadder and more depressed than I already was.

The evening wasn't without repercussions on the home front. Mom attempted to guilt-trip me right before I left by insinuating that what I was doing was unbecoming behavior for someone who was engaged and that I was in some way cheating on Brad. I'd never heard her talk to me like that before, so I was a bit upset—even a little angry that she would think I would do anything to jeopardize my relationship with Brad. Her words really stung. As untrue as I knew they were, they planted a tiny seed of doubt in my mind that would soon germinate, take root, and start to grow over the next few months.

A New Reality

After that night, on weekdays, I simply got up, went to my college classes, played cards in between, studied, came home, wrote Brad letters, studied some more, went to bed, and did the same thing the next day. On weekends, I hung around the house, trying to stay as busy as possible. Then, as the weeks slowly dragged on and I had a lot of free time to think without Brad at my side daily, a new reality set in. I realized that even though I loved him very much, it was a fairy-tale notion of love. Brad was my Prince Charming, and I was his princess. At a very impressionable time in my life, he'd rescued me from the depth of trauma and unhappiness and taken me to the height of love, happiness, and joy in a world where we never disagreed or argued. When I began to look at things realistically, I started feeling like I wasn't ready or mature enough to settle down into the responsibilities of marriage, let alone a family, which I knew he wanted. My mind went into overdrive, thinking through all the possible scenarios and actions I could take.

Brad and I wrote almost daily. In my letters, I started expressing my concerns and describing my anxieties, insecurities, and loneliness. They were parts of me he'd never really seen. I'd never wanted him to see them. I still didn't mention anything about my dysfunctional relationship with my parents. In return, his letters tried to keep me positive, raise my confidence, and assure me that everything would be okay as soon as he was home from sea duty and back by my side.

Sadly, my self-doubts continued to increase. I was on edge most of the time, and I found myself irrationally angry with Brad for abandoning me, becoming more upset as each day went by. I was lonely and needed companionship. In a weak moment, I'd been tempted by and confusingly attracted to someone else, which made me feel ashamed and bad about myself. I began to think I didn't deserve Brad's love. I was constantly battling all these feelings, which were increasingly overpowering my psyche and what I knew deep inside was love for Brad. But as the weeks went by, I could tell I was losing the battle. I just wasn't strong enough to keep all the negative feelings from burrowing into and infesting my mind.

A Painful Breakup

After two months, which felt like an eternity, Brad came home for a few days of leave. He arrived back on base late into the night but was at my parents' front door at the crack of dawn the following morning. I skipped classes, and we spent the entire day trying to reconcile my feelings with his and overcome my pessimism with his optimism.

There were angry, hurtful words, accusations hurled at each other, and lots of crying. I was especially blindsided when he told me that his friends told him that proposing to me was a big mistake because I wasn't the right one for him. I was totally crushed when he told me he should have listened to them.

Yet there was also a lot of reminiscing, laughing, hugging, and kissing. I knew deep down that Brad had done nothing wrong. He was the real deal, and this problem was all me. After it was said and done, it was still obvious how much Brad loved me. Though there'd never been anyone for me but Brad, it was obvious that my love for him had been entirely overridden by my fears, anxieties, insecurities, and feelings of unworthiness, which had resurfaced when he left for sea duty. Even worse, I knew that those feelings and the loneliness that would come with the long seven-month separation that still lay ahead would be near impossible for me to handle. There was a high probability that I'd give in to a weak moment and cross a line I would never be able to forgive myself for. I just couldn't do that to Brad or to myself.

By the end of the day, we both realized I was no longer the same person I'd been when he left a mere two months earlier. Even though my love for him had been deep, intense, and very real, there was now something different about it that I didn't understand and couldn't explain. I just knew there was only one decision I could make to save us both from an even worse and inevitable pain down the line.

That Friday evening, I called off our engagement, gave Brad back the engagement ring, and broke up with him. The pain tore deeply at my heart, as I'd never expected my feelings for him to so quickly change the way they did. I'd never expected to hurt him as much and as deeply as I felt I had. As painful and upsetting as it was for me, it became even more so. As upset, saddened, heartbroken, and pained as Brad also was, he told me he understood. Whether he really did or not, I never knew. Yet, in my heart, I knew he deserved so much more, so much better than what the eighteen-year-old in me could possibly promise to give him, especially feeling the way I did at that point in time.

We decided before he left that night that it would be best to tell my parents together about our ended engagement. While we both tried not to get too emotional when we told them, Brad broke down crying right away, which set me off crying too. We were both a complete mess, yet my parents' reaction made it even worse for me. They immediately turned toward me, and Dad asked, "What did you do to screw things up this time?" Mom angrily blurted, "How could you do that to him?"

I was taken aback by their reaction, and a sense of disbelief raced through my mind. What about my feelings? What about what I'd been going through? What about my pain? With my history with them, I should have anticipated a negative response. Yet, in that instant, I was totally taken by surprise at the depth of disappointment, disdain, and blame they threw my way.

Right at that moment, Brad decided it was time for him to leave. So we walked out to his car together. Without a word, he gave me a big hug and a quick kiss. Then he jumped into his car and drove away. I don't know what I was expecting would happen at the exact moment he left, yet it all happened so fast. I had no time to tell him how sorry I was and ask for his forgiveness. I didn't even get a chance to say goodbye.

The Immediate Aftermath

For a long while, I stood outside, crying, alone with the consequences of the life-changing decision I'd just made. I turned back toward the house, dreading what was going to happen next in the lion's den I thought awaited me inside.

Thankfully, my parents didn't say a word as I headed straight upstairs to my bedroom to be alone in my pain and sorrow.

The next day, I skipped classes again. So I had one more day plus the weekend to try to pull myself together enough that I wouldn't break down every five minutes. By Monday, I was totally drained and exhausted. Yet, I knew I needed to get back to my classes. Although thoughts of Brad continued to surface for quite some time, I forcefully pushed them out of my mind. That was the only way I was able to cope with all the wonderful memories of our time together and thoughts of our painful breakup, and still function daily.

For the first week or so, my parents mostly ignored what was going on with me since I mainly stayed in my bedroom when I was home. That was okay with me, since crying or showing emotions in our house was seen as a sign of weakness, and my parents pretty much frowned on it. However, the fact that they never mentioned Brad's name around me ever again hurt a lot. It was as if that part of my life had never existed, invalidating my very real, deep, and intense feelings of love, then pain. My feelings were of no matter or consequence to my parents. That's when I vowed to myself that whenever I finally escaped the dysfunction at home, I would never let my parents in on what was going on in my life, no matter how hard things were or how bad they might get.

For the immediate future, though, I continued to live at home through the winter and spring quarters at college. And I worked in my parents' store over the summer. Although they still made it clear that I was no longer their responsibility and could do whatever I wanted, they continued to have a very strong emotional and mental hold on me. They critiqued and criticized the things I did and the people I associated with, and they wanted me to do what they thought I should do—of course, always with my best interests in mind. If I didn't follow their instructions, I knew I would pay the consequences in some way or form. I just needed to make it through until the timing was right for me to move out.

Chapter Seven

NAVIGATING LIFE ON MY OWN

When I first started college, I was always with Brad when I wasn't attending classes, playing cards between classes, or studying at the college library. I spent the least amount of time on campus as was necessary. Still, college itself was an intriguing, eye-opening experience, especially since I'd been extremely controlled growing up, had become engaged while still living under my parents' roof, and had never lived away from home. To say the least, I was still very impressionable, idealistic, and totally fascinated with campus culture.

In 1970, Skagit Valley College was a small two-year community college with a diverse environment full of recently graduated high school students, hippies, Saudi Arabian foreign exchange students, and Vietnam vets. With the enormous social, sexual, and musical revolution of the times well underway, along with the fallout of the unpopular Vietnam War, it was a culture in which booze, pot, drugs, and casual sex went hand in hand with attending classes, studying, and going to campus church services on Sunday mornings.

Now, without Brad in my life, I found myself absolutely overwhelmed yet completely drawn into the campus culture itself. It was enticing but scary as I continued to deal with all my anxieties, insecurities, and low self-esteem, which had increased even more now that I was on my own with no one to depend on but myself. My habit of smoking cigarettes, which I'd started in high school but given up when I was with Brad, returned with a vengeance. Instead of smoking a few cigarettes a day, I was smoking a pack a day to try and keep myself calm. My appetite decreased, and I started to lose more weight.

It wasn't long before my friends and those in the card group, which I'd decided to continue participating in, also noticed I was no longer wearing my engagement ring. Most of them politely tried not to bring up the subject outright, but it was very uncomfortable for me. At that point, I was in no frame of mind to explain the missing ring or all the other changes that were becoming outwardly evident with me. I finally decided to address the situation with a few key people, and word spread fast through the grapevine. Thankfully, all the tiptoeing and rumors about me quickly became old news.

It was in this new chapter of my life that, despite my best intentions, I gradually began losing my way on the path to where and who I was always meant to be. I started reverting to my old ways of thinking of and about myself. I just didn't have the strength or resources to stop the regression that was taking over my thoughts.

Chapter Eight

A NEW LOVE INTEREST

Bob

Several weeks later, Bob—the guy I'd ridden with on the card group's car run—invited me out for a drink. My feelings were still like an open, raw sore, but I was lonely and figured I had nothing to lose. We compromised, though, and went out for coffee instead. As we got to know each other more over the following weeks, I found he had tremendous focus and was working toward a degree in law enforcement. He often came across as serious, responsible, and meticulous about certain things. However, I also saw he was personable and playful when he wanted to be. He was completely different from Brad, yet someone I felt comfortable and safe around. Also, he was fun to be with in a low-key way. I even started smiling and laughing again. Deep inside, I knew it hadn't been that long since my breakup with Brad. But I couldn't explain it or help it. I sensed I was already beginning to fall for him.

We soon started seeing each other exclusively in what felt like an enjoyable, mellow, and down-to-earth relationship. Apart from going to a couple of parties and some picnics over the course of a few months, our relationship consisted of more than just enjoying each other's company. We mainly played hearts between classes; studied at the library together; hung around campus with either my friends or his best friend, Marv; and went to a few places with a married couple he was good friends with.

The Parties

The first party we went to was one that Marv invited us to. It was somewhere out in the boonies, in an area I was unfamiliar with, and I didn't know anyone except Bob and Marv. We were all crowded into this small house, there was lots of booze, and most everyone was smoking pot. I was very uncomfortable, battling an anxiety attack that I could feel coming on, and I wasn't enjoying myself at all. Consequently, we left not too long after we arrived. I felt bad leaving so early, but I was extremely nervous, stressed out, and claustrophobic, and I needed to get out of there right away. I always tried to keep my anxieties under wrap when I was around other people, especially Bob now, and deal with my emotions when I was by myself. But in this situation, that was impossible to do. Bob said it was okay, but I'm not sure he knew exactly what was happening to me. I finally made up a story about having a migraine headache coming on and feeling nauseous, so he took me home with no further explanation necessary.

Then we went to a weekend lake party that one of my high school girlfriends invited us to. It was an early summer party where he met a few friends of mine for the very first time. It was a nice, sunny day. We swam, attempted to water ski, barbecued, and visited, and the whole group of about a dozen of us spent the night sleeping on bunk beds in a one-room dorm-like cabin. We had a lot of fun, but there was an issue that came up that night between Bob and me that almost ruined our weekend, not to mention our relationship.

It was one of those sleep-in-your-clothes slumber parties, and the number of bunk beds was limited. Bob and I ended up on a top bunk in the corner of the room, with me up against the wall under a blanket and him on top of the blanket on the outside of the bunk. I thought it was a rather good choice because I'd slept in the buff whenever possible since middle school because of my sensitivities to regular cloth fabric rubbing against my skin during the night. After the lights were all turned off, I discreetly stripped down under the blanket for comfort, though only to my skivvies due to the circumstances. Bob was mortified, and I thought he was going to come totally unglued. In my mind, it wasn't like anyone could or would see me or that anything inappropriate was going to happen between us, especially in a room full of people. I just needed to be comfortable enough to sleep, and no one was any the wiser or ever said anything to me about it. I think Bob spent the whole night worrying that someone might see me and get the wrong idea. That's when I first realized it was very important to him to maintain a good impression or image around others. Meanwhile, I was more interested in discreet comfort, not that either point of view was bad. They were simply different.

Taking Things to Another Level

In late spring, when it felt like our feelings toward each other were beginning to turn into love, we became intimate. For me, it felt like a pleasurable sexual experience with someone I cared about, yet without the heights of being made love to that I'd previously experienced. Thinking that would eventually come as time passed, especially as we'd started talking about love and perhaps eventual marriage, I accepted it for what it felt like then.

Then, when we were leaving campus and saying goodbye to everyone one day, someone asked what we were headed off to do. Without blinking an eye, Bob told everyone we were going back to his place to have sex. This time, I was the one who was totally mortified! Although my views about sex are based on my own spirituality (there's no judgment or shame in a God-given pleasure between two consenting individuals) as opposed to most religious beliefs (total abstinence with no sex before marriage), I was still a very private person. When it came to what one did behind closed doors, it was no one's business except mine and the person I was with. Although I'm sure he meant it as a joke, I was thoroughly shocked at his crude announcement. Afterward, I think he knew I was unhappy about what he said, but the matter was dropped.

Changes Ahead

Aside from his best friend, Marv, who was a first-year student like myself, and the married couple he was fairly close with, Bob never introduced me to his family or any of his friends outside campus. Although he knew most of my campus friends, I never introduced him to my family either, or to any of my friends outside campus, except the few he'd met at the lake party. At the time, this arrangement seemed to suit us both, although the subject of love and perhaps eventual marriage had already been discussed. If there was a red flag with this arrangement, I simply didn't see it or want to see it.

Bob was a year ahead of me, and I knew he had to transfer to a four-year college in the fall. Still, it was disheartening when I found out late in spring quarter that he was transferring to Washington State University (WSU), across the mountains in the eastern part of the state. I was apprehensive about what would happen to us with him moving that far away. Flashbacks of the loneliness, anger, and abandonment I'd felt when Brad left for sea duty began reeling through my mind. Yet Bob told me he planned on coming back to the valley for a weekend every four to six weeks, so I hesitantly convinced myself that we'd be able to maintain that kind of long-distance relationship. With that in mind, we continued to enjoy our time together through the summer, and I put aside all thoughts of him going away.

That summer, Bob took the job as live-in dorm monitor in the only dorm at the time, which was right across the street from the college. The dorm consisted of a two-story building—females were housed on the first floor and males on the second floor—and a long row of dorm apartments for males who owned cars. The live-in dorm monitor's apartment was on the first floor and next to a common area where everyone could mingle, watch TV, play games, read, or study. It was also next to the door that led into the hallway to the female rooms and just past the stairs that went up to the males' rooms. The job itself didn't appear to be that hard, more like babysitting college kids. His job was to enforce the house rules, including curfew, and make rounds several times during the day to ensure females stayed off the second floor, even though males were allowed in females' rooms with doors left open until a certain time at night. After curfew, he'd make rounds again to ensure there were only females on the first floor and only males on the second floor. The job also entailed just being there in case of a building or medical emergency. Consequently, he spent most of his time that summer at the dorm, which at least gave us a place to hang out together whenever I wasn't working for my parents.

Bob's Big Move, My Big Move

The third week of August, Bob transferred to WSU in Pullman, moved into an apartment close to campus with two other roommates, and started his fall classes the following week. It was bad enough that I became extremely depressed when he left. Worse was that he found out prior to leaving that he'd be away WAY longer than we originally planned for his first stint in Pullman. Instead of four to six weeks, he wouldn't be able to come back until his Thanksgiving break, which was about twelve weeks away. All I could do at this point was keep busy and try to hold things together on my end. Initially, even though we had no classes together, his best friend, Marv, was still attending Skagit Valley College, and I'd occasionally run into him, which helped keep my connection to Bob alive.

At least one good thing came out of Bob's big move across the mountains. With the start of my classes still a few weeks away, his move gave me the time and initiative to finally make my own big move away from home. Although my parents weren't too happy about it, I co-rented a room in the dorm across from the college, where Bob had been the live-in dorm monitor. I shared it with a good friend from high school to help keep costs down. Even though it meant I was without a vehicle (because I had to leave my parents' car behind with them), everything I needed was within walking distance, so it didn't bother me. The one downside, however, was that it meant both my living expenses and my tuition were now coming out of my college fund, almost doubling per quarter the amount I was using out of what remaining monies I had. Yet the newfound freedom I imagined it would give me was priceless.

However, living away from home for the first time in my life wasn't at all what I thought it would be. With its strict rules and regulations, the dorm felt even worse than home at times. Also, not long after we moved in together, it became apparent that even though we were good friends, my roommate and I weren't suited to be roommates. I was doing okay academically, but I found myself having a difficult time socially. I was anxious and depressed a lot of the time, and it was much like high school all over again, except I had only myself to rely on.

Surprising Bob

About a month after Bob left for WSU, Marv caught up with me between classes and suggested it would be fun to make the six-hour drive and surprise Bob that coming weekend. He asked me to go along, supposedly to keep him awake during the long drive. I was SO excited, and Marv knew how much I was missing Bob.

We left after classes on Friday afternoon and arrived around ten that night. As it turned out, though, surprising Bob wasn't a very good idea. It was Father-Son Weekend on campus, and while Bob's father wasn't there, his two roommates and their fathers were there. So the apartment was a bit crowded. We were able to spend a little time together over the weekend, but Bob seemed distant, uneasy, and a bit put off by our surprise arrival. He said he was only trying to be polite in front of his roommates' fathers and make a good impression. Knowing Bob, I figured that most likely was true. With all my insecurities, though, it felt like it was more than that, even when he took me alone on a personal guided tour of the campus. Although we hugged, kissed, and held hands, when it came to sleeping arrangements, Bob didn't think it was appropriate for me to just fall asleep (fully dressed) with his arms wrapped around me on the couch or for us to sleep on two separate bunks in a room with the door open, where we could at least talk. That wouldn't make a good impression! I mean, it wasn't like we were going to have sex, especially with seven of us in the small apartment! I just wanted to be as close to him, physically and emotionally, for as long as possible before the long eight weeks ahead until I'd be able to see him again. Instead, I was relegated to spend two nights by myself in a tiny room on a bottom bunk with the door closed.

In my mind, considering the way we'd always communicated and related to each other before he went to WSU, his attitude and actions that weekend were confusing and upsetting to me. In fact, his reaction made me feel like I was an intrusion into his new and different life at WSU, even as he kept telling me how much he loved me. He kept apologizing for everything, but I knew it wasn't his fault. I should never have let Marv talk me into surprising him! We should have planned for a weekend that would have been more convenient and fun for everyone. But the damage had already been done to my psyche. By the end of the weekend, I was already feeling a little angry and abandoned, and I had a gut feeling that something wasn't right.

Unfortunately, a lot of things were left unsaid when Marv and I headed back early Sunday morning. While Bob and I agreed we were both looking forward to seeing each other during Thanksgiving break back in the valley, I couldn't shake the unsettling feeling of dread deep down inside.

Sadly, our time apart and the short weekend together made me realize that while I loved Bob, it was a love I wasn't vested in to the extent or depth of feeling I sensed he was. After obsessing and agonizing over it for several days after I got home, I knew for certain that a long-distance relationship with Bob, or anyone else for that matter, would never work for me. I wanted someone who would be close by, physically and emotionally, as shallow as that may have sounded or looked to those around me. While I was extremely disheartened by how I felt, I was thankful he hadn't asked me to marry him. We weren't even engaged yet.

Since we weren't writing or calling each other, I knew I wouldn't be able to say anything to him until we talked face-to-face during Thanksgiving break. I was beside myself, not knowing how I would handle things until then or how I would even break it to him when we did see each other. It was never my intention to hurt him, but I knew he would be devastated. I dreaded having to explain everything to him. I was in the same position as before. I felt terrible about breaking things off—first with Brad and now with Bob. What was wrong with me? Why did I feel this way?

Chapter Nine

RELEASING A REBELLIOUS CHILD FROM WITHIN

My insecurities and social anxieties started bubbling to the surface more often and greatly intensified once I returned from WSU. I avoided Marv, since I just couldn't talk to or face him at that point, feeling about Bob the way I did then. I embarked on an uncharacteristic rampage, making new friends who lived more on the edge. These were the kinds of people I'd never felt comfortable being around before. I started drinking and smoking pot, mostly to relax and help ease my insecurities and anxieties. All I wanted was to get to the point of being numb to all the different kinds of pain that had taken over within me. It felt like my emotions were spinning out of control, and my behavior, at times, was totally inexcusable. I couldn't seem to help myself and was unable to slow the downward spiral I felt I was getting caught up in.

Dale

I wasn't into hookups or one-night stands and wasn't even looking for a relationship with anyone. After all, I still hadn't even faced breaking up with Bob when he was to return at Thanksgiving—something he didn't even know about yet. But from the very first time I saw Dale, I was thoroughly intrigued by him. He was known campus-wide for his good looks, incredible charm, and fast lifestyle, and he had quite a reputation as a real "love 'em and leave 'em" type. He even had an estranged wife who'd moved back in with her mom.

I initially saw him at the college library, sitting across from a gal I presumed was his most current love interest. A few days later, when I was studying at the library again, I saw them sitting next to each other a few tables away. This time, I noticed he would often glance over at me and flash a quick smile. Then, several days later, while in the library once more, I heard the chair next to me slide away from the table. When I looked up, there he sat, staring at me with that same smile he'd flashed at me a few days earlier. He introduced himself, asked me my name, and wanted to know if I wanted to go grab something to eat or drink. My first thought was how full of himself he must be! Yet I was curious about this guy I'd heard rumors about, so I agreed. Over a cup of coffee, we had a somewhat flirty conversation. I must say, I was quite flattered by the interest he seemed to have in me. He even walked me back to the dorm afterward. As he said goodbye and walked away, I wasn't exactly sure what to think about him.

Later the next day, Dale showed up at the dorm with a beautiful bouquet of flowers for me. I couldn't believe it! No guy had ever brought me flowers before, and it made my heart melt. Afterward, we took the winding dirt road that led up to the top of Little Mountain, parked the car, laid back on the windshield, and talked for several hours as the sun set and stars came out. I had a great time. It was nothing like what I'd expected from all the rumors about his bad-boy reputation. It turned out he was a Vietnam vet, and I sensed that underneath his notorious reputation, he was just another young guy who'd never grown up beyond the brutality and horrors he'd witnessed on the front lines. From that night on, things moved quickly.

I knew from the onset that, in addition to smoking pot, he used and occasionally supplied students with speed under the radar, as a lot of students used it to help them study. I suspected that, for Dale, however, it was more about feeling alive and staying awake to avoid the haunting dreams he experienced whenever he closed his eyes and tried to sleep.

Not long after he started spending time with me at the dorm, a guy who was upset at me for turning him down for a date found out about Dale's reputation of supplying speed to other students and turned his name in to the dorm monitor. After that, Dale was banned from the dorm and dorm property, with the threat of having the cops called if he was ever caught there again. That didn't deter Dale, however. He'd wait around the corner until he saw me come out of the dorm, quickly drive up so I could jump into the car, then peel out of the parking lot before anyone caught him on the property. All we had to do was find somewhere else to spend time together. Sometimes that would be the house he rented with another army buddy and his buddy's girlfriend, who Dale couldn't stand. Most times, though, it was out on some kind of adventure.

While I didn't like that he took speed, he didn't mind that I didn't. I truly understood his need for escape and was more than willing to overlook that part of him in return for a small taste of his adventurous side. And spending any kind of time with Dale felt like an adventure because he was as fearless as they came. He loved driving his '66 Mustang at dangerously high speeds, spending time in the outdoors and open spaces, and pushing himself to the limit. Strangely enough, during my adventures with him, he always made me feel safe even as I was scared out of my wits the majority of the time.

The most memorable of those adventures began one sunny, warm Friday afternoon in early October. We drove up into the mountains on an old logging road, parked at a trailhead, and started on what should have been a short hike to a waterfall he wanted me to see. Unfortunately, although it was only a short hike, the last part of it was quite an uphill climb, and I was no longer in the best of shape. So my headway going up was slow and unsteady. He was very patient with me, but it became apparent by the time we finally made the falls that we wouldn't be able to make it back down and out before dark. At first, I totally freaked out, as we had just a little water left, no snacks, and no flashlight. Plus, the temperature as the sun went down over the mountain dropped quickly, and we only had light jackets. Yet it was like some kind of autopilot kicked in with Dale, and I found myself surprisingly feeling quite safe and protected. He spotted a small hunting cabin in a meadow way down below on the other side of the falls, and he decided we should go for it. Carefully working our way over the top of the falls, Dale grabbed my hand and guided my every step since it was a long way to the bottom if I were to slip. Then, with Dale forging a trail as we headed downward, we slowly made our way to the cabin just as dusk approached.

It was an old, shabby one-room cabin with a huge fireplace and several mattresses scattered about on the floor. There were no bathroom facilities or water, and nothing in the cupboards except an old can of Bisquick and a roll of foil. We could tell it was used only a few days out of the year during hunting season. Dale quickly brought in wood, and, as smokers, we carried lighters, so getting a fire started was no problem. We pulled one of the mattresses directly in front of the fireplace and lay spooned together for warmth, taking turns every half hour or so at being the one closest to what little heat the fire emitted. The wood seemed to burn way too fast, and every hour or so, Dale would go outside to find more wood to keep the fire going. Despite his best efforts, it was a long, bone-chilling night, and I was the coldest I'd ever been in my life.

Hunger never even entered our minds until the next morning. Throwing caution to the wind, we mixed the last of our water with the old Bisquick and fashioned the lumpy dough into something that slightly resembled a biscuit, attempting to cook it on foil with the last of the embers from the fire. It wasn't fancy, or even tasty, for that matter. But it was at least some kind of nourishment, which we needed for the trip back out.

As soon as it was light, Dale checked out our surroundings and discovered that just across the river, which meandered through the far end of the meadow, was the old logging road we'd taken to the trailhead. Unfortunately, the river was high banked. There was no way to safely reach the water, which would have been too cold, deep, and swift to wade across anyway. However, he did find a large cable pulley setup suspended high across the river, complete with a bucket large enough to hold one person. It dawned on us that this cable pulley setup must have been how the hunters got across the river. But our immediate problem was that the bucket was tied to a pole on the other side. So, dangling himself high above the river, Dale slowly and carefully shimmied on all fours across the cable to the other side, untied the bucket, hopped in, then pulled himself back across.

It wasn't without incident, however. Although it didn't seem to faze him at the time, on the way across to get the bucket, Dale had gotten a long and rusty sliver of cable embedded in his calf. Before we could do anything else, we had to get the sliver out and stop the bleeding. He sent me across the river in the bucket first, then pulled the bucket back over for himself. Together, we both managed to pull him over, then tied the bucket back to the pole the way he'd found it. Getting across the river had been a tiring ordeal, and we were hungry and freezing, and Dale's leg was now bleeding again. With his arm around my shoulder for support, we slowly limped down the road a few miles until we finally came to the trailhead where his car was parked. What a beautiful sight!

Once warm inside his car, we headed down the mountain, found the nearest place to grab some food, and proceeded to stuff ourselves. Dale never complained about his leg, though I'm sure it hurt and needed medical attention. In fact, we both ended up laughing about the situation we'd gotten ourselves into. Later, he dropped me off at the dorm where, ironically, it turned out no one had even known I was missing. Apparently, neither one of us mentioned to anyone that we were going on a hike that afternoon. My roommate assumed I'd gone home for the weekend, while my parents assumed I was staying at the dorm. It was an adventure that could have had a much worse ending!

To say the least, my time with Dale was intense and electrifying. It was also short-lived, as I could already feel his restless soul aching to move on and share his adventures with someone else. Although we had feelings for each other, our relationship had always been about the adventure, with no pressure or commitment. Yet there was no denying there had also been an underlying sexual tension between us that we'd never acted on. That is, not until the day we decided to end things with an afternoon of purely physical sex under an army parachute canopy that was draped from the ceiling over his bed. It was a chance for him to keep his "love 'em and leave 'em" reputation intact and a gratifying release for both of us from our fun and adventurous time together.

As things turned out, though, he didn't shut me out of his life like he did the other gals. Dale always told me I was special, different than the others, and he became like a big brother to me. A few months later, he reconciled with his wife, and I also became friends with her. Until they moved to Portland a few years later, he would periodically stop by, no matter where I was living or who I was with, just to make sure I was doing alright. Regardless of what else was happening in Dale's life, I always appreciated that he cared enough and kept checking up to see what was going on in my life.

Gary

After my short time with Dale and the change in our relationship, I found myself aimlessly drifting through the days when I wasn't in class or doing homework. I had girlfriends I did things with, yet deep down, I felt lonely, sad, and empty.

One day, I noticed this guy I hadn't seen before standing around and watching the people playing hearts in between classes. A few days later, he started playing hearts, and that was my introduction to Gary. We instantly clicked, and it wasn't long before we started spending time together outside of playing cards. I always had the impression that he was a Vietnam vet, but he was quite private about his time before college, so I never pressed the subject. He was just a sweet, kind, reserved, and quiet guy who was different from anyone else I'd ever met.

For several weeks, since he was living northeast of Everson with a young couple he was friends with, we spent time with each other only weekdays on campus. Eventually, one Saturday afternoon, a good friend who also lived at the dorm offered to lend me his car if I wanted to go spend some off-campus time with Gary. He said I could stay out as late as I wanted if his car was back in its parking spot when he got up in the morning.

I called the number Gary had given me to where he was living and, though he wasn't home at that moment, the couple he lived with knew who I was. They told me he'd be home soon and that I should come on up. They said he'd be glad to see me and proceeded to give me directions to their place. It was a crazy idea, since Gary had no clue I was coming, and I momentarily had flashbacks from when I'd surprised Bob. Yet I couldn't resist and was excited about seeing Gary on his own turf. I took off right away before I changed my mind and drove the forty miles on winding back roads to get there.

I was a little disappointed that he still wasn't there when I arrived. But it wasn't long before he showed up, and I'm glad I risked surprising him, as he was happy to see me.

We kicked back, smoked a joint, drank a glass or two of wine, and spent the time getting to know each other better. We totally lost track of time, and when I finally got ready to leave, not only was it dark out with no moon, but it was also very foggy. Since it was also a long, winding drive back and it was late, Gary asked me to spend the rest of the night there with him.

I don't know if it was the joint, the wine, or the weeks of being physically attracted to each other with no outlet, but that night, we ended up having sex on the small, lumpy couch he slept on in a family room that doubled as his bedroom. We curled up next to each other on the couch afterward, and he fell right asleep. As for me, it was a short, restless night of barely any sleep at all. In the back of my mind, I was really worried about making sure the car got back to its parking spot before my friend woke up the next morning.

In the morning, we were still fogged in. But Gary handed me a nice, hot cup of coffee on my way out the door. I left at dawn and was able to get the car back in plenty of time, which was a huge relief. Having now driven that route myself, though, I didn't know how Gary could stand that long, winding drive back and forth to campus. Not long after, he found a small rental house in Mount Vernon, which gave us a comfortable place to spend all the free time we wanted in total privacy.

After that, we'd spend several evenings a week at his place, smoking a joint, drinking wine, and playing cards, which was his favorite pastime. The strange thing about Gary was that he appeared to genuinely enjoy my company when I was with him. I also sensed at times that he would be just as content to be alone, living quietly inside his head. We did have fun together, though, and continued to occa-sionally have sex, though we were more like friends with benefits than a couple. Still, I could always rely on him when I needed someone to hang around with, be with emotionally and physically, or simply talk to when life felt chaotic and out of control. At the time, he was the peace I needed, and, though never serious, it was the kind of relationship we both seemed to get something out of. It was comfortable with no commitment. In essence, Gary was the calm before the influx of storms that were soon headed my way.

Breaking up with Bob

Bob and I hadn't communicated since the weekend I'd surprised him at WSU, so when he returned for Thanksgiving break, he came to see me at the dorm. Before I could even say a word, he told me it was a good thing I was at the dorm where I belonged and not out running around with someone else. I was taken aback by his comment and demeanor, which was a side of him I'd never seen before. It came across as a bit scary. That's when I found out he'd already seen Marv, who, it turned out, had been following me and filled Bob in on all my activities since our weekend at WSU. It was apparent from some of the specifics Bob was spewing at me that Marv had kept a very close eye on me—where I'd been day and night, who I'd been with, and what I'd been doing. Not just once or twice, but during the entire time without my even knowing it. I was totally freaked out that I'd been stalked and my privacy violated! I've always believed it was initiated by Marv's misguided loyalty toward Bob rather than something Bob asked him to do. Either way, it was too creepy for me to process right then and the least of my worries at that exact moment.

Instead, I felt terrible and truly remorseful. My gut feeling was that I should have been stronger and never left anything unsaid that weekend at WSU. I should have broken things off with him then. If I had, Bob wouldn't have felt (rightfully so) as betrayed, angry, and hurt as he did, and things would have never gotten to that point. I told him all about my anxieties, insecurities, and doubts, and about my inability to handle this long-distance relationship. I took full responsibility for my actions since I'd last seen him, and we verbally went back and forth at each other for quite a while. Finally, I ended things between us, and we said our goodbyes. When he left, I was relieved that it was all over with, yet I felt awful about the way it ended. I never intended to let it all happen the way it did. I didn't even understand what made me feel the way I did or do the things I'd done. All I knew was that I couldn't help the way I felt when he was no longer around or able to spend time with me. Was I so shallow that I could deeply care for or love someone one day, then, just a short time later, no longer care for or love them at all? What was wrong with me?

A Visit from Brad

A few days after this, I had a totally unexpected phone call from Brad. He was being discharged from the navy and had been in touch with my parents to get my current phone number, hoping he would be able to get ahold of me so we could talk. Luckily, I was at the dorm when he called, and we set up a time when he could actually come see me after classes the next day. It had been almost eight months since I'd last seen or heard from him, and I was confident that I'd finally gotten over him. Still, I wasn't quite sure what seeing him again would do to me. I did want to see him, though, if nothing more than to say what I'd wanted to say when we'd last parted. Instead, the moment I saw him, all the memories of our time together instantly came flooding back. I knew then that I still had some strong, unresolved feelings for him and even began second-guessing my decision to let such a wonderful man go in the first place.

He seemed as happy to see me as I was to see him. It was a beautiful early December afternoon, and we took a long hand-in-hand walk, talking about what it was like for him to live and work aboard ship and how college and dorm life was going for me. It felt so comfortable, so familiar. He asked me if I was happy despite the events of the last few months, and it seemed like I was as happy as I deserved to be, so I told him yes. When he went to leave, though, I was taken by surprise when he didn't say goodbye. Instead, he just gave me a long, soft, sweet, loving kiss, got in his car, and drove off. The hopeless romantic in me wondered if that kiss meant Brad wanted to see me again despite all that had happened while we were apart the past eight months. I even momentarily dreamed what it would be like to try to rekindle what we'd had before he'd left for sea duty.

When I called to talk with Mom several days later, I was stunned to find out that Brad had stopped by their place the day after he'd seen me to pick up the things he'd stored there, say his last goodbyes to them, and let them know he was moving to California the following day. It hit me then that when Brad and I had seen each other and talked, he'd said nothing to me about moving to California, even though he must have already known. While that last kiss meant for me that I still had some lingering feelings for Brad that needed to be dealt with, that last kiss for him was his way of saying a final bittersweet goodbye to me without speaking a single word.

Once I recovered from the shock of Brad's unexpected reappearance and immediate disappearance—and despite my momentary relapse into fairy-tale dreamland—I knew that breaking up had still been the best decision for both of us in the long run. Yet once again, I felt sad and abandoned even though I knew I had no right to feel that way anymore. Once again, I never got a chance to say how sorry I was or ask for his forgiveness. Once again, I didn't even get a chance to say goodbye. Only this time, there was something deep within my soul telling me I would never see or hear from Brad again. I had myself one last long cry fest, then I buried those happy and wonderful yet sad and painful memories of Brad deep down inside my heart once and for all.

A Place of My Own

After that, I found I could no longer handle the restrictive environment of the dorm or the tension that had gradually built up with my roommate. For the first time in my life, I just wanted to live alone. Much to my parents' disapproval, I immediately found a small furnished studio apartment that was just a few more dollars a month than I was paying to live in the dorm. It was only a mile from the college—well within walking distance—and there was a small store and laundromat right across the street. The downside was that it was, to say the least, a dump in an apartment complex well-known by the police for various criminal activities. Yet it was affordable, and I was desperate to escape my current living situation and mindset. Also, I honestly felt it would be easy enough to keep to myself and stay out of trouble and other peoples' business.

Pretending Nothing Happened

I rented the apartment on a Friday, knowing I'd have to go the next day to give it a deep clean before moving my things in. I figured it would take me most of the day. So, knowing there would be no food on hand, I arranged to have my friend—the one who'd lent me his car to go see Gary in Everson—bring me something to eat later that day. It was late. Instead of bringing food, he showed up with a bottle of wine, saying we'd have a quick drink to celebrate my new apartment, then we'd go get something to eat. Even though I was starving, I didn't say anything. He poured us each a glass, we toasted my new living arrangements, and I started sipping my wine.

Whether it was the wine on an empty stomach or something else, it wasn't long before my head started spinning and everything went black. The next thing I remember was briefly waking up, lying flat out on the kitchen table, my legs spread apart and dangling over the edge of the table. I fought to get up, but my friend was leaning over me, buttoning up my open blouse and trying to zip up my jeans. I blacked out again, then there was another brief memory of being hit on the head with something hard, and I was out again. The next thing I remember was waking up in bed the next morning in my dorm room with no one around. I felt sick to my stomach, had a massive headache, and had no idea how I got there.

While my mind couldn't remember much, my body had a memory of its own. I knew something had happened the previous night. Yet I couldn't say the words out loud. (Sexual assault? Rape?) I couldn't even think about it, as that would make what had happened real. And who would even believe me if I said something? After all, I was the one who asked him over, though it was only to bring me something to eat. I didn't refuse the drink he poured me even though I really wanted something to eat. And those who later saw me being carried rag-doll style into my dorm room most likely assumed I was passed-out drunk. That was apparently when my head hit the doorframe. He'd flung me into the room, threw me on the bed, and high-tailed it out of there before the dorm monitor caught him.

I felt thoroughly ashamed, like it was all my fault. Then I momentarily panicked as another thought irrationally flashed through my mind! That is, until I remembered I was taking birth control pills even though this happened during the five days I wasn't taking them that month. Still, I just couldn't believe this had happened to me, let alone he'd done it! We'd been good friends for such a long time, and I really trusted him. It was all too confusing, and I was in no shape to process it anyway. This had come so totally out of nowhere! Now it all felt like a terrible nightmare that I couldn't wake up from.

When I saw him that afternoon, I couldn't bring myself to say anything about what had happened the night before, and he acted like nothing had happened. Since we never spoke about it, for me, it became a deep, dark secret that I never shared with anyone, not even Gary. The only way for me to deal with it was to simply pretend nothing had ever happened.

While we continued to have several classes together after that, my trust in him had been shattered beyond repair. I physically distanced myself from him as much as possible in class and went out of my way not to run into him anywhere else on or off campus. In my mind, it was an emotionally and mentally devastating event that led to the end of what I'd always felt was a good friendship.

That evening, despite a wicked hangover, I packed up what few personal belongings I had at the dorm and was able to get a hold of Dale, who helped me take what little stuff I had to the apartment. Strangely, once Dale left and I was alone with only my thoughts, I realized I still cherished the feeling of having a place of my own. No matter what had happened there the previous night, I was bound and determined to think of it as my sanctuary. Yet mere days later, another incident rocked my sanctuary to its core.

Bob Returns to the Valley

Bob, who was back in the valley for winter break, somehow found out where I was living. He showed up drunk on my doorstep about two in the morning, having obviously been dropped off there since his car wasn't parked anywhere outside. He was pounding on my door, upset and yelling incoherently. I wasn't sure what to do, but I didn't want anyone to call the police. I finally opened the door before it broke down, and he stumbled forward into my apartment. In all our time together, I'd never seen Bob drunk, so this version of him, in addition to all his ranting and raving, was terrifying. I couldn't understand anything he was saying, and he wasn't in any shape to hear anything I had to say. I felt trapped and wasn't sure what to do, going into panic mode with each passing minute!

Before too much time passed, he finally slid down onto the floor and passed out. Keeping my distance and eyes on him from across the room until I felt it was safe enough to leave, I grabbed my purse and ran the mile to Gary's house. I frantically pounded on the back door, as I knew he was home, though most likely sound asleep. I was too scared to leave and had nowhere else to go. Since the door was unlocked, I finally let myself in. By this time, Gary was awake. When he saw me, despite the time and lack of expla-nation about why I was so upset, he had me slip into bed with him, where I spent the remainder of the night wrapped in the safety of his arms. In the morning, he drove me to class. When I returned to my apartment late that afternoon, Bob was gone. I never saw him again after that night, yet it was a reminder of just how vulnerable I continued to feel after less than a week in my own apartment.

A Continuing Downward Spiral

From then on, my emotions and actions rapidly fluctuated from one extreme to another. While I kept up with my studies, I constantly dealt with the need to be left alone and the need to have someone around. Gary's companionship helped at times, but things just didn't feel the same anymore. There was never an actual breakup. We just gradually started seeing each other less and less, eventually parting ways except to say hello when we'd run into each other on campus. I suppose it should have been sad, but it didn't seem that way. It seemed more like the result of our relationship, or whatever it had been, running its full course. It was time to move on. What I hadn't realized until then, though, was how much I'd relied on him. Now that he was out of my life, I was once again feeling lost.

Regardless of how independent I thought myself to be by having moved into my own apartment, inside, I was scared and unsure about whether I could handle everything on my own. Underneath it all, I felt emotionally starved for companionship, desperate to have a sense of belonging somewhere, wanting to be with someone I could be close to, feel safe with, and depend on. Unfortunately, I continued to be very naive in so many ways, as well as extremely and unrealistically idealistic, which, combined with everything else, kept me spiraling downward in a self-destructive manner for the next three and a half years.

Chapter Ten

FALLING IN LOVE WITH THE GUITAR MAN

I first met Dave when he accompanied Dale on one of his regular visits to make sure I was managing okay in the apartment. It was late December 1971, and Dave was a musician who had recently returned to the valley from California. That night, he just happened to be tagging along for the ride with Dale for something to do to fill his time. I wasn't at all sure about this tall, muscular man with the long, kinky hair who'd accompanied my friend. He was funny, witty, and friendly, with a slight hint of playful intimidation. Although he was intriguing, Dave and Dale were only there for a short while, and I didn't think anything more of it after they left.

The first week in January 1972, Dave popped over one day by himself just to say hello. Unfortunately, I was sick and feverish, barely able to make it out of bed to answer the door. Instead of leaving, he offered to stay and fix me something to make sure I was at least getting some liquids down. He wanted to know that I was going to be okay before he left. Even though I was anxious about being sick and alone in my apartment with this man I'd only met briefly once before, I didn't have the energy to resist his offer. I don't remember much about that day, but I know he stayed, took care of me, and spent the night sleeping in a chair across the room until my fever broke the next morning. And then he left. Later, all I could think of was how nice it was, gallant even, that he would take the time and make the effort to care for someone he'd just met. That, and the fact that he was a guitarist, which tapped into my love of music, was the hook in our relationship. It was the beginning of it all for me.

Over the course of the next month, Dave and I spent a good amount of time together when I wasn't in class or studying. He gradually opened up to me about himself, sharing small bits and pieces at a time. He was twenty-five, had been adopted at birth, had an older sister who was also adopted at birth, and had been raised in the valley. His adoptive parents still lived close by. He'd been married before, and he had an ex-wife and a young son who also lived in the area. He'd attended Eastern Washington State College as a music major, then chose the life of a guitarist who played odds-and-ends gigs wherever he could find them.

He came across as a romantic, often writing poetry for me based on song lyrics he'd heard or written himself. He had a very charismatic personality, introduced me to people in his inner circle who otherwise wouldn't have given me the time of day, and opened my eyes to the very different lifestyle of a musician. He encouraged me to accompany him to his gigs so I could see and hear for myself the world he was deeply immersed in. And I loved watching him play, listening to the music he made, and seeing for myself what an incredibly talented guitarist he was. It was like his body, mind, and soul melded into one when he played his guitar.

Most of all, though, I couldn't believe that he wanted me to be a part of his music world—a world that took me back to the music heaven I'd escaped to during my high school years. Finally, I had the feeling that I belonged somewhere with someone I thought I could trust and who could make me feel safe. I fell fast and hard for the guitar man, and we quickly took our relationship to a whole different level by moving in together after knowing each other for only two months.

I decided that my parents should meet Dave before I informed them that we were moving in together. So Mom invited us over for dinner one night. I knew things were off to a bad start when Dad gave Dave money to run to the store to buy some beer, and he didn't come back right away. After the first half hour with no Dave back from the store, out of nowhere, Dad told me, "You know, there's more to a man than what's between his legs." I was absolutely taken aback by his remark. I didn't know what to say, so I just walked away and went into the other room.

Dinner was ready a short while later, and there was still no Dave. I could tell Mom was seething and trying to keep her anger under control. Thankfully, Dave turned up about fifteen minutes later. His excuse for taking so long was that he'd run into someone who potentially had a gig for him, and they went to grab a beer at the bar to briefly talk things over. Then time got away from him. I don't know whether that was even true or if my parents believed him or not, but he was on his best behavior the rest of the evening. They soon warmed up to him, especially after he got to talking about how he loved playing rhythm and blues and jazz, my parents' favorite types of music. We never did get around to the part about us moving in together, and considering what happened to begin with, that was fine with me. I was just thankful that the evening turned out as well as it did.

BELIEVING LOVE WILL CONQUER ALL

Already deeply and emotionally drawn into this relationship—and refusing to see things for what they really were outside of his music—life with Dave was truly a major disaster from the time we moved in together. I was in love with this charismatic man, as he claimed to be in love with me too. I became totally embedded in a naive fantasy that love would conquer all and everything would be okay. Whether it was our living arrangements, money, the way he treated me, or the multitude of bizarre predicaments I found myself in because of our relationship, I was always more than willing to overlook and forgive him no matter what, just so I could be in his life.

As soon as we moved in together, there were several things I immediately found out about Dave that I would continually have to deal with in order to stay in his life. I understood and accepted them at the time. But deep down, I always felt I could change them for the better as our relationship progressed. These things were his drug habit (speed), an issue with intimacy, his car, and an extremely dysfunctional relationship with his mother.

When I met Dave, aside from smoking cigarettes, I knew he also drank, smoked pot, and used speed, which he claimed intensified his guitar-playing experience. As for me, I'd been smoking cigarettes on and off since my senior year in high school and was no stranger to drinking or smoking pot by then. Legal or not, it was a part of the college culture, and not much surprised me anymore when it came to those things. I was never one to do drugs myself except for experimenting with speed a few times with Dave. But it raced my heart so fast that I thought I was going to die, and the crash was absolutely awful. So that was it for me on the drugs. The only thing I was really concerned about was Dave's speed habit, and with that came an unrealistic notion that I would be able to help him quit the habit.

For all his outward affection (hand-holding, hugs, kisses, and cuddling), Dave had a serious issue when it came to actual intimacy. We hadn't yet been intimate before we moved in together. After we started living together, we slept in the same bed, but our schedules were almost opposite so often that we were seldom in bed at the same time. When we did sleep together, we didn't have sex unless he initiated it (which was rare). If I attempted to initiate sex, he would push me away or pretend to be sleeping, a rejection that made me question my self-image and lowered my self-esteem. I convinced myself that the speed was causing the problem. So, for the time being, I let it ride, thinking it would change for the better once I was able to get him to quit his speed habit.

When it came to his car, Dave was quite possessive, almost to the point of being obsessive about it. I wasn't allowed to drive it except in an emergency, since he felt like he needed to be on call twenty-four hours a day in case someone called him for a gig. It didn't much matter to me when we lived close to the college or my job because I was already used to walking. However, when we lived in Big Lake and I worked in Anacortes, or when we lived in Mount Vernon and I started attending Western Washington State University in Bellingham, it was more of a hassle. Consequently, I hitchhiked a lot of the time unless he knew for sure he was free to take me or pick me up. It was a totally different social climate in those days, and it was quite acceptable to hitchhike. I really didn't mind. Considering all my anxieties, it completely surprised me I wasn't afraid to hitchhike, but I honestly wasn't. As a result, I was able to put the car issue on the back burner for the immediate future.

The biggest problem was dealing with the dysfunctional relationship between Dave and his mother. His father was a very laid-back, soft-spoken man who took life in stride. His mother, on the other hand, was extremely and excessively overbearing. His father dealt with her by strictly tuning her out. In response to that, she focused all her attention on Dave. (His sister married young and moved out of the area.)

No matter where we lived, Dave's mother would show up on our doorstep at least once or twice a day in addition to phoning once or twice a day to find out "what's what." We even moved once without telling her where we were living, just to get some peace and quiet. But she spent days driving up and down the streets in the entire area until she located Dave's car. She was relentless about bringing him groceries, buying him clothes, and filling his gas tank whenever it was empty. She also paid for his car insurance and occasionally gave him cash, always with the ulterior motive of getting him to do what she wanted when she wanted it.

Even though this situation benefited him, since money was short, it was a true love-hate relationship that, for the most part, he hated. He wanted to break the cycle but never seemed to be able to while he lived in the valley and close to his parents. I always felt she tolerated me more than she liked me. Essentially, I'd become a part of Dave's life, so by default, I'd become a part of hers too.

Aside from those issues, it was simply the march of time that brought up all the other issues, which became intertwined with each other—issues I had no clue about before we moved in together. Throughout it all, though, I truly believed he was a good man at heart, love would conquer all, and I could eventually help him overcome all his issues. That in and of itself became the pattern and definition of our life together for the next three years.

CRAZY LIVING CONDITIONS

The first place we rented, in March 1972, was great: a furnished one-bedroom house just a few blocks west of the college in Mount Vernon. I'd given the rent money to Dave to take to the landlord. But I didn't know until a month later, when we were evicted, that he'd spent it on his drug of choice—speed. I believed him when he said he really WAS going to pay the rent with money he expected to make by playing gigs that month. Then, when he got no gigs, he was afraid I'd leave him if he told me right away. So I let it go. Since we were basically broke after that first month, we moved in with friends for a few weeks until we felt we'd worn out our welcome.

From there, we slept in/lived out of the car for a short while with what few personal possessions and clothes we owned, along with Dave's guitar. Everything was stuffed either in the trunk, on the back seat window ledge, on the floor in the back seat, or on the floor of the front passenger seat. Since I was shorter, I slept in the front seat with my legs under the steering wheel, and Dave stretched out in the back seat. Thankfully, an acquaintance who was renting a farmhouse a short distance north of the community college gave us permission to park our car in their field. That way, we were safely off the streets and wouldn't be bothered by the cops. Dave dropped me off at the college early in the morning so I could clean up, change clothes, and make it to my classes on time. He'd either go to rehearsals, go house-hunting, or find friends to hang with during the day. Then he'd pick me up at the college in the late afternoon. We'd drive around to different places or visit with friends the rest of the time.

Dave didn't want anyone to know about our living circumstances, so we pretended all was well when we were out and about. With no place to rest comfortably or stay warm at night, and with no money coming in, it very quickly became apparent we were getting nowhere with our situation. My anxieties increased with each passing day, and I was close to a breaking point.

Finally, Dave caved and asked his parents if we could stay with them until we could afford a place of our own. (They were already aware that we were living together.) Of course, the answer was yes. His mother was totally delighted to have him under her roof again. However, I had to bite my tongue most of the time so as not to say anything or get in the middle of all the nerve-wracking arguing and bickering that went on between her and Dave. In the end, we managed to get along fairly well under the circum-stances, and it was only a few weeks before we were able to change our living arrangements.

OPPORTUNITY OF A LIFETIME

Not long after we moved in with Dave's parents, I had what I believed would be the opportunity of a lifetime—an offer to take a trip to Europe for three and a half weeks with my parents and sister. Dad told me he would pay my airfare, and I would be responsible for only a quarter share of the hotel, transportation, and food expenses. Those expenses, he said, could be deducted from my college fund so I wouldn't have to come up with any money up front. It sounded like a fair deal, so I accepted his offer.

I was able to finish my college classes early and take advantage of summer break, so the timing was perfect. As I'd vowed before, though, I never let my parents in on what was going on in my life. Although Dave and I had finally told them in mid-March that we'd rented a house together, they had no idea what our current living conditions were. (They never asked, and we never said.) So, when they offered to pay Dave to stay and watch their house/business warehouse the whole time the four of us were gone, it was a blessing in disguise.

As it turned out, Dad had planned and booked the entire trip himself from a *Europe on $5 a Day* book—everything, including the airline tickets, train passes, bus tickets, and all the hotels we stayed in. It was a jam-packed, whirlwind trip through England, France, Belgium, Holland, Switzerland, Austria, France, and Italy, with longer stays in London, Paris, Florence, Venice, and Rome. Although I really enjoyed all the places and sites we visited, I was totally overwhelmed and extremely exhausted by the end of the trip. Plus, I really missed Dave and was more than ready to be back by the time we got home late in June.

On the afternoon we returned to my parents' house, Dave and I left immediately and rented a motel room in Burlington to have some privacy and catch up on everything that had happened since we'd last seen each other.

Frustratingly, the motel was just the first of constant moves from place to place for the next year. As it turned out, we ended up living in the motel for a month until we found this great deal (or so we thought) in a furnished studio apartment in South Mount Vernon. That, however, only lasted for a month. It was a very hot summer, the apartment was a converted attic on the top of an old brick building, and it was like living in a brick oven that never cooled down, even at night.

From there, we moved into a communal house near Big Lake with five other people. The owner, one couple, plus Dave and I each had our own bedrooms on the main floor, while the other couple had the basement. We all had assigned daily cleaning chores as well as designated nights for cooking for everyone and doing dishes. The downside was there was no running water or heat. But at least the electricity was hooked up for the lights, stove, and refrigerator. There was an old well on the place, so we'd haul buckets of water in for cooking, washing dishes, bathing, and flushing the toilet. But the rent was next to nothing, so it was well worth it. We managed to stay there for two months, until the late fall weather turned too cold and we couldn't handle the lack of heat.

We moved again, this time renting a furnished one-bedroom house beside Max Dale's restaurant in Mount Vernon. Amazingly, we stayed there three months before we finally moved into a two-bedroom house in West Mount Vernon that Dave's folks had recently bought as a real estate investment.

A FINANCIAL BLOWOUT

Unbeknownst to me beforehand, there was also a long-term financial blowout because of my European trip, which affected Dave and me tremendously during that crazy year of moving all over the place.

Dad had originally told me he would pay my airfare for the trip. All I would be responsible for was a quarter share of the hotel, transportation, and food expenses, and those would be taken out of my college fund, which he still had control of. Before I even agreed to go, I calculated the balance of what I was still owed. According to my calculations, even with a worst-case scenario of spending on the trip, I'd still have enough money left over to last me the remainder of that school year at Skagit Valley College and part of my first year at Western Washington University, plus living expenses. Aside from the lure of the trip itself, that's why I agreed to go in the first place.

But when we returned from our trip, Dad told me that my total share of the expenses was coincidentally equal to the entire amount left in my college fund. According to all the expenses he said he'd kept track of, my college fund was now at a zero balance. He never did provide me with a written account of expenses, but I'd learned from experience that you didn't question or argue with Dad, ever. Later, I learned he'd deducted all the trip expenses for the four of us as a business expense on his income tax return that year. He always had an angle when it came to saving himself a buck.

Consequently, finances were always a sore point throughout my time with Dave. While I attended college, he seldom worked outside of his music gigs, which paid very little. I turned to Grandpa, and he agreed to lend me the tuition money, as well as some living expenses, as long as I was going to college. There were a few times when we were eligible for food stamps. But it seemed like what little money we had on hand—which I was either borrowing or working for between quarters at school—had a habit of disappearing quickly. At one point, I discovered that the collector coins I'd put away for safekeeping were gone. Dave denied any involvement, and I chose to keep an open mind, especially since we were living in the communal rental house at the time. Sometimes at work, I'd find the money till didn't balance at the end of the day, and it always seemed to be on the days Dave happened to stop by. He suggested that he was probably distracting me while I was working, and I was simply giving customers back incorrect change on their purchases. I convinced myself that could very well be true. So, again, I gave him the benefit of the doubt. Regardless, all the shortages were automatically deducted from my take-home pay, which meant less money coming in.

THE MINI-WOODSTOCK EPISODE

Through word of mouth, Dave heard about a free one-day mini-Woodstock at a farm near Snohomish where a bunch of local bands were going to play. The day of, we headed out there to enjoy the festivities, and though it was only midmorning, it was already packed. We parked outside the barbwire fence and headed inside the gate, and even though we were way at the back, almost against the fence, we could still hear everything.

All was going well until about an hour into it when there was a big commotion right behind us. We turned to see what was going on, and Dave suddenly took off running toward the group of people. I blindly followed him, not knowing what was happening. It turned out that the person in the middle of the commotion was a former bandmate of Dave's I'd never met. He looked to be high on drugs and apparently had tried to commit suicide by slashing his wrists on the barbwire fence. He was bleeding profusely, but I could see the cuts weren't too deep.

Dave jumped right in and, with the help of a couple of

guys who donated their shirts, quickly wrapped the guy's wrists to help stop the bleeding. He then dragged him to our car and heaved him into the back seat. We jumped in, and off we went to what I thought would be the hospital. Instead, Dave decided to drive back to our place, since his friend was really high on drugs. Dave didn't want him arrested or put in a seventy-two-hour mental lockup for an attempted suicide.

I was terrified and panicking, as I thought the guy would die on us! We made it to the house, though, got him inside, and settled him onto the couch. We stopped the bleeding and managed to get his wrists cleaned up, then we wrapped them with the few medical supplies we had on hand. He'd been passed out since we got home, so we watched him for several hours. He'd occasionally wake up, but only for a few minutes, and mumble incoherently. We could at least tell by then that he was starting to come down from being high to just being totally exhausted, so we let him sleep.

That's when Dave said he needed to go to the store to get a pack of cigarettes and would be right back, leaving me alone with this person whose name I didn't even know. When the guy finally woke up the following day, I had to explain who I was and where he was because he couldn't remember anything from the day before. After a cup of hot coffee, he called a friend to come pick him up and thanked me for helping him out of the situation as he left. The reason he thanked ME was that Dave had never returned home from the store. In fact, he didn't return home for three days!

I was a nervous wreck, not knowing where he was, what he was doing, or why he didn't come back to help! When he did get back home, all he said was he had things on his mind that he had to think through. I was torn up inside, not knowing whether to be angry that he'd left me to deal with the situation on my own or relieved that at least he'd finally come home safe and sound. When I tried to talk to him about it, he cut me off with the attitude of "I'm not going to talk about it ... end of conversation."

Unfortunately, that was only the first of many times that Dave would go out for a pack of cigarettes and not show up at home again until two or three days later. It was gut-wrenching and nerve-wracking whenever it happened. I'd worry the whole time he was gone that something terrible had happened to him, because he'd never call. Then he'd show back up like nothing happened and refuse to talk about it other than to say he needed to clear his head. It got so I'd never know what to expect, though, since there were times he'd say he was going out for a pack of cigarettes and would come right back.

QUESTIONING MY NOTION THAT LOVE WILL CONQUER ALL

From the time we moved in together, our relationship took on a life of its own at an extremely fast pace, with a lot of things happening all at once. At the same time, I was trying to balance what was going on at home with attending college full-time and keeping up with my studies. It got to where I had absolutely no time or energy to really question or deal with all the chaos that would gradually become a norm in our relationship. And still rattling around in my mind was the notion that love would conquer all as Dave continued to profess his undying love for me. To say the least, however, it wasn't very easy.

Once, I surprised Dave by getting a ride to a gig he was

playing, only to find out later that one of his loyal friends smuggled the woman Dave had brought with him that night out the back door and given her a ride home. I don't think that was the first time or the last time he'd ever done that, but I never knew for sure.

One morning, I woke up to find Dave wasn't in the apartment. A while later, I heard his voice and laugh coming from the apartment next door, where one of the "ladies of the night" lived. When I went and knocked on the door, she denied he was there, even though I could hear him in the background. I told her to tell Dave I was leaving for a walk and would be back later. Shortly after, as I was walking down the street, I saw him drive past me. When we both finally returned home later, I asked him about it. He denied ever being in her apartment or driving past me. I knew it was a lie but didn't feel like pressing the issue any further, as he always had a way of turning things around and making me feel like I was imagining things.

Many times, he'd tell me he had a rehearsal or was playing a gig, but I'd find out he was simply hanging with friends in order to hide from his mother, avoid a confrontation with me, or get out of helping with any kind of chores (cleaning, laundry, groceries, etc.).

When he'd take me out for the evening or to a party, he'd usually go off with some of his friends, saying he'd be right back, then leave me to fend for myself. Often, it happened in a place where I knew only one or two people, and it was rather awkward for me. He would eventually return, although it was never right away.

Dave was an extremely trusting person and generous to a fault. He made friends quickly with what always seemed like the lost souls and addicts of the world. Friends and even people he'd just met were always welcome in our home at any time, day or night. There were times it felt like our home was a revolving door of people who stopped by for a visit, food, or a place to crash for the night—and sometimes for all three, and always at our expense. At first, I thought it was an admirable quality in Dave—that he put himself out there, perhaps helping these people in some way. That is, until I later realized it was a bit narcissistic and more about him and what he got out of it—pot, speed, music contacts, favors to be collected on later, you name it.

Dave liked to entertain and cook for everyone, and he was a good cook. Yet he also expected me to help entertain and feed everyone while they were at our house. It didn't matter if it was during the day and I was studying, or if he woke me up at three in the morning even though I had classes later. The expectation was that if I was home, it was my responsibility as well as his to entertain. In the beginning, I didn't mind most of the time, as I felt like I'd finally been accepted as part of the group. Other times, it was a bit unnerving, as a few of these people eventually fell victim to suicide, death by drug overdose, or an unexplained disappearance and were never heard from again. The hardest part was that there were many times I never knew when, who, or how many people would be hanging around or sleeping on the floor when I'd leave in the morning or come home in the late afternoon.

DEAD OR ALIVE?

One night, we went to a party at a house in Clear Lake that I wasn't familiar with, and I didn't know anyone there. Dave immediately headed out back with a guy I didn't recognize, but they never came back into the house. After quite a long while, I went looking for him, but he was nowhere around. That was when I noticed the car was gone. Thankfully, by that time, Dale had shown up with a few of his friends, and he gave me a lift back to where we were living at the time.

When we got there, Dave's car was sitting out front, which was out of character. So Dale went inside with me to see what was going on. I immediately went into panic mode because Dave was lying limp, face down on our bed! Dale rolled him over to find his breathing extremely shallow and his pulse nearly nonexistent, but at least he was alive.

I felt we should call an ambulance, but Dale convinced me that Dave would eventually be okay. Then, always like a big brother, he stayed there to calm me down and make sure Dave came out of it. It wasn't until a few hours later, when Dave's breathing became more regular and his pulse increased a bit, that Dale said he was out of the woods and finally left.

As for me, I was up the entire night making sure Dave kept breathing and stayed alive. The next day, he confessed to drinking a couple of beers while simultaneously taking speed with quaaludes (a sedative/muscle relaxer) when we were at the party. After that, he couldn't remember anything, let alone how or when he got back to our place. Although the incident scared both of us, it didn't scare him bad enough to change his drug behavior.

Deep down, a part of me knew I should have left him by this point since we weren't even married. Still, I loved the musically brilliant lost soul of his and desperately believed things would change for the better if I just hung in there with him long enough. Besides, it was too hard to believe that I might have made a mistake—that I deserved better.

. . .

ONE OF THE LOWEST POINTS

One of the lowest points in our relationship came when we were both arrested in December 1972 in a massive drug sting operation. The bust was based on information obtained by two undercover snitches. They'd been working to help the county indict an Anacortes doctor who'd been rampantly writing methamphetamine prescriptions for young people in the valley.

We got involved in the sting operation due to events that had occurred several months earlier. One night, Dave wanted to go to this particular tavern in Anacortes, telling me he was meeting someone who had information for him about an upcoming gig he was going to play. When we arrived, the tavern looked crowded. He said he was only going to be in there for about ten minutes, so I waited in the car. A short time later, he came out with two guys he'd just met and wanted to go somewhere private to smoke a joint. Since my parents were away on a trip and I had a key to their house, we went and sat in their living room and passed a joint between the four of us as we talked about anything and everything. Afterward, we all left the house at the same time. Dave and I went our way, and the two guys went theirs. We didn't think anything of it. After all, that's another thing Dave did—he'd meet new people, share a joint, part ways, and never see them again.

Then came that fateful day in December, which started with a phone call from Dad. That was strange in and of itself, since he never called me. He said that the Anacortes police wanted to ask us some questions about a case they were working on. He wasn't sure what. He said they could come see us at our house in Mount Vernon or we could stop by the Anacortes Police Station any time that day. Dad was aware that Dave usually had weed around, so he suggested it would probably be best if we went to the police station. So, early that afternoon, we headed in that direction.

When we showed up at the Anacortes Police Station, the first thing they did was separate Dave and me into two rooms. They confirmed my identification (although they had my last name as Havens and thought I lived in Bellingham), asked a few questions about some doctor, then placed me under arrest, charged with possession and distribution of a controlled substance. To wit, marijuana. It turned out that the two guys Dave met at the tavern several months before were the undercover snitches. To get the warrant, the police had interpreted our sitting at my parents' house with the two snitches as possession (Dave provided the joint) and distribution (Dave invited them, and we all touched the joint as we passed it around).

My initial thought was *You've got to be kidding!* My next thought was *So much for Dad not knowing what this was all about.* He had inside knowledge about the drug sting all along and knew what was going to happen. I was scared and beside myself with the onset of a panic attack about to overtake me. I had no idea what was happening or why and what this had to do with some doctor. Nor did I understand the extent of what it was all about, since the drug sting rounded up around thirty people.

After I was able to get my panic attack under control, they took my purse and cigarettes away. I was handcuffed with my arms behind my back and put into the rear seat of a patrol car. Dave was already in there, also with his arms handcuffed behind his back. At least our fingertips could reach far enough to touch, and he tried to calm me down, telling me everything would be alright, as we were driven to Mount Vernon.

I was dropped off at the Mount Vernon Police Department. I would later learn that Dave was taken directly to the Skagit County Jail. I was still very anxious and starting to feel sick to my stomach, but there was nothing I could do about my circumstances. I would soon find out that I wasn't the only one either. There were two other women already there, also picked up as part of the drug sting.

It was now early evening and apparently too crowded, thanks to the drug sting, for us women to be booked into the county jail. That was why they put us in city lockup for the night. But the city lockup at that time had no accommodations specifically for women, and the police weren't quite sure how to handle the situation. They ended up putting us all in one cell, where we were each given back our cigarettes as well as a pillow, a small blanket, and a thin mat to sleep on. None of us had eaten since morning, so they fed us TV dinners with pop, followed by breakfast rolls with coffee the next morning. Not long after breakfast, they came with the transport van to take the three of us to the county jail, just a few blocks away.

Once there, we were processed. I was taken to the women's section, which was on the top floor of the county courthouse. It was nothing more than one giant cell with barred windows way up high on three of the walls, about ten bunk beds already made up, a single commode stall, a sink, and a shower. There were five other women already there, and I was instructed to pick any empty bed that hadn't been claimed. Thankfully, there was a bunk bed more off by itself, so I claimed its bottom bunk and settled in. As I checked the place out more, the women introduced themselves. That's when it dawned on me that the two other women I'd been with in city jail the night before hadn't been brought in, which seemed strange to me.

Shortly after I arrived, I was taken to a room where

two detectives interrogated me for the longest time, asking me all these questions about some doctor I had absolutely no answers for. I didn't know this doctor, I'd never even seen or met him, and I didn't know anything about prescriptions for methamphetamines. That's when I learned Dave hadn't been in the tavern that night to talk to someone about a gig. He was there to get a prescription for methamphetamines from the doctor they were investigating. Even though I'd been sitting in the car the whole time, they assumed I must have known what was going on. They never asked or talked about the marijuana charges. They talked only about this doctor. Then they left without answering any of my questions, and I was taken back to the women's section.

That entire day, I was never shown any papers or legal documents, received no phone calls, and had no visitors. The only people I saw or conversed with were the other women in the cell and the lady who brought us our meals. My insides were torn up, my anxieties were out of control, and I was smoking cigarette after cigarette as I tried to stay calm. More than that, though, I was getting upset and a little angry that no one would tell me what was going on.

The next afternoon, I was told I had a visitor and was taken to the same interrogation room I'd been in the day before. I had no idea who was coming to see me. Much to my surprise, it was Grandpa. I felt embarrassed and ashamed, as I could see the tears in his eyes. Yet I was so happy it was he who'd come to see me. I hoped that maybe he could tell me what was going on. He didn't lecture me but did sternly tell me that I needed to come clean with whatever I knew about this doctor. I told him I didn't know ANYTHING. After that, his tone softened. He said my bail had been set early the day before at $500, but Dad was refusing to post it, so Grandpa was going to post it himself first thing in the morning.

The following morning, when my bail had been posted, however, it was Dad who'd posted it. He was sitting in his van in front of the courthouse, waiting for me. He never said a single word to me the entire ride home. There was no "Hi" or "Are you doing okay?" Nothing. Yet it was the best thing he could have done right then, as far as I was concerned. He pulled up to the house, I hopped out of the van, and then he drove off.

Shortly after that, Dave's dad posted his bail and dropped him off at the house. I was happy to see him but still confused about what was happening. He held me for the longest time and told me everything would be okay. As always, I believed him. I was too tired and didn't want to think otherwise right then.

That was the day I discovered two things about Grandpa that I never knew, and it made me love him that much more. The first was that he used to be the Skagit County deputy sheriff, so he really was trying to help me when he came to see me. He knew I wouldn't dare lie to him, so when he sternly told me I needed to come clean about what I knew, he wanted the detectives behind the mirror to know I wasn't lying when I told them I didn't know anything. The second was how much influence he had with Dad when push came to shove. I can only imagine what Grandpa must have had over him that would make the autocratic narcissist cave and post my bail.

My parents and I were not on the best of terms for a good while after that day. Apparently, news of the drug sting made the headlines in the local paper, along with some of the names of people who were arrested, mine being one of them. Dave and I did see them later in the month when he and I went to my grandparents' house for our family Christmas dinner celebration. It was kind of strange, since NO ONE in the entire family said anything regarding our arrests, acting like nothing had happened and everything was fine. It turned out to be a nice Christmas, normal as usual for my family, with things swept under the rug.

Ultimately, it was Dave's parents who hired an attorney for both of us. Life went on as normally as it could, though on a much more somber note. I was able to finish fall quarter at Western Washington State University (where I'd transferred after Skagit Valley College), but because I was in limbo regarding the charges against me, I ended up dropping winter quarter until we knew more.

JUST WHEN I THOUGHT IT COULDN'T GET WORSE

A month later, while he was still out on bail, Dave got drawn into a dispute our neighbor was having with an ex-boyfriend. She asked Dave to go along with her to pick up her remaining belongings at this guy's house. A fight broke out between the ex-boyfriend and Dave, resulting in Dave being shot. Fortunately, it was a through-and-through shot in his upper thigh, and no arteries were hit. Unfortunately, Dave was the instigator of the fight, and he sent the other guy to the hospital. So he was once again arrested, this time on assault charges. Unbeknownst to me and complicating matters even worse, this wasn't the first time he'd been arrested or served time for assault. His parents bailed him out. I was soon to learn they'd done that several times in the past.

. . .

OUR WAKE-UP CALL

Those last two months were my wake-up call, and I was prepared to finish sorting things out, figure out where I was going to live, and end it with Dave for good. But after coming home from being bailed out, Dave promised me he'd change, saying I was such a good influence on his bad behavior and that this whole situation was his wake-up call.

Although a part of me was skeptical, the other part of me was happy and truly believed he'd finally gotten to a turning point in his life. Plus, I felt I needed to see things through with him as we awaited word on our arrest charges. Although he still drank every once in a while and smoked pot occasionally, he quit taking speed. So that was definitely a step in the right direction as far as I was concerned.

When we finally met with our lawyer, it seemed the two undercover snitches the sheriff's office had used were strangely no longer around to testify. However, enough information had been obtained from the other people arrested that the doctor was formally charged without us getting involved. The lawyer had a plea deal in mind and would ask that my charges be dropped altogether. Dave's would be a combination of a misdemeanor marijuana and an assault charge, and he would ask for three months of jail time with one year of probation. The lawyer also hinted that the prosecutor and judge would probably be more inclined to accept the deal if we had a permanent residence, Dave had a job, and we were married.

A RENEWED SENSE OF LOVE = MARRIAGE

Around this same time, Dave's folks had invested in a rental house in West Mount Vernon, and we became their first renters. Between his parents, my parents, and our friends, we were given enough kitchenware and furniture to fill the house with all we needed. On one hand, it made things worse when it came to his relationship with his mom. As she lived quite close by, it was easier for her to drop in on us at any given time, several times every day, with all her demands. On the other hand, it was a relief to finally settle down into a permanent residence, as this was the eighth time we'd moved in the past year, not including the short stint of living out of our car.

Not long after we moved into the house, we were feeling a renewed sense of love for each other. So Dave decided to take the lawyer's hint to heart and talked to me about marriage. Although he never outright asked me to marry him, I amazingly found myself saying yes when we discussed getting married. So, when his gunshot wound had healed enough, Dave got a temporary job at the local cannery, and we surprised everyone and got married. All we had to do then was wait for news on the plea deal.

Our wedding took place on the afternoon of March 3, 1973. My parents hosted the wedding at their house, so it was a small, simple ceremony with a short reception after-ward—almost identical to my sister's the year before, right down to the same minister and the same relatives on my side of the family. It took place in their living room with just enough space for Dave's parents, his aunt, my parents and grandparents, my aunt's family of five, plus two friends of Dave's (his best man, AKA my big brother Dale, and with his wife), and two friends of mine (my maid of honor and another girlfriend). My long, straight hair was braided on each side and pulled back into a further braided tail, and I wore a purple hot pants outfit with knee-high black boots. Dave had shoulder-length kinky hair and wore a white silk Nehru jacket with a gold trim collar and matching white slacks. The only hitch was that Dale, the best man, had our wedding rings (matching silver rings with green opals). He'd stopped on his way to the wedding to visit some friends and lost track of time. He and his wife finally showed up a half hour after the wedding was supposed to start. However, once they arrived, the ceremony itself was short and to the point. Within minutes, we were married. It felt like the happy occasion I'd hoped it would be.

Later that evening, some friends of ours had a party for us in this huge, very old farmhouse they were renting as part of the shift they were making to become self-sufficient and live off the land. They had no electricity or running water (although they did have an indoor composting toilet). And there were lots of oil lamps and candles, which made for a festive atmosphere. Also, there was more than enough food and drink to feed a large crowd, which came in handy, as almost everyone we knew showed up, along with a whole bunch of uninvited people who simply crashed the party.

Among the ones who crashed the party was Marv, Bob's best friend. I froze, and my heart started racing as soon as I saw him come through the front door! His eyes scanned the room until he saw me staring at him, then he casually strolled over to where I was standing and said, "I had to come see it for myself with my own eyes. I can't believe you did this to Bob and actually married this guy!" Then he walked away, mingled for a minute or two, and left. It all happened so fast that I was shocked and speechless, unable to say anything to him or move from the spot I was standing in. I hadn't seen or heard from either Marv or Bob in over fifteen months. We had no friends in common that I knew of. How on earth did he even know Dave and I had gotten married, let alone that day? Visions of being stalked once again momentarily flashed through my mind. However, I soon gathered my wits about me and was able to once again move around and mingle. After all, the whole thing had happened in less than three to four minutes, and I was determined to not let him ruin my wedding day for me!

Eventually, as the party continued into the wee hours of the morning, I got so tired that I finally curled up in a chair and went to sleep. The next morning, I saw that Dave had finally passed out on the couch and was still sleeping it off. It was definitely a memorable wedding day, though not necessarily for the right reasons.

THE GOOD TIMES

By May, the doctor was prosecuted, and the court had agreed to the plea deal our lawyer had presented. Dave started serving his three-month sentence at the Skagit County Jail in June, and I was able to visit him twice a week. With time off for good behavior, he only had to serve ten weeks, which was great. Happily, he was released just prior to my twenty-first birthday on August 27, 1973, which we celebrated with a family BBQ potluck in the large back-yard at our house with the summer sun shining down on us. It was a wonderful day—the beginning of a new life for Dave and me.

I had started back at Western Washington State University in spring quarter and continued through summer quarter while Dave had been serving his time, so I was still on target to graduate the following June. I worked in the cannery later that summer until the beginning of fall quarter to make some extra money. Dave took on small gigs with some local musicians, which helped him stay focused, although he still rarely got paid more than travel and drink expenses. Yet we were able to coordinate our schedules a bit better with the one car, so I didn't have to hitchhike as much.

The only out-of-the-ordinary thing that happened during this time period was that Dave suddenly became quite interested in finding out information about his biological parents. He'd told me when we met that he'd been adopted at birth, and that was all. But the way he was talking made me wonder if his parents had ever shared his adoption records with him or if he knew only that he was adopted. It took a while, but one afternoon, he came home with a copy of his birth certificate (he never told me how it came into his possession). It indicated that his birth mother was Native American and his birth father was Caucasian. Then that was it. The birth certificate disappeared, and he never spoke of it again.

On our first wedding anniversary, March 3, 1974, we celebrated with a wonderful dinner at Hope Island Inn, then we privately renewed our commitment to each other and our marriage. We topped the evening off with a homemade cake I'd made in the shape of a guitar. I was happier than I'd been in a long time and was feeling like things had gone surprisingly well this last year. I was looking forward to spending a happy life with my guitar man.

SLIPPING INTO OLD HABITS

Unfortunately, it wasn't long until those happy feelings started to deteriorate bit by bit. I could tell by late spring 1974 that Dave was beginning to slip into his old habits. He'd finally gotten his chance to become a member of his favorite blues and jazz band in an Everett tavern and was happy to be playing music on a full-time basis. Not only were they the house band for the tavern, but they also played gigs in other local taverns and venues. While it meant he stayed busy, he was gone at least four nights a week and rarely brought home any money or wages to show for it. In addition, it meant he spent a lot of his days either sleeping or rehearsing. So we saw less and less of each other, as I was busy finishing up my last quarter of college. That's about the time I found out that his drinking and pot smoking had increased substantially and that he'd once again started to use speed.

There was also the other issue that had been there from the very beginning, which now I could no longer ignore. While Dave was outwardly affectionate and romantic, especially when we were around other people, he had very real and deep intimacy issues. His relapse with speed had reduced his already extremely low sex drive to nonexistent, at least with me. He wouldn't talk about it and denied it was even an issue. That was the end of the discussion in his mind. I was a married woman at the young age of twenty-one, and lack of any intimacy in my life was heartbreaking. Still, I was bound not to give up on him and thought that after I graduated, we would have more time together to work through this issue.

THE BIG MOVE

After I graduated in June with a bachelor's degree (major in sociology, minor in psychology), I started job hunting and interviewed for a counselor's position at a boy's home in Everett. I was offered the job, but before I could start, Dave surprised me with a major announcement. It turned out he'd been offered a job opportunity. But it meant moving to Oklahoma. The tavern owner was from there, and he wanted to open an establishment in his hometown, taking any of the band members with him who wanted to come. I was terrified of leaving the familiarity of the valley and wasn't thrilled about living in Oklahoma. But Dave was so excited about the potential for his music, and I thought perhaps moving away from all the bad influences in the valley might actually be a positive thing for our marriage, so I agreed. I figured I could find a job in my field anywhere we lived.

We gave our notice to his parents so they could rent the house out and spent the next several weeks packing and preparing to move. Everything was right on schedule when, at the very last minute, the entire deal fell through. The tavern owner decided to keep the tavern in Everett and have the band stay on there. Since our house was already being rented out and I had no job yet, we decided to make the best of the situation. In late July 1974, we started looking for a place in Everett, thirty-five miles away from the valley, so Dave could be closer to his music gigs. After a few days of looking at various apartments, we settled into a small unfurnished two-bedroom apartment in a large apartment complex in North Everett. Although the rent was higher than I thought we could afford or needed to pay (there were other places just as nice and less expensive), Dave insisted we move there. So, move there we did, with a rental truck full of all our furniture, personal belongings, and the four cats we'd acquired over the past year.

I had a little money left out of the college money I'd borrowed, so at least we had enough for the first month's rent. Dave started working as a bartender at the tavern and playing in the house band. As before, however, he wasn't bringing in much money. So right away, I needed to find a job, anything, to get us through a few months of rent until I could find something in my field of study. Luckily, within a few weeks, I was able to find a temporary day job fifteen miles away in Lynnwood at a place called Condon King. It was a manufacturing outfit that made free-standing fireplaces. They were closing down operations in the area, so I was hired to work only three months to do a closeout inventory.

One positive thing that happened at this point was that Dave's parents bought him another (used) car, which meant each of us finally had our own vehicle to drive. Even though it was technically not mine, having an extra car helped relieve some of the pressure of our daily life in this new, totally overwhelming environment I now found myself in.

OFF TRACK ONCE AGAIN

Sadly, distance from the valley didn't help, and life with Dave never did go well or get back on track after we moved. My life went from something I was at least familiar with to something totally unfamiliar—a nightmare I wasn't prepared for.

It turned out that the apartment complex Dave insisted we moved into was where many of the band members and several tavern regulars lived, so he already knew a lot of people. However, with my time split between working full-time and the new, ever-present expectation that I accompany him whenever I could when he played, there was little time left for me to make any friends of my own. I went with him as much as my work schedule permitted, but it was very difficult. Plus, I learned very quickly that I didn't fit in too well with the circle of friends that now surrounded him.

Going to the tavern with Dave presented its own set of unique problems for me. On the one hand, when Dave went on breaks, he always went off with other people to drink or smoke, and he ignored me. On the other hand, he didn't want me to feel alone or bothered during the evening, so he usually had one of the regulars watch over me, dance with me, or play a game of pool with me. Worst of all, the wives and girlfriends of the other band members felt I thought I was too good to be associated with them. One night, they cornered me in the tavern bathroom, letting me know I wasn't being very friendly. They intimidated me both mentally and physically to set me straight on how things were going to be. Truth be told, the loud music, large crowds, and constant sense of being isolated and/or watched over made it difficult for me to relax and get to know anyone there.

I also took issue with things I was now seeing firsthand that went on at the tavern all the time. Being that it was a Black-owned tavern in an isolated part of town, the Everett police tended to have a hands-off approach to anything that went on there. Underage drinking was rampant, drugs were more out in the open, and wives were occasionally shuffled out of the picture so that men could openly bring in girlfriends. It was definitely much different than anything I'd seen or experienced at college. I was uncomfortable, which was something I struggled with on an ongoing basis.

Ever since our move to Everett, Dave had put on an "all is great with us" attitude around his friends, showing outward affection toward me when they were around. When it was just the two of us, however, he'd become increasingly controlling and argumentative. It was as if he always wanted me around when I wasn't working but paid no attention to me when I was there. By this time, we hadn't been intimate in over eight months, and I felt more like a piece of property than a wife. To make matters worse, I had no one I could talk to or confide in about my situation—no family, old friends from the valley, no one. I was too embarrassed, ashamed, and emotionally defeated by the situation that I'd gotten myself into and couldn't bear the thought of retreating from my unrealistic belief that I could change Dave's behavior for the better.

One day, not long after I started working at Condon King, Dale momentarily popped back into the picture out of the blue. He was up from Portland, found out from Dave's friends in the valley where we now lived, and unexpectedly dropped by to see us. We'd been out of touch ever since he'd moved. Not surprisingly, he and Linda were on the outs again, although they remained married. Instead, he'd brought his most current squeeze with him on a whirlwind trip to the area. He must have immediately sensed that things weren't quite right, because he left her to entertain Dave and took me outside on the apartment steps for a talk. As we sat there together, his arm wrapped around my shoulder in a brotherly hug, I broke down and told him everything I was feeling, including how I felt about living in Everett, how I was immersed in Dave's world, and how uncomfortable I was with the whole situation. We both knew he was only able to listen to me vent and couldn't help in any way. Besides, he was heading back to Portland that evening. Yet I was so glad Dale was there for me once again, with his big-brother mentality, as venting to him really helped clear my mind. After he and I went back inside, we all visited for a while, and before I knew it, the time had come for them to leave. Then, as Dale gave me a great big bear hug on the way out the door, I immediately felt a profound sense of sadness and grief, as I knew deep in my heart that it was the last time I would ever see him.

. . .

THE BEGINNING OF THE END

Even after venting all my feelings to Dale and being clear on how I felt, I absurdly continued to believe that Dave and I hadn't hit total rock bottom as far as our relationship went. So I kept holding on by a thread just to make sure there wasn't something in our marriage that would give me hope that it could still somehow or in some way be salvaged.

While the job at Condon King was relatively easy, it wasn't the most pleasant work environment for me, and it just added to the stress of daily life. To begin with, there were only eight employees remaining to help close out the business. The younger lady in the office took an instant dislike to me, suggesting to one of the warehouse supervisors that I be given some of the worst and dirtiest jobs when I finished inventorying. On top of that, I was the only female working in the warehouse, and I felt like most of the guys resented my presence, thinking I was just some stupid kid who had no business being there. If it hadn't been for the older lady in the office and the other warehouse supervisor, who treated me with some degree of respect, it would have been an almost impossible environment to endure. Granted, I did get a chance to learn how to drive a forklift, spot weld, and grind metal, which gained me a few job skills. And we definitely needed the money, so I continued working there until the job itself ended the last week of October.

The first of November, I was hired as the assistant manager at Pizza Hut in Lynnwood. I was ecstatic, as the pay was good and the job was varied, with more responsibility. Finally, I had something to look forward to that brought me a little more happiness in what was turning out to be a pretty bleak way of life.

I was so excited about starting the day after I was hired. They even scheduled it so I could attend an all-staff meeting to get to know everyone before starting my first shift that next morning. That night, before we left for the tavern, for whatever reason, Dave warned me not to say anything to anyone about getting this new job. He insisted that the owner would cut his bartending hours back and pay him less, as if his job depended upon what job I had or how much I got paid. I didn't understand his reasoning, but I was in a good mood and didn't want to argue, so I agreed not to say anything.

That night, as we got into the car to head home from the tavern, I was talking to Dave about who knows what. I don't even remember. As I turned to look toward him, out of nowhere came a fist into my face. It made contact on my cheekbone, just under my left eye. Although it was quite painful, I was even more pained by the shock of him hitting me and confused about what had just happened. It turned out that apparently, over the course of the evening, I'd inadvertently said something related to my new job to someone, and it had gotten back to him. In his mind, I'd done something he'd specifically warned me not to do, and that justified his actions. The next morning, I went to my first staff meeting with a black eye.

While on some unconscious level, I must have known it was unhealthy, I'd always accepted the emotional and mental abuse he'd thrown my way. When it came to physical abuse, however, I had no idea how to handle it. I'd known since his last brush with the law that he had a violent streak, though I rarely saw it myself. And I never thought in my wildest dreams that he'd turn it toward me. For the first time in our relationship, I was terrified of what he might do to me now that he'd taken that first step. I'd put up with a lot the past few years in my twisted fantasy that love would conquer all. But that night, I knew for sure I no longer felt any love toward Dave. I just couldn't take any more! My self-esteem was at its lowest point ever, and there was absolutely no one I felt I could turn to. And in that moment, my fear of staying in this dysfunctional marriage became greater than my fear of leaving it. I didn't know how, when, or where I would go, but I knew I had to get away before it was too late.

I never said a word to Dave about leaving him. But after that night, I started distancing myself from him as much as possible. Working at Pizza Hut became my respite from life at home. I liked the job and even made a few casual friends with a couple of the employees, although I was careful to keep my personal life under wraps. I was too scared and embarrassed to trust anyone from work with the details. The best part of my job was that scheduling shifts was my responsibility, so I gave myself as many swing shifts as possible, making it impossible for me to accompany Dave to the tavern most of the time. Yet the more I pulled away, the more he tried to pull me back in, and things got much worse than I could ever imagine.

Although it calmed my nerves, I decided to quit smoking pot altogether, no matter how much Dave coerced me. I also developed an aversion to all the drugs he had around the apartment. In response, he began physically restraining and drugging me without my consent.

It all started one evening when he set up an ambush for me as I walked in the door after work. He had a friend, who was tall and very strong, jump out from behind the front door and grab me as soon as I walked into the apartment. This guy yanked my arms behind me, twisted my wrists upward to hold me down, and locked me into a painful position that I couldn't get out of. Dave grabbed my chin, pried my mouth open, and stuffed what I would later find out was psychedelic mushrooms down my throat. Then his friend let go, and I dropped to the floor. It all happened so quickly that there was nothing I could do to stop it! I crawled to the couch, pulled myself up onto the cushions, and tried to process what had just happened. I was freaked out, not knowing what would happen next. Then, about twenty minutes later, I went into a panic attack as I started hallucinating. That lasted for the next couple of hours. I could hear Dave and his friend laughing and joking with me as my heart raced out of control. The whole ordeal scared me even more than I'd been before! Unfortunately, this wouldn't be the last time this happened.

There were times when we'd go to dinner at a friend's house, where I would inevitably find out too late that the food had been spiked with pot or hashish. Other times, he'd spike my food at home with who knows what kind of drugs, all without my knowledge. Each time, I was left to deal with the high or hallucinations on my own. It got so I was afraid to eat anything he cooked that wasn't already prepackaged or that I couldn't fix on my own from items I'd just bought myself.

One afternoon, I overheard him tell a friend that I needed to get pregnant—that having a baby would solve any problems we were having. Since by this time we hadn't been intimate for over ten months and I was convinced he was impotent from the drugs he'd been using, I wasn't sure what he had in mind. It made no difference, since I was on birth control pills. But after that, I became hypervigilant and wouldn't let him or anyone he knew come near me or touch me if I could possibly help it.

For months, my life was an unpredictable living hell.

Aside from drugging me against my will, he'd get angry and throw things at me. Mostly, he'd miss, and things would just break against the walls, like my beautiful Tiffany lamp. I'd saved for two years to buy it and could only watch as it was shattered beyond repair. Other times, he'd simply physically intimidate me with his stature, temporarily restrain me with his strength, or play mind games with me. His unpredictability and increasing anger got to the point where I became totally frightened to be around him.

With the exception of all the times he drugged me with someone's help and the "get pregnant" episode, everything happened when we were alone, with no witnesses. If I'd called the police, it would have been my word against his, and aside from the black eye in November, he was always careful to leave no bruises. Mainly it was pure emotional and mental torture, which wasn't visible and couldn't be proven. It had truly become a test of wills between us, and I was a nervous wreck just trying, in my mind, to stay safe and alive. I knew I hadn't yet saved enough money to leave him, but I wasn't about to give up.

At some point along the way, I realized that Dave wasn't the kind of person who would actually take the time or make any effort to actually stalk me when he was angry, so total avoidance became my best defense. My problem was I had nowhere to go except work and no one to talk to or turn to. All my clothes and belongings—my cats, everything I owned—were in our apartment. I often felt like a prisoner in my own home, hypervigilant 24/7, and could never relax.

It was during this time of living hell that God blessed me with a guardian angel to help guide me through this whole nightmare. While I knew that dealing with Dave was ultimately something I had to do myself in my own way and in my own time, it was good to know someone was there if or when I needed to ask for help. And it wasn't long before I needed some help in a way that only reinforced the reality that Dave had never considered my needs.

I was driving home around twelve thirty one night after working the closing shift at Pizza Hut. I ran out of gas on the freeway just as I was coming into Everett (the gas gauge never worked in that car). It was the height of the gas shortage crisis, and there was only one gas station that stayed open all night. It wasn't too far from where I was, so I walked there, intending to borrow a gas can and buy some gas. Unfortunately, they had no gas cans. I knew Dave was at the tavern until around two thirty, but if they were playing a set, he wouldn't take my call. I also knew that if, by chance, they were on a break and he did take my call, he wouldn't leave the tavern to get a gas can until he was done playing for the night and ready to leave. By this time, I was SO tired and wanted nothing more than to go home and fall into bed.

After tossing it around in my mind for a while, I found myself calling my guardian angel for help. In spite of being woken up from a deep sleep at that late hour, this kind person brought a gas can, bought me some gas, took me back to the car, poured the gas into the tank, and sent me on my way home. I was beyond grateful that someone cared enough about me to help out when I really needed it.

AN UNNERVING CHANGE OF TACTICS

After our second wedding anniversary, Dave's angry tactics abruptly changed. Now when we were alone together, he was just dismissive of me, telling me to stay out of his way and saying that he couldn't stand the sight of me. Since I'd been in a constant state of fear for four months by then, I was more than happy to oblige by either keeping myself holed up in the bedroom when I absolutely needed to be at the apartment or leaving when I sensed that the tension in the apartment was too much to handle. I didn't trust this change in his behavior, and I was always afraid it would switch back in an instant to what it had been before. His new behavior was unfamiliar and felt too much like the calm before a storm. It was a welcome change, but because of his unpredictable behavior, I remained constantly hyper-vigilant, just in case.

By mid-March, we were keeping different hours and living totally separate lives. He gave his friends very plausible explanations when it came to my obvious and frequent absences at the tavern. A part of me hoped he would move out and finally give us both some peace from the constant tension. Realistically, though, I knew that would never happen as long as I was the one paying the rent and the bills. I was still a few months away from having enough extra money to move out myself, so there wasn't much I could do except stay as safe as possible and bide my time, making myself as scarce as possible whenever there was a high probability our paths would cross at home.

Insanely, while we were keeping different hours and living different lives, appearances still meant a lot to Dave. He wanted other people to think we were together and for things to appear to be okay between us. He always insisted that we keep up the "all is well" facade in front of his friends. While most didn't have a clue what was happening, there were a few who knew exactly what was going on but stayed silent. They either condoned it, were too loyal, or were simply too afraid to confront Dave about his behavior. Dave also felt we should keep up the "all is well" facade with family, whom we very rarely saw or even talked to after moving to Everett anyway.

The people coming and going every once in a while—the ones who came to be fed and crash on the floor for the night—also continued, making it appear that "all was well" on the home front. As time went on, I recognized fewer and fewer of these people and often felt like a stranger in my own home. But I learned early on never to say anything or let on in any way that things weren't "all is well," whether it be in front of his friends or our family. Otherwise, I'd pay for it dearly later on when Dave and I were alone.

I do have to admit, there were times when the nice, gallant, caring Dave I'd met in the very beginning would shine through even during the worst of it. He was still charismatic and a charmer when he wanted to be, and, surprisingly, he would (on occasion) continue to profess his undying love for me. Sadly, I no longer cared anything at all about him. I neither loved him nor hated him. I only feared him. I knew going along with whatever Dave wanted was the only way I would survive until I could get away from him. Deep down, I'd known that ever since the very first time he hit me the previous November. The subsequent months had only reinforced that time and time again.

THE BITTER END

It was the first part of May, and I was extremely apprehensive, but I knew it was now or never. Dave and I had been at my parents' place in Anacortes for the afternoon, and in the car coming back, I decided to carefully approach the subject of my leaving.

When I first mentioned it, he shockingly said he couldn't understand why I wanted to leave him. In spite of everything that had happened, he was in total denial of the whole situation. So I started going down the list, as diplomatically as I could, talking about the things that were least hurtful first. Ironically, right after I said how I didn't like it when he took me out somewhere and left me sitting while he took off with other people, he stopped at a tavern to get a drink, and the first thing he did was walk off with some guy he'd just met then headed out the back door with him, leaving me sitting alone at the bar. I couldn't believe it. I didn't know whether he was absolutely clueless or simply baiting me.

He returned about an hour later, and we left the tavern. Then he turned off the main highway and took the narrow, winding back roads to Everett. Then he restarted the conversation by trying to convince me to stay. I attempted to stay calm, reminded him of all the slights and abuses I'd experienced at his hands over the past couple of years, and held my ground, all the while hoping I could get through this without making him angry. Then, all of a sudden, he slammed on the brakes, throwing us forward into the dash (this was before seat belts), and claimed his undying love for me as we sat stopped in the middle of the deserted road. I couldn't believe that despite everything I'd said to him, nothing had sunk in. Not once did he ever acknowledge, admit to, or take any responsibility for the things I'd talked to him about. All he could talk about was how much he loved me. I was totally speechless.

After a bit, when I didn't say anything or respond to his declaration of love, he turned to me and blurted, "So, is there someone else?" By his tone of voice and the way he said it, I could sense he was getting agitated. It was also at that moment that I realized he was incapable of ever admitting he'd done anything that should even remotely make me want to leave him. The only thing in his narcissistic mind that would make sense to him was if there actually was someone else in the picture.

In my heart, I knew the answer was no. I'd decided six months earlier that I was leaving him and had been secretly working toward making that happen ever since. I knew my reason for leaving was his mental, emotional, psychological, and physical abuse. It wasn't because there was someone else (even though I admittedly had started to become close to my guardian angel). But I knew that if I truthfully said no, he would continue trying to suck me right back into the nightmare of a life I'd been living and there would be no reason for him to ever let me go. Ultimately, there was only one answer that would allow me to finally escape this abusive nightmare. So, regardless of what I knew was the truth, I said yes.

Immediately, I could tell he was hurt, upset, and simmering with anger. But underneath it all, I was so angry at having to lie my way out of this dysfunctional marriage that I didn't care what he was feeling. I wanted to knock him down a notch, make him hurt just as much as he had made me hurt these past few years. Besides, I'd just handed him the only excuse his mind would accept in order to allow him to let me leave and still save face. I knew he would make himself out to be the good guy, the victim in it all, and I would be the one blamed and held responsible for tearing our marriage apart.

There was an uncomfortable silence. Then, after what seemed like an eternity, he slammed his foot down on the gas pedal and tore off down the winding back roads toward home. He started speeding really fast, passing what few cars there were like they were standing still. There were times I thought for sure we were going to miss a corner or hit a tree, and the look on his face was so intense, distant, and enraged. I was too scared to say anything or even cry, afraid he'd kill us both if he was distracted. It took no time at all to make it back to the apartment at those high speeds, and, to my relief, we made it in one piece. I sat there shaking uncontrollably for a minute before I got out of the car and slowly headed toward the apartment. Dave, on the other hand, had immediately jumped out, gone in the apartment, grabbed his guitar, and was already headed back to the car. As I quickly moved off to one side to stay out of his way, he climbed back into the car and tore out of the parking lot without saying another word to me.

There was no going back now. At this point, I really had no idea what was going through his mind or what would happen if I was still there when he returned. I packed a small suitcase, wrote him a note saying I'd be back in a few days so we could talk more when things had calmed down, then moved into an old sleazy motel (which was all I could afford at the time) where he couldn't find me. Although he knew where I worked, I'd already figured out that he wasn't the type to stalk me. And it was a given that he'd never dare show up at the Pizza Hut, since there would be witnesses to anything that might transpire between us.

The hardest thing about actually leaving Dave that night was admitting defeat—in essence, acknowledging that he'd been using and abusing me from the very beginning. We'd been living together for three years but were virtually nothing more than roommates that entire time, with me being the one footing the bills the majority of the time. My emotional starvation and my need to belong, fit in, and be accepted at all costs had made me a willing accomplice. I was as guilty as he was of enabling this to happen. I couldn't help but feel that it was my fault for bringing on myself the things that had happened to me. I was crushed by the fact that no matter what I did or how hard I'd tried, I could never change the situation for the better.

THE AFTERMATH

I was fearful at first but returned to our apartment a few days later when Dave was supposed to be there so we could talk. As I suspected might happen, he'd ducked out on me, but it was very apparent he'd moved on with his life. He already had a lady friend living there. Her clothes were hanging in the closet next to mine, and all her personal items were in the bathroom next to mine. While I was totally relieved on one level, I was angry on another over being taken advantage of one last time. I'd just paid the rent and utilities for May. Plus, I'm sure Dave's lady friend was eating the food I'd bought and using items in the apartment that were mine.

The next day, I called Dave and set up another meeting at the apartment. He did show up this time. Since he'd asked his girlfriend to make herself scarce before I got there, things remained fairly calm. We talked about my leaving and how we'd divide up all our things. We decided it was easiest to just take what we'd each brought into the relationship and marriage, then trade back and forth for items we'd accumulated together. In the trade, I got the extra car in return for the new elaborate deluxe stereo system I'd just started making payments on and would continue to pay off as part of the car trade. Afterward, I gave notice on the apartment and utilities so I wouldn't have to pay anything past the end of the month. My only problem was figuring out where I was going to store all my things and whether I'd continue living at the motel for a while or try to find something I could afford. At no time did I ever consider moving back to the valley. I wasn't about to give my parents the satisfaction of telling me how much I'd screwed up again.

The next week, when I felt things had calmed down enough to bring up an actual divorce, I called Dave. We met at the apartment to talk. I could tell he wasn't in the best of moods, so it was a very short and to-the-point exchange of words. I told him I wanted a divorce, and his reply was that he didn't have a problem signing divorce papers. But I would have to pay for it myself. End of conversation. Sensing his dark mood, I quickly picked up a few more clothes and personal items to get by with for the time being and left as fast as I could. I knew I had a few weeks yet to deal with everything else that was mine, but now was definitely not the time.

Because I couldn't afford an attorney, it took another six weeks or so before I had the time and money to pick up and fill out all the paperwork myself. Then he had me meet him at his new apartment in North Everett so he could sign the papers. I was a little apprehensive about meeting him on his turf until I arrived and realized he was now living with yet another lady friend and her young daughter.

After he signed the divorce papers, I gave him the phone number where I was now living in case he had any questions about the divorce. In return, he gave me our photo album, a signed copy of a record the band had just released, and a sealed letter addressed directly to me from his mother. Immediately after leaving, I opened his mom's letter and found a very detailed letter accusing me of stealing a long list of items from Dave, including the car. She demanded that they all be returned to her immediately. I sensed that Dave knew nothing about the contents of the letter. To me, it was simply her way of taking back the control over Dave she'd lost when we moved to Everett. By this time, I knew what she was capable of, and all I wanted was to have things completely over, including getting her out of my life.

Later that week, I addressed each item on her list, noting whether an item no longer existed (it had either been broken or long since disposed of) or was something we'd traded for that I was going to keep regardless. I also indicated what Dave had taken in exchange. I then packed up the remaining items and shipped them to her. As for the car, I had no choice but to return it. I'd not yet had time to transfer the title into my name and didn't notice that, along with Dave, she was listed as co-owner. So even though Dave was okay with signing it over, she wasn't about to sign it over to me or even give me the opportunity to buy it.

At this point, the only thing I'd shared with my family about the situation was that Dave and I were separated and getting a divorce. Fortunately, my wonderful grandfather came to my rescue on short notice when I told him about the car situation. A few days later, I made arrangements to meet Grandpa in the valley and had him follow me to Dave's parents' house. I parked the car in their driveway, handed the keys to Dave's dad, who'd come out to see who was there, then turned around and left without ever saying a word. That same day, Grandpa took me out to look at cars until we found a used Toyota Corolla that I could afford. He paid cash on the spot for it, so I was able to drive it home that day. I faithfully made payments on the car and the college and living-expenses loan until it was all paid in full.

A few weeks later, I ran into the tavern owner's wife at Fred Meyer in Lynnwood. She said she couldn't believe that I'd left Dave. She'd always thought I was "one of them." This coming from a woman whose husband would send her off to her mom's for a month every so often and move his girlfriend in while she was gone. Also, it was apparent from our conversation that Dave had indeed played the victim card in order to save face and made sure the story of our breakup reflected that I was the bad guy, the one who'd destroyed our marriage and left him for someone else.

Incredibly, while his version of our breakup was circulating with his friends both in Everett and the valley over the next few months—and while he was living with his new lady friend—Dave called me several times, always after the bar closed at two o'clock. He'd be drunk and/or wasted, crying and asking me out for lunch, dinner, dates—anything so that he could see me. I'd listen to his ramblings for a little bit, turn him down, then hang up. His efforts to reconnect were exhausting! I eventually looked through our photo album and realized that all the pictures and happy smiles were reflections of times and people I no longer recognized. I finally listened to the record the band had recorded. While I could still feel Dave's soul in the music, it no longer meant anything to me beyond the fact that he was a great guitarist.

Thankfully, shortly after our divorce was final on September 29, 1975, his calls finally stopped. I learned later that this was when he moved back into the rental house in the valley that his folks owned, where we'd previously lived. It was only then that I really truly felt safe at last. I buried the memories of our time together deep down inside my heart.

After taking a good look at my current situation, I realized that in the last five years, I'd given away too much of myself and my time to other people. From my first love (Brad) through my hard love (Dave), I'd gone from the highest point in my life to the lowest point in my life, plus everywhere in between. I'd veered way off track to the point

I didn't even know who I was anymore. I felt years older than I actually was, and any innocence I'd started out with had been eroded away over time. I mostly felt naive, gullible, and inexperienced when it came to becoming the true me and forming healthy relationships, let alone with someone I could depend on, feel safe with, be close to, and give my love to.

Chapter Eleven

MY GUARDIAN ANGEL

The Beginning of a Friendship

Back in late December 1974, while I was living a nightmare with Dave and in constant survival mode, my personal life outside home took a very unexpected turn.

It was a few days before Christmas when I crossed paths with someone I'd previously met but never imagined I'd ever see again. This chance meeting came about seven weeks after I'd decided to leave Dave, and over a period of time, it eventually led to a relationship that neither one of us had anticipated or planned. It just happened. Yet, considering the timing and circumstances of everything, we've both always believed that God had a plan in mind for us. It started when our paths crossed again that Christmas. This someone was the man I would eventually call my guardian angel.

I first met Leo when I worked at Condon King. He was my supervisor for a while, one of only two people who treated me nicely, like an equal, and didn't talk down to me like I was some stupid kid. At some point, I found out he had a free-standing fireplace for sale, and, knowing my parents wanted one, I hooked him up with them. As a result, he ended up both selling it to and installing it for them. When the time came, I picked up the parts and pieces at his house. I still remember his wife's and kids' peering eyes staring out at me from their front window. Leo followed me to my parents' house in Anacortes with the fireplace in his utility trailer and did the installation in one day. It felt pretty good to help my parents get a fireplace and help Leo make some extra money for his family. Although I knew him and talked a bit with him while I worked there, it never dawned on me after I left Condon King that I'd ever see anyone I worked with there again, let alone Leo.

Then came that fateful night a few days before Christmas, for which I have solely his kids to thank because they chose to eat at Pizza Hut over Shakey's that night. I was working my shift at Pizza Hut, and in walked this man with three kids in tow. I immediately recognized the man as Leo, my former supervisor at Condon King. It was a surprise to see a familiar face from outside my current work and home setting, and from what I could tell, he was just as surprised to see me. We chitchatted for a bit, they ate their pizza, then they left.

After that, Leo came by a few more evenings between Christmas and New Year's to grab a bite and catch up on things that had happened since I'd last seen him at Condon King in October. He told me his marriage had been on the downswing for some time, but it had gone from bad to worse with something that happened over Thanksgiving, the last straw in his mind. He moved out the week after Thanksgiving, was in the process of filing for divorce, and had stayed at a hotel in Everett the first few weeks. Then he'd gone to stay with his best friends, who lived closer to his house and the kids in Mountlake Terrace. At that time, his wife, Gloria, had taken the kids to Canada to visit her mother the week of Christmas and New Year's Day, so he was staying at the house until they returned.

I told him a little bit about my current situation but kept the conversation light. Then, after those few visits right before New Year's Eve, he stopped coming by. I was a little disappointed, but it was very understandable, considering both our situations at that point. I was just glad we'd both had someone to commiserate with for a short time during what had become a dreary and sad Christmas season.

In late January 1975, who should come walking into the Pizza Hut out of the blue but Leo. It was like having a long-lost friend reappear in my life, even though I barely knew him. He'd been in a sledding accident shortly after the last time he'd come by and busted his jaw, broken off his front tooth, and sustained a large gash above his right eye, requiring a forehead full of stitches. His entire face was bruised and swollen from hitting a stump head-on. He said he'd wanted to stop by but really didn't want anyone to see him until his face had healed up enough and his tooth had been replaced.

I was glad he was okay but found myself even happier that what little I'd shared with him about my situation hadn't scared him away. That night, he filled me in on new details since I'd last seen him in December. His divorce papers had been filed, he'd started a new job at Olympic Foundry in South Seattle, and he'd settled into a furnished one-bedroom apartment in Lynnwood. I sensed he was relieved to not be living in a constant atmosphere of tension with Gloria. But at the same time, he was having a really hard time, as he missed his kids something terrible.

Although he had joint custody, his work schedule meant they could only stay with him on weekends. He said it was cozy with the four of them in his one-bedroom apartment, yet it was evident he was a family man at heart and loved spending time with them whenever and wherever he could.

After that, he came in several times a week after work to grab something to eat and visit with me when it wasn't too busy. I gradually found myself baring my soul to him about some of the things that were going on at home and my plan to leave as soon as I could afford to. It felt good to talk honestly with someone about what was going on. More than anything else, I needed a friend I could trust and confide in, and he seemed to fit the bill. I also sensed that he needed someone to talk with, someone who understood at a certain level what he was going through. He even gave me his work number and home number just in case I ever needed someone to talk with.

The Guardian Angel Emerges

Over the next month or so, my home life continued to be an unpredictable and total nightmare that I still didn't have enough money to escape from. By then, Leo had become quite aware that I was having a difficult time holding it together. Yet, I continued to make it clear that this was something I needed to deal with on my own. The only time I broke down and called him was when I ran out of gas on the freeway on the way home from work. Thankfully, he was able to help.

In spite of making it clear I needed to deal with things on my own, Leo decided to give me a key to his apartment. He said that if I ever needed a place to go to feel safe while he was at work, I could go there. Although I was apprehensive at first, his trust and protection toward me meant a lot. And when I finally did start using his place as a haven, it was a relief to have somewhere to go besides hanging out at work before or after my shift, wandering through the mall, or sitting parked in the car somewhere to stay out of Dave's immediate presence.

From that time forward, when Dave was up, about, and at home in a foul mood during the day before my work shift started, I spent my time at Leo's apartment. In exchange for a safe place to be, I would clean up the apartment and do dishes when I was there. One day, I brought a box of Fruit Loops with me so I'd have something to snack on. Leo took notice, and after that, he started keeping Fruit Loops stocked at the apartment. It was kind of silly, but it became a private joke between the two of us.

As more time passed, Leo let me know that if I needed to, I was also welcome to come there even after he got off work if I didn't feel safe going home. So once or twice a week, for a few hours after my shift was over, I would stop by until I knew Dave had left to go to the tavern and it was safe for me to go home. Sometimes Leo was there, and sometimes he'd be working his second job spraying textured ceilings for his friend, Bob Diveley. When he was there, though, his company was quite a refreshing change from the abuse I was experiencing at Dave's hand.

The Building of a Friendship

As time went by, I found myself looking forward to the evenings I spent at Leo's apartment when he was home. It was more than just being thankful for a safe haven in the midst of the abuse or wanting to escape the reality of my situation. I could actually start to relax when I was there.

Plus, it gave us time to get to know each other a little better, and it was fascinating to hear more about his life, which was so very different than mine.

Leo was born at home and raised in a very rural area of Alabama where they had no running water or electricity. His family moved around a few times, but mainly they lived and farmed in an old community in the hills, where his family and one of his mom's brothers still lived with his wife and five kids. The nearest town, grocery store, and school were a two-hour drive on old dirt roads, although the church they attended every Sunday was only an hour's drive. On July 4, 1950, the house his dad had built on their farm burned down. While they were all able to escape, they lost everything except the clothes on their backs and the old pickup. After that, they left the farm behind and moved closer to town, utilities, and school. Leo worked hard, first on his dad's farm, then in high school, when he drove a school bus route, worked part-time at the local mill after school and on weekends, and picked cotton during the summers. Although he belonged to Future Farmers of America and played football and softball in high school, he was quite shy and didn't date much. In his junior year, he joined the Army Reserves. At the end of his senior year, he was discharged and enlisted in the US Navy just prior to his graduation. The day after graduation, he left for boot camp in San Diego and, with no regrets, never returned to live in Alabama.

After three months of boot camp, he was stationed at NAS Whidbey. About a year later, he met his wife, Gloria, in Vancouver, Canada, where the guys went on weekends since the drinking age was only nineteen there. After a short courtship, they were married. And not long after, he was transferred to California and Nevada for training and sea duty aboard the USS *Coral Sea*. Over the years, they had three kids: the oldest son and daughter born in California, and the youngest son born in Everett, Washington. While he and Gloria stayed married for fifteen years, aside from the kids, he realized they had nothing in common, although they did square dance together for a while early on. However, she didn't like hiking, camping, or fishing, and he didn't like watching soap operas or playing bingo.

He was also tired of constantly moving when she wasn't happy with where they lived or couldn't get along with their neighbors. He often worked two and sometimes three jobs at a time to keep up with her spending. And he was exhausted with her unfounded extreme jealousy, constant yelling, and loud arguing, as well as the endless personal put-downs he endured from her. Apparently, the worst was when Gloria would get mad at him, pack the kids up while he was at work, then take the train to Vancouver, Canada, to stay with her mother, simply leaving him a note telling him where they'd gone. He never knew when it was going to happen, although he finally learned that he just had to wait for her to get mad at her mother, at which point she'd call him to drive from Everett to Vancouver and pick them up and take them home.

In 1973, the buildup of stress, plus a pack-a-day smoking habit, landed him in the hospital for surgery to remove a bleeding ulcer and a small portion of his stomach. The doctor told him to quit smoking and lower his stress level to keep it from happening again. He quit smoking right afterward, but lowering his stress level was challenging because nothing at home changed. Ultimately, they tried marriage counseling a few times, but that didn't help, as Gloria always needed him to be solely at fault for every-thing that was wrong.

At their last Thanksgiving together, she got mad at him and locked herself in the bedroom right before company was to arrive, but not before telling the kids that he'd poisoned the turkey he was cooking for dinner. That was the final straw for him. He didn't feel like the kids deserved to be in the middle of their marital problems any longer. Consequently, he moved out in the first part of December and filed for divorce, requesting joint custody of the kids.

As we continued getting to know each other, it was apparent that even though we came from totally different backgrounds, lived under very different circumstances, and were almost a generation apart in age, we had similar beliefs, values, and interests in life. I truly enjoyed his company and the depth of his soul. Plus, he seemed to enjoy my company too.

Up to this point, we were very careful, and Leo was the only one who knew about me spending time at his apartment. We'd never been seen or gone anywhere together in public, I never came around on weekends when his kids were there, and I always cleaned up after myself so there was no trace I was ever there. I kept the curtains closed if I was by myself, and if someone knocked on the door, I didn't answer. Nor did I ever answer the phone if it rang. If Leo was home and someone came over when I happened to be there, he would have me slip around the corner behind the bedroom door to protect my identity. It wasn't because we had anything to hide. It was simply a matter of practicality that neither one of us needed any more drama or complications than we were already dealing with in our respective lives.

Yet it was touch and go at times for Leo to keep it that way. His soon-to-be ex-wife, Gloria, continued to be quite jealous even after he'd moved out and was waiting for the divorce to be finalized. She had her married girlfriends stop by when he got home from work, fishing for information on what he was up to, asking if he was doing okay, and trying to find out whether he was seeing anyone. Then there were her single friends who would stop by when he got home from work to see if he was interested in dating. Gloria herself would even show up via taxi or a friend. She'd had a driver's license in Canada but refused to get one in the US. Regardless, her visits were always unannounced and on the pretense of talking about the kids. But they more so to check up on what Leo was doing or see if he had someone there with him.

One time, I'd just gotten off work and was there taking a shower to get the fast-food pizza smell off me when I heard Leo come home from work. A few minutes later, as I was getting dressed in the bedroom, there was a knock at the front door. It was Gloria. He blocked the doorway so she couldn't come in. He asked what she wanted, reminding her that she was supposed to call before coming over.

Although I couldn't hear the entire conversation, I did hear, "So, are you too embarrassed of me to introduce me to your new girlfriend?" That meant she'd been waiting outside somewhere close and seen me go in or even known there was someone there. Still, Leo kept his cool and held his ground in the doorway. After a few more minutes of conversation, she finally left. Ironically, we were only friends at the time, but he felt it was none of anyone's business but his own that he was providing a safe place for me. I was just thankful to him for giving me a safe place where I wasn't being tormented and for keeping my identity to himself for the time being.

More than Just a Friendship

One night in mid-April, Leo invited me out for dinner the coming Saturday night. This meant I would be meeting his kids, as he wanted me to come to his place first so we could go in one car. His invitation took me by surprise, and I was anxious at the thought of going out in public together. It was only dinner, yet in my mind, it created a dilemma on so many levels. There was no denying we'd started to have deeper feelings for each other, something neither one of us had ever planned on happening. But we knew we needed to proceed slowly and cautiously. For one thing, Leo's divorce wouldn't be final for a few more weeks. And even though Dave no longer cared what I did and we were living our own separate lives, we were still legally married and occupying the same apartment. Interestingly, the much bigger issue was making sure Leo and I weren't simply getting sucked into rebound feelings with all the loneliness and emptiness we'd both been dealing with. Neither one of us could afford to be hurt any worse than we already had been. And, specifically with Leo, there were the kids to consider.

Ultimately, I met his kids that Saturday night, then the two of us went out for dinner in Seattle while his older son babysat. It was nice to be treated like a lady for a change, with dignity and respect, and not like someone's piece of property. I had a wonderful time, and Leo was a perfect gentleman. As a result, that was the first of several times we went out in public together. It was also the first time I spent a little time with him and the kids at the apartment on either a Saturday or Sunday.

Around this same time, Leo wanted to introduce me to his best friends, Bob and Renee. It felt a little awkward, since he'd apparently already told them a lot about me. Yet all I knew about them was they'd known Leo for a long time, had helped him (both emotionally and financially) when he moved out of his home with Gloria, and that Leo worked part-time for Bob spraying textured ceilings. I was hesitant to get too friendly since I wasn't sure exactly what this was Leo and I were getting ourselves into. However, I was pleasantly surprised at how friendly and accepting they were toward me right from the very start.

In addition to the deep, budding friendship Leo and I had, there was also no doubt as time went on that a physical attraction had developed between us. We were two lonely people craving emotional, mental, and physical connections that neither one of us had experienced in a very long time. I don't remember exactly when we were intimate for the first time, though I know we both felt awkward and nervous to begin with. What I do remember was how incredibly satisfying and wonderful it felt to be made love to, something I hadn't felt for several years.

The week after his divorce was finalized on May 2, 1975, Leo rented an unfurnished two-bedroom house in Lynnwood so he and the kids would have more space to move around in. It was an interesting little house, and, in the beginning, the only things he had were a small black-and-white TV, an army cot he slept on, a set of gold silverware a friend had given him, and a bird mobile that the previous tenants had left behind. Later, he bought a few dishes, a sofa-sleeper couch with a matching chair, and bunk beds so the kids would all have a place to sleep when they came over. I knew money was tight for him, since he was working full-time at Olympic Foundry and for Bob on Saturdays, along with occasional evenings after work. However, he was so much happier and way more at ease than I'd ever seen him before.

A Crazy Whirlwind of Events

From there, the next several weeks were a total whirlwind of events that probably made the outside world ask, "What the hell ARE you thinking?" When I finally left Dave and moved into the motel the first part of May, Leo emotionally supported me through the process. Although he wasn't at ease with the motel's location and reputation, he knew it was all I could afford. By the end of May, I knew I needed to get all my things out of the apartment in Everett. Considering that Leo and I were now seeing each other almost daily, we did what any practical and sane person would do. We decided we should pool our resources, live together, and see where things took us over the next several months while we were both adjusting to our new lives.

Again, it wasn't what we'd planned or intended, but it resolved a few immediate problems. Leo needed furniture and more household items, and I needed a safer place to live. This way, we would be able to see each other every day. But would I be able to live with him and still move forward with discovering the true me? I didn't know. How could I have known? My head was still reeling from my mere escape from my situation with Dave and the initial relief that came with it. And I didn't know where else I would go or what else I would do. However, because of the way Leo and I were starting to feel about each other, it seemed like a perfect solution for both of us at that moment. Toward the end of May, I finally moved out of the motel with my few belongings and moved in with Leo.

While we already knew we were sexually compatible, I'd never spent a night just sleeping next to Leo. By then, I'd been sleeping alone for such a long time that I wasn't sure what to expect or how I would feel about it. Yet that very first night, when we finally settled in on his tiny army cot, I fell asleep wrapped in the cocoon of his arms and against the warmth of his body. I felt so incredibly content, cared for, and protected—something I'd really been missing in my life. It was nice to know it was still possible for me to find the qualities I was looking for in a man, as well as a man with those qualities who also wanted to be with me.

Over Memorial Day weekend, I planned a time when Dave and his lady friend would be gone from the apartment. Leo rented a U-Haul for me, and we drove to Everett and packed up all my personal belongings, furniture, and the cats. Then we moved everything from the apartment to his house. It was unbelievable how fast this had all taken place. We were now officially living together! Although we laugh about it now, it was truly like jumping from the frying pan right into the fire, and it would test the strength and endurance of this relationship we found ourselves in, whatever it was.

Chapter Twelve

LIFE WITH LEO

Getting Used to New Dynamics, Rules, and Boundaries

It was one thing to live together as a couple and have very strong feelings toward each other. It was another thing to figure out what it meant to be a couple, especially in the early stages of a relationship. The word *commitment* was too scary to even think about, let alone say out loud. Plus, Leo had already made it very clear to me that he would live with a woman but would never marry again. Neither one of us was sure where all of this was headed, but we were at least willing to see where it might lead.

The one thing I picked up on right away was that the kids would always be his main priority, which was understandable. The second, but more important, thing was that in his mind, there would always be more than enough room for his feelings for me and his love for his kids to fit into his concept of family.

The first several weeks until school was out, we had the kids only on the weekends, just like the arrangement he'd had before. It was during this time of picking up and dropping off the kids that I finally met Gloria face-to-face, as opposed to her just hearing about me from the kids. While it was only for a few brief minutes, I immediately sensed the depth of her anger and bitterness toward Leo. It was vaguely concealed under her forced smile and an attempt to be amicable since the kids were right there. Although it was uncomfortable all the way around, it was good to finally get past that initial introduction so that everything was now out in the open.

While the kids already knew me by then and we all seemed to get along, they didn't know the twenty-four-seven me. On the flip side, I hadn't been around kids hardly at all up until then, let alone three all at once. This was a perfect way to test the waters and make sure moving in together was going to work out for the five of us. Even though I was a bit anxious, it was a good adjustment time for all of us, and I naively thought things would work out okay.

However, I also knew it wasn't going to be easy, especially for the kids, as their parents' divorce, my coming into Leo's life, and a new household dynamic with all its baggage attached had come about in a very short amount of time. At thirty-seven, Leo was still trying to come to terms with the fallout from his fifteen-year marriage. At twenty-two, I was not only trying to process my abusive marriage and impending divorce but also adjusting to a family household so very much different from the one I was raised in. At the same time, James had just turned fifteen, Laurie was twelve, and Richard was six, and they were having to get used to living in two completely opposite types of households every week.

It wasn't long before I realized my new life was much more difficult than I anticipated it would be. I had a new boss at Pizza Hut who had a much different view of how to run things and decided to take over scheduling the shifts herself. Consequently, I ended up working more inconsistent shifts, often back-to-back, with much longer hours than ever before. I was also sleeping less as I was dealing with middle-of-the-night phone calls from Dave. Meanwhile, I really wanted to make sure I could spend time getting to know the kids better and work into a consistent routine with them on the weekends.

Because of all this, my anxieties became front and center most of the time, and I was exhausted from all the chaos and change I'd moved into. Yet I already knew that I was falling crazy in love with Leo. I'd never met anyone who was so honest, trustworthy, kind, compassionate, understanding, and patient. Plus, he had such a wonderful sense of humor that even during the worst of times, he could make me smile and laugh. He truly possessed all the qualities I'd been longing for in a relationship. So I was determined to stick around to see how things played out. He always told me, as we concentrated on dealing with all the chaos, that "our time will come."

Not long after school was out, I quit my job because work hours and ethical differences had put me at odds with the new manager at Pizza Hut. Once Gloria found out I wasn't working, she decided that all three kids should spend most of that summer at their dad's as she looked for a new place to live. Sometimes it would be all three kids, sometimes it would just be Laurie and Richard, and sometimes it would be only Richard. Regardless, it was the perfect time for the kids to get to know me better and for Gloria to see how I was with the kids to help ease her mind over any concerns she might have.

That's when things really started to change. Leo wanted

a different kind of home atmosphere for the kids than they'd had when they'd lived with him and Gloria. He was determined that when they were with us, there would be no more loud arguing, yelling, screaming, or temper tantrums, which appeared to have been the standard when they'd lived with Gloria. In addition, at our house, the kids all had age-appropriate assigned chores to do, set bedtimes, and consequences for not following the rules. Previously, these things had been almost nonexistent. I'm sure the kids didn't like this change much, as it was an ongoing struggle to keep the rebellious attitudes and behavior down to a minimum. It was difficult, but Leo was trying to create some consistency in their lives and teach them some rules, manners, and respect when it came to the new household dynamics.

Leo and I continued to get along good, not that we didn't have our share of arguments. We both had to learn how to argue in a healthy way with each other, and not the way we'd argued in our past relationships. Also, there was always drama between Gloria, Leo, and the kids, with me being drawn into it all due to my simply being there. If it wasn't the constant battle over all of them trying to break us up, it was the battle between Leo and the kids or myself and the kids over new and different house rules, chores, and boundaries. It was frustrating for me and a whole different type of chaos than I'd ever experienced.

But I was determined to not let Leo slip away, as I felt deep inside there was something very special about him. I didn't want to lose him because of my anxieties and insecurities. It really didn't help that Gloria started perpetuating the lie to the kids and anyone else who would listen that I'd stolen Leo away from her. According to her, that was the reason for the breakup of their marriage, something she fabricated in her mind to excuse her own behavior and inability to take any responsibility for their marriage failing. That was my introduction to how vindictive and angry she was toward Leo and how determined she was to destroy our relationship and Leo's relationship with the kids.

As the newbie living in the household, I was beyond shocked in the beginning of our twenty-four-seven time together. As an outsider looking in, I sensed that James was intelligent, angry, and wrestling with his sexual orientation. Laurie was defiant and manipulative, and nothing was ever her fault. Richard was very anxious, quite timid, and desperately wanting to be with his dad. I was totally unprepared for all the types of rebellious behavior, especially someone going through our personal belongings and some of them mysteriously disappearing right under our noses. Then there was our personal mail being read, the kids balking at doing chores, the constant reporting to Gloria about what went on in our household, and (in the beginning) James running away to Gloria's in the middle of the night, after which she would call Leo to come and immediately pick him up regardless of the time.

Leo and I were aware that all these things were happening, yet he carefully picked the battles when it came to what to confront and what to let ride for the time being as he attempted to bring some consistency into the kids' lives during this difficult adjustment period. After a while, James stopped running away, and our personal belongings disappeared less often. However, getting the kids to do chores was always a struggle, and the older two never stopped feeding Gloria information about us and what went on in our household.

Leo and I also found ourselves having to set up some new boundaries that the kids had no reason to adhere to when he and Gloria had lived together. One thing was the notion of our privacy, as the kids had a habit of barging into our bedroom day or night when the door was closed, even though we'd asked them to knock first. We finally had to put a lock on the inside of our bedroom door so they would learn to knock first until it eventually sank in, and we no longer used the lock.

After that, we started working on boundaries regarding spending time together. We purposely set up times when they did activities and went places only with Leo, times when they did activities and went places only with me, times when we all did activities and went places together, and times when Leo and I did things together by ourselves. That way, the kids knew they would be included in most activities but that there would also be times when Leo and I needed alone time to go out or do things together as adults. Again, this was something the kids weren't used to, but it sank in over time.

As summer progressed, we took the kids camping; went on picnics; spent time with Bob and Renee, who had a son about the same age as Laurie; and spent family time with all the kids. Even though we managed to get along as best as could be expected, it was an emotional summer. I must admit there were times I questioned myself as to why I stayed and put up with all the chaos. I often felt anxious, overwhelmed, and like I was constantly being disrespected and tested to the limit by the two older kids. Yet all I had to do was look at Leo, hear his voice, and be around him to remember why I'd been so drawn to him in the first place. He was worth it to me. Thankfully, I didn't give up, and we survived that first summer together.

When school started in September, James and Laurie went back to living with Gloria full-time, and we returned to the previous schedule of having them on weekends only.

On the other hand, by mutual agreement, Richard continued to live with us, and I enrolled him in first grade at Lynnwood Elementary School, about a mile from the house.

The Negative Impact of Gloria's Temperament

Unfortunately, Gloria had an unpredictable temperament that continually and negatively affected our household that first summer, even when the kids weren't with her. One time, the kids were sent to stay with us because Gloria was checking into the hospital for a "nervous breakdown." The first night she was in the hospital, she called and asked to talk with the kids. Then she proceeded to tell them she wished they'd never been born, then hung up. So there we were, trying to calm down three upset and crying kids and saying she didn't mean it, though there were times I believed she did because of her actions. She called again the next night to talk with the kids, and this time, she was as happy as could be to talk to them. There was no acknowledgment of her previous night's comment that caused the kids so much pain. It was as if she'd never talked to them the night before.

Then there was Gloria's ongoing feud with her neighbor lady and son, which led to a scary series of events for us even though Leo no longer lived there. It started way before Leo ever moved out and always involved some kind of drama between Gloria and this lady, along with James and the lady's son. One time, the son hit James over the head with a lead pipe. Another time, he threw a brick through the kids' bedroom window. Leo never knew what precipitated those events (he'd be at work when he'd get the call), but he felt sure it wasn't without provocation from either Gloria,

James, or both. Police would be called, and things would supposedly get straightened out, but no matter what, the ongoing feud continued even after Leo moved out.

About a month after I moved in with Leo, we got the first anonymous phone call from someone who threatened to kill the kids, then hung up. We had an unlisted phone number, so we weren't sure who was calling or if it was even intended for us, but it was very unnerving. To be on the safe side, Leo called the phone company and had the number changed to another unlisted number. About a week later, we got another call from the same anonymous person, who was again threatening to kill the kids. This time, Leo and I went down to the police station and filled out an incident report. They had us call the phone company and change to a third unlisted number, then they put a trace on our line. Sure enough, about a week later, we received another anonymous call. Only this time, the police were able to trace it and find out who was making the calls. It turns out it was the neighbor lady and her son, who were still feuding with Gloria. She kept getting our unlisted phone numbers because she had a close friend who worked for the phone company who would pass the information on to her. Both the lady and her son were charged and prosecuted, although we never did find out what their sentences were. What we did know was that the calls stopped, and we were finally able to get closure on this horrific invasion into our lives. The kids had never answered any of those calls and were oblivious to the nightmare that happened during this period of time.

A Surprise Visit from Dad

A week or so after school started and a few weeks prior to my divorce being final, the phone rang one night. It was Dad. I was totally shocked, since neither he nor Mom had bothered to call to find out how I was doing since I'd separated from Dave in early May. I'd called a few times and given them the address and phone number of where I was living. But the calls were never reciprocated, and as I'd vowed a few years earlier, I'd never let them in on what was going on in my life, no matter how hard or good things were or might get. They knew nothing about what had transpired to cause me to move out and divorce Dave, let alone anything since then. Yet now, Dad was sitting just a few miles away, parked at a gas station, and insisting he needed to come by the house to talk to me about "something important." But he didn't have my address with him. He asked if I could come meet him so he could follow me to the house.

What could I say? I knew he wouldn't be able to find the house if I just gave him the address, as it was somewhat hidden in the woods at the end of an unmarked dirt road. Plus, it was already dark out. The thing was, while I'd told him and Mom I was living with a friend, they had no idea it was a man, let alone a man with children, and let alone someone they'd already met. I took a long, deep breath and finally told him that I'd meet him there in about ten minutes. After I hung up, I immediately went into a full-blown panic attack—ranting, raving, and totally freaking out. Leo had never seen me this way before, and I felt sure I was scaring both him and Richard. I just couldn't help it, as I wasn't prepared to do this, even though I'd already committed myself to it.

Panic attack or not, I needed to do this. So, after loading

Richard into the car, Leo drove me to the gas station, where I quickly jumped out and climbed right into Dad's van. Unfortunately, I could already see he'd recognized the driver, and the very first thing out of his mouth was, "What have you done this time? I suppose you went and got yourself knocked up." I yelled, "No!" But he was already following up with a lecture, asking, "How stupid could you possibly be?" After that, it became "Blah, blah, blah," since I was no longer listening. Instead, I found myself once again feeling like that young eighteen-year-old breaking up with Brad, as I was taken totally by surprise by Dad's reaction to my current situation and his disappointment in me. So, as Dad followed Leo's car, all I did was sit in silence as he droned on and on until we arrived at the house, where at least I was back in my own comfort zone with Leo by my side.

Ironically, once we were inside the house, Dad never said anything more to me about my living situation or anything else, for that matter, about Leo and me. He just got right to the point. It turned out that the "something important" he needed to talk to me about wasn't the need to talk. Instead, he needed my signature on some paperwork he was doing to set up their business as an LLC. After he briefly explained what HE needed ME to do (always the autocratic narcissist) and got my signature on the paperwork, he simply turned around and left. Still no "Hi." "How are you doing?" "What's new?" Nothing. Yet it took hours for me to come down from my panic attack and all the ranting, raving, and freaking out I'd done. And for what? I didn't understand why I was still so reactive to this man or why his thoughts and opinions continued to affect me so much!

An Important Decision to Make

After my divorce was finalized at the end of September 1975, Leo and I started to look more seriously at where our relationship was headed. It had begun with a friendship and gradually grown into a sweet, adoring love over the months we'd been living together. Now it felt like a deeper love was developing between us. Yet I didn't know exactly what that meant to Leo. He'd always been clear that he'd live with a woman but would never, ever get married again. Life had been nothing but a crazy whirlwind of events since we'd been together, which made it difficult to envision if a future commitment was even possible. Still, we were in love. And, call it old-fashioned, but just living together didn't feel like a true commitment of that love. It was decision time for both of us. So, after some serious discussion and against all odds of it lasting, we decided to get married.

We knew the planning would be easy. We didn't want the attention a wedding would create, since Gloria had somehow gotten it into her and the kids' minds during the past summer that we were already married. Also, it was a second marriage for both of us, so we wanted a very plain, simple, and extremely private ceremony with only ourselves and two witnesses. Consequently, it was just a matter of looking at upcoming weekend dates that would work for us and Gloria, since all three kids would be staying with her.

Shortly after that, I started having full-fledged anxiety and panic attacks. Self-doubt set in, and I wasn't sure if I was doing the right thing. I couldn't fathom what Leo saw in me. I didn't know if I was ready or good enough to step into the role of wife, homemaker, and stepmom in a way he would continue to love. I didn't know if I'd be able to handle everything this marriage entailed, complete with what I felt was a totally dysfunctional family, even though it was quite different from my own family's dysfunction. I wasn't sure I could deal with it all. Yet I kept coming back to the fact that I was deeply in love with Leo and truly wanted a life with him.

One of the scariest things for me was knowing this was a decision I was making completely on my own. Leo and I had kept our personal lives to ourselves since we met, and very few people even knew we were a couple, let alone living together. If it hadn't been for Dad's surprise visit in mid-September, I wouldn't have yet told anyone in my family since I especially didn't need to hear any more of Dad's rude, crude remarks. For the time being, I didn't feel like they deserved to know any more about Leo's and my relationship status other than what little Dad might have picked up the night he surprised us.

Not long after Dad's visit, Mom reached out and invited Leo and me for dinner at their place in Anacortes. I sensed she wasn't happy with me because Dad had told her I was living with a man and wasn't even divorced yet. Not only that, but this man was the same one who'd sold them and installed their free-standing fireplace the year before.

It was a bit awkward at first, but she eventually started warming up to Leo. Dad, on the other hand, couldn't care less one way or the other because he'd figured I'd already screwed up again anyway. We stayed mainly on neutral topics that night, which helped, and Leo and I didn't mention that we were planning on getting married. All in all, it went as well as we could have hoped for.

The New Man in Gloria's Life

Sometime in the fall, Gloria met Jim at her favorite drinking hole, Harvey's Tavern. In October, he moved in with her at the apartment she'd eventually moved into in Edmonds. He was a tall, heavyset, rough-looking bullshitter who'd just gotten a huge work disability settlement and was no longer working. Leo was initially concerned about how Jim would be with the kids (much the same as I would think Gloria had been about me), since he'd been married twice before and had at least three kids we knew about who didn't live with them. However, we thought that at least things might settle down with Gloria now that she had a man in her life. Only time would tell what it was going to be like.

Sadly, in November, we found out exactly what it was going to be like. We'd already planned with Gloria and Jim that we'd have all three kids for Thanksgiving Day. The kids would then have Thanksgiving dinner with Gloria and Jim over the weekend. A few days before the holiday, Jim called Leo to say he wanted to meet with him privately the night before Thanksgiving at Harvey's Tavern to discuss how the kids were doing. Although Leo wasn't thrilled about going to the tavern, he agreed because it was about the kids. Leo told me he didn't know how long it would take, but he'd be home with the two older kids as soon as he and Jim finished their talk.

A little while later, Gloria called me. She said, "You need to come get your husband. He's drunk and can't drive home." I thought Jim and Leo must not have talked very long. Also, Leo never drank that much, so it was strange that he was drunk. But Richard and I headed over to Gloria's apartment to see what was going on.

Once we got there and I saw where Leo was, I immediately got Richard out of the car and into their apartment. Jim told me that Leo had too much to drink at the tavern, so Jim had driven him back, propped him up in the driver's seat of his car, rolled down the window so he'd have some air, then had Gloria call me. Strangely, though, Leo's car was parked so the driver's side of the car was directly facing the apartment window, but it wasn't in a marked parking spot. And when Richard and I had arrived, Gloria, Jim, and the two older kids were staring out the front window, keeping tabs on their "drunken" man in the car, although no one had been out to check on him since Jim had left him there.

As the five of them continued to watch out the window, I ran over to check out the situation. Leo was passed out and partially slumped over in the seat. He'd been puking his guts out, as it was all over him, the car, and the outside of the car door. I propped him back up and tried several times to rouse him without success. I became worried that he might have suffocated on his own vomit. Finally, he woke up long enough to mumble something incoherent to me, but at least I knew he was alive. I drove my car up next to his so my passenger-side door lined up with his driver-side door. I then managed on my own to lift and wrestle Leo into my car, close the door, and leave his head hanging out the window while I went to ask Gloria and Jim if they would keep Richard for the night. Of course, they had no problem with that. They said we could come pick up the kids in the morning before our Thanksgiving dinner and pick up Leo's car at the same time. So I locked his car and left it as is before I left. Gloria and Jim thought the whole thing was funny, saying he was a lightweight and couldn't hold his liquor.

I slowly made it home with Leo leaning his head out the

window the whole way, although he'd periodically lift it to try to mumble something to me. I parked the car as close to the front door as I could get, went and unlocked the front door, and turned to go get Leo. But before I knew it, he'd managed to open the passenger-side door and ran through the front door, straight toward the bathroom. In the few seconds it took me to go back, close the car door, and make it into the bathroom, he'd already passed out in the bathtub.

At that point, although he did look kind of cute curled up in the bathtub, I was mad at him for choosing that night to get drunk. We still had things to do to get ready for our Thanksgiving dinner the next day, which, in addition to the kids, would include Bob, Renee, and their son Robert. I didn't relish doing everything by myself. However, things had to be done, so I put a pillow under Leo's head, covered him with a blanket, and finished up while constantly checking on him to make sure he was still breathing. I finally went to bed at midnight, leaving him snoring away in the bathtub.

After I got up the next morning, I waited quite a while before I finally woke Leo up, as we needed to go get the kids and his car, then get back in time to get dinner ready before our guests arrived. He had a terrific headache and wasn't in the best shape, but I was still a little mad at him and not very sympathetic. That is, until he told me his side, the REAL side, of the story. Then, everything I'd felt was a little off and odd the night before suddenly made sense.

According to Leo, he'd driven himself to Harvey's Tavern, where he found Jim waiting in the parking lot, apparently having walked there from their apartment. As they sat down, Jim motioned to the waitress, and she immediately came with their drinks. Before Leo even finished that first drink, however, she was back with a second round, and Jim hadn't even started to talk about the kids yet. That was when Leo began to feel lightheaded and dizzy. He got up to head for the bathroom, and that was the last thing he remembered. It seems Jim had gotten his friend, the bartender, to slip a Mickey into Leo's drink, supposedly as a joke. Yet Leo and I knew it was no joke. This had been planned with Gloria well ahead of time to pull one over on Leo in front of all their friends at the tavern so they could see who the "better man" was.

We both realized how deep Gloria's vindictiveness and anger toward Leo still was and how much she wanted to destroy his relationships with the kids and me. The difference now was she had Jim to help her do the dirty work. Despite it all, we made it through Thanksgiving, and life went on. We were just a little more cautious than ever when it came to Gloria and Jim.

Informing Our Parents about Getting Married

Right after Thanksgiving, we went to see my parents and finally told them about our plans to get married. Mom gave Leo a look of disbelief while Dad didn't say anything at all. Although it was very clear they weren't overly enthusiastic, they also didn't voice any objections. As for Leo's parents, who lived in Alabama, he'd already written to them about me. When he called to tell them we were getting married, they were happy for us. After that, they started writing to me. I, in turn, would write back, send pictures, and let them know what was happening in our lives and with the kids. Unfortunately, I wouldn't meet them in person until the following December.

Chapter Thirteen

MARRIAGE INTO A READY-MADE FAMILY

A Wedding and a Honeymoon to Remember

Our wedding took place on December 12, 1975. It was a Friday night after Leo got off work. At first, we weren't sure I was going to make it, since the night before, I had the worst stress-induced asthma attack I'd ever had. I ended up sleeping propped up in bed on several pillows so I could breathe. I was sure Leo thought I wouldn't make it through the night without him having to take me to the ER. Yet I made it through the night no worse for wear and woke up to a wonderful romantic note that Leo had left for me on the dresser before he went to work that morning. My asthma didn't return, and I made it through the whole day entirely on sheer adrenaline.

The wedding took place at the Edmonds Wedding Chapel. Bob and Renee picked us up and were our two witnesses. We exchanged ten-dollar K-Mart special gold wedding bands, and it was over in less than ten minutes. There were no pictures, no reception, and no wedding cake.

Our marriage certificate was our only memento of the occasion. In our minds, it was absolutely perfect and memorable.

In fact, the whole honeymoon weekend was memorable in many ways. We dressed simply for the ceremony. Leo wore brown slacks, a yellow shirt, a brown tie, a brown houndstooth jacket, and cowboy boots. I wore a blue floral jacket top with a matching skirt, a handmade blue veil, and open-toed black shoes. It started snowing just as Bob and Renee came to pick us up to go to the wedding chapel, and it was coming down heavy. I slipped on the ice as we got out of the car at the chapel, but Leo caught me before I hit the ground. Fortunately, the ceremony itself went off without a hitch, except for Bob jokingly whispering, "Sucker, sucker," into Leo's ear right before it started.

Unfortunately, the Seattle restaurant Leo had picked out for the four of us to eat at afterward, which had a beautiful and romantic atrium, was still open, but the atrium area was closed. So we ended up having dinner in a Denny's-like atmosphere. On the way back, it snowed so much that by the time Bob and Renee got us home, they couldn't get the car all the way up the hill to our house, so we had to carefully walk, more like slide, up to the house to change clothes so we could head out for our honeymoon.

We'd planned a short weekend honeymoon in Victoria, Canada, so we headed to my parents' house in Anacortes. We'd planned to spend the night with them before catching the early-morning ferry to Vancouver Island. On the way out of town, we first drove to the post office to mail our handwritten wedding announcements so that family and friends would know we'd gotten married. However, the drive to Anacortes ended up being a nightmare in what turned out to be one of the worst snowstorms in Washington history. Instead of taking the normal time to get to

Anacortes, it took several hours. We didn't arrive until around midnight, only to find my parents had drunk the bottle of champagne they'd gotten for us and had already gone to bed. Then it was a short night, since we had to catch the seven o'clock ferry to Vancouver Island. We had a great day in Victoria, just walking around sightseeing. Then we had a wonderful dinner that night at our hotel. However, on Sunday morning, I unexpectedly started hemorrhaging very heavily, and Leo spent an hour trying to find a pharmacy. He had a hard time, since blue laws were still in effect in Canada, and only pharmacies were allowed to be open. We later caught the ferry back to Anacortes, stopped at my parents' house so I could rest a bit, then drove home, picking up Richard along the way. The next day, things were back to normal. Leo went back to work, Richard went to school, and I went to the doctor, only to find out the hemorrhaging was a result of my high stress levels and everything was okay.

The only negative aspect surrounding our marriage was that a notice of marriage licenses was automatically published in the local newspaper. Although Gloria didn't get the newspaper, a friend of hers did and saw the notice the week after we got married. She called Gloria when she saw Leo's name to see if that was her ex. Gloria immediately recognized both our names and called Leo, wanting to know why he hadn't told her we were getting married. Of course, she couldn't really give him much of a bad time since she'd concluded in the first place that we were already married. However, she wanted him to know she wasn't pleased that she'd been left out of the loop.

Christmas with My Family

From as far back as I can remember, the Christmas tradition in my family meant celebrating at my grandparents' house on Christmas Eve. We'd have appetizers, drinks, and Grandma's home-cooked dinner. Then dishes were washed by the young ones in the family, after which we'd all sing Christmas carols together, open presents, and finish up the evening with coffee or juice and homemade Christmas cookies. As a young child, I always looked forward to this Christmas Eve tradition with my grandparents. Even as the family grew extensively over the years, I still looked forward to everyone getting together to pass on this tradition.

The first year Leo and I spent Christmas Eve at my grandparents' place (the kids were with Gloria), it had been only two weeks since we'd gotten married. No one except my parents had met Leo. So it also became an informal wedding reception, with Christmas and wedding presents intermingled. The evening went well—better than I expected, as the extended family tended to welcome newbies very slowly and with some initial apprehension. However, Leo charmed them all, especially Grandpa, who took to him right away and loved and treated him like the son he'd never had.

We drove home late Christmas Eve and were joined by the kids the following morning for a Christmas Day celebration. There were just the five of us, and it was fun having our own time together, eating dinner, and opening presents. I hoped we'd someday be able to start our own family traditions. But for this year, our first Christmas together, it felt like a good beginning.

Gloria's Vindictive Deception

The first week of February 1976, Gloria and Jim decided to move to North Dakota without the kids, so James and Laurie came to live with us. Because they'd been living in Everett at the time, the kids had to change schools midyear. Gloria and Jim's move didn't last long, and they returned to the area in the latter part of March, then got married on April 9, 1976. Since summer vacation was only a few months away, the kids continued living with us so they didn't have to change schools again during the same school year. After school was out in June, James and Laurie went back to live with Gloria and Jim, while Gloria felt that Richard should continue living with us. And as before, the two older kids lived with them but still spent a lot of time with us over that summer.

While Gloria and Jim were in North Dakota, Leo started receiving certified letters from the State of Washington Office of Enforcement. According to the state, when Gloria initially filed for welfare, she'd claimed that she wasn't receiving child support and didn't know where Leo lived, which wasn't true. She always knew his address, home phone number, and work phone number, as she called him all the time about the kids and money. However, the state had no address on file for Leo, and she wouldn't provide them with one. So they'd paid her the child support he supposedly wasn't paying. She received these additional payments from February 1975, the month after he filed for divorce, through July 1976 (four months after the first registered letter arrived). The kids had been living with us most of the time, and Gloria and Jim were in North Dakota for over seven weeks. So we had no idea any of this was going on until these certified letters started arriving. When the state finally "found" Leo, we started sending them detailed letters, and they began investigating more thoroughly in July 1976. We produced all the documentation, copies, and receipts Leo had. But, after two more years of sorting it all out, we still ended up paying the state back a certain amount of money that Leo couldn't prove he'd already paid because, in the beginning, he'd naively paid her quite a bit in cash.

Again, Leo decided not to get into it with Gloria over the whole thing, since she most likely would take it out on the kids. In fact, he had it in his mind to never say anything bad or negative about her to the kids, even though she constantly said things about him in front of the kids. He'd always felt that he needed to be the better person in every situation we encountered with her. In my mind, though, it was just another opportunity for her to get back at him in her vindictive way. It drove me absolutely nuts and raised my stress levels through the roof. It was so hard to keep my mouth shut. I did, though, because I didn't want to make waves with Leo, the kids, or Gloria. I was still the newbie in the house and had enough on my plate without adding anything more to it.

The Constant Shuffle of Kids Comes to an End

Right before school got ready to start, Gloria and Jim decided they only wanted to have James live with them full-time. So Laurie, as well as Richard, continued living with us, and we enrolled Laurie at the nearest middle school. That lasted less than three weeks before Gloria called and said James was creating problems for them by living there. Instead, they decided Laurie should live with them. Consequently, James came back to live with us, Laurie went to live with Gloria and Jim, and we enrolled James at Lynnwood High School. I'm not sure how the kids felt about it, but we knew this constant shuffling had nothing to do with the kids and everything to do with Gloria. It wasn't good for the kids, but we weren't sure exactly what we could do about it.

Then, on Saturday, September 23, 1976, without any prior notice, Gloria and Jim surprised us by coming over with legal papers already drawn up. She'd signed full custody of James and Richard to us. At the time, she told us and the two boys that signing over custody was just tempo-rary. She said she'd file for custody again when they were older. Yet in that same custody agreement, Gloria also signed full custody over to me rather than back to herself in the event anything ever happened to Leo.

About six weeks later, Gloria called and said Laurie was now creating problems for her and Jim by living there. They decided Laurie should come live with us, and Gloria followed up on November 22, 1976, by signing over full custody to us. At that time, Gloria repeated to Leo, me, and all three kids that signing over custody was just temporary. She claimed that when they were older, she'd file for custody of them again. That never happened. Also, as with the boys, in that same custody agreement, Gloria also signed full custody over to me rather than back to herself in the event anything ever happened to Leo.

That meant we now had full legal custody of all three kids. They permanently lived with us, and Leo was no longer responsible for paying Gloria child support. Leo and I were thrilled that we finally had all three kids with us and the issue of constantly moving them back and forth finally over. We had high hopes that this arrangement would benefit the kids and us emotionally and mentally, creating more consistency and less disruption in our lives.

After we got full custody of the kids, things seemed to settle down. Gloria and Jim would occasionally take the kids for a weekend day, an overnight stay, or a weekend stay. We'd also take Jim's two boys, who were living with them by then, for an occasional weekend day. Life fell into a half-way-consistent pattern for the next few years, although I was always on high alert for the next drama to appear.

I really loved Leo, but even after getting full custody of the kids, I came to realize that to James and Laurie, I was merely another person in the house—someone their dad happened to be married to. The best I could expect was that although they would never really love me, maybe not even like me that much, we would hopefully be able to get along well. They might even come to respect me over time. Fortunately, Richard was young enough when he first came to live with us that I already felt like I was part of his family.

Meeting Leo's Parents

I met Leo's parents shortly before Christmas 1976, when they came to spend three weeks with us. Although it created cozy living conditions, with the seven of us in our small house and only one bathroom, we made it work. And I was so happy they were staying for Christmas and New Year's, making it a special time for all of us.

I was immediately taken by their down-home country ways and loved listening to their thick Southern accent. I was fascinated to learn about their lives and more about Leo's upbringing from their perspective. We saw them only in the evenings and on weekends for the first nine days. Then Leo took the week off between Christmas and New

Year's, and the kids and I were off on Christmas break, so we actually got to spend quite a bit of time visiting. We took them to see the Ballard Locks one Saturday as the salmon were running at the time, but mostly we stayed home and prepared for the holidays.

On Christmas Eve, they joined us at my grandparents' place so they could meet my family. They had a wonderful time, especially visiting my grandparents, who were very close to their age. The only strange thing that happened was I thought Grandma was going to pass out when she saw Leo's dad. Her face turned ghost white, and she immediately headed off to the bedroom, returning with a picture in hand. When she turned the picture around, we saw that it was of her dad, my great-grandfather in later years, and he looked exactly like Leo's dad. They could have been twins! Other than that jaw-dropping revelation, it was a very enjoyable Christmas with all the family together.

The most exciting thing to happen while they were there was that our hot water tank, which the kitchen counters were built around, exploded and flooded the kitchen on New Year's Day. No stores were open, so all that we could do was turn off the circuit breaker to it and mop up the floor with as many towels as we could rummage up. Early the next day, Leo and his dad tore the kitchen counters and cupboards apart to get the old tank out. We bought a new tank when the store opened. Then they installed it and rebuilt the cabinets and counters good as new in one day. Thank goodness for experienced carpenters in the family!

The Good Times Always Outweighed the Bad

Money was always really tight for us, even though Leo worked off most of our rent doing odd jobs for the landlord and working for Bob Diveley's textured ceiling business, in addition to his full-time job at Olympic Foundry. I received unemployment checks at first, and when they stopped, I babysat the neighbor girl and delivered phone books to bring in some extra money. Leo also put in big gardens, and we raised chickens, ducks, and rabbits for food and eggs. Still, we often lived paycheck to paycheck and rolled our loose change to buy milk. The kids got reduced-price lunches at school. Yet we always had a roof over our heads, food on the table, and clothes to wear, so we never considered ourselves poor. Although it was nerve-wracking for me, especially since it reminded me of my past financial issues with Dad and Dave, Leo always found a way to make and stretch the money out to cover our bills. I knew then that I would always be able to depend on him to do whatever it took to provide for his family. Yet it continued to elude me as to what I'd ever done to deserve such a great man.

As time went on, Leo and I took square dancing lessons together, then belonged to a square dance club in Everett for a few years. The two older kids took lessons and joined a teen square dance club. Richard wasn't old enough or interested in dancing, but he accompanied us to our dances and played square dance caller. Eventually, James learned how to square and round dance call, and he called at some of the teen dances. We also went camping and fishing a great deal during the summers and spent a lot of time with Bob and Renee on the weekends. We usually spent Saturday nights playing pinochle with Bob and Renee while the kids played games or watched TV. Richard joined Cub Scouts when he was old enough, and I became a den mother while Leo became Scout Master for Richard's troop. We later became friends with another couple, Ken and Dodie, whose son was the same age as Richard. We'd have dinner together at their place and go camping together, along with Bob and Renee. Despite everything else that might have been going on, we had plenty of good times together as a family and with friends.

The kids also became part of my family, although it always felt like the older two resisted forming any kind of meaningful relationship with either me or my family. However, Mom did take to Leo over time, and we visited my parents more often, taking the kids with us when we went. We and the kids spent Christmas Eve with my grandparents, Easter with my aunt's family, and Thanksgiving with my parents whenever visitation with Gloria wasn't an issue. We often went camping with my grandparents. Sometimes my parents joined in, and we'd try to get the kids involved as much as possible. The bottom line was they were always welcome to join whatever we did with my family. I wanted my family to get to know the kids, since they were now part of my life.

Olympic Foundary Perks

The one nice thing for Leo and me during our bouts of being stretched financially in those early years was that Leo's job at Olympic Foundry came with perks. He was in charge of shipping and receiving, which meant the big trucking companies competed with each other to get the shipping contracts from Leo (i.e., Olympic Foundry). For several years, we were wined and dined by many different representatives of the shipping companies—fancy restaurant dinners and parties, major league football tickets, chartered fishing trips, you name it. It meant we did things and went places we could never afford to do on our own. It was a time to dress up and rub elbows with people who would spare no expense to make the customer (Leo) happy in order to gain the shipping contracts for the companies they represented. Eventually, the trucking companies put a stop to those perks, but it was fun while it lasted.

Will It Ever Stop with Dad?

Even after I married Leo and the kids became part of the family, Dad continued his disparaging remarks to me, which made me try to limit the interactions we all had with him. Thankfully, Leo and the kids weren't there to hear one of the worst things to come out of Dad's mouth, which happened at my great-aunt's funeral.

My dad's aunt moved from Iowa in the mid-seventies and came to live with my parents so she could be closer to her only remaining sibling (my dad's dad). She was a retired schoolteacher, never married, had no children, and was getting up there in age. Although I didn't know her well, I'd visit with her when we'd go to my parents' house, as I loved her tales of travel over the years, as well as her keen sense of humor. She lived with my parents for a few years until she passed away on July 3, 1977. Her funeral was set for two days later.

Dad, being the executor of her estate, took care of everything, including her funeral service, where he acted as greeter, usher, main speaker, and minister. Being it was a weekday, Leo was at work and the kids were at Gloria's. So I took a bereavement day from work and went by myself. It was a hot day, and I'd worn a sleeveless, loose-fitting slim black dress. It was nothing fancy or distasteful, just comfortable. As soon as I entered the small chapel where the service was being held, Dad walked up to me and said, "Didn't you have anything else to wear? You look like a whore!"

Not only was I totally embarrassed by what he said, but it felt like his voice carried throughout the entire chapel for everyone to hear, making me want to crawl away and hide under a rock! I was also angry at him for saying anything at all about how I was dressed, as I looked around to see that, apart from my dress being a bit shorter than other women's dresses, it wasn't that different from what they were wearing.

Consequently, I stayed for the short service out of respect for my great-aunt but sat in the back corner pew and left immediately after to avoid my dad. Unfortunately, that also meant I missed spending a little time visiting with my grandparents afterward. However, I was in no mood to see or speak to anyone by then anyway. At age twenty-five, I'd thought I'd finally escaped from being the brunt of his sexist remarks, but no such luck.

Having a Baby?

In the spring of 1977, as our household and financial situation began to stabilize enough, Leo and I decided we wanted to have a baby of our own. We also decided we weren't telling anyone that we were even going to try to have a baby. After all, at that time, we had no idea if it was even possible, since Leo had undergone a vasectomy right after Richard was born.

After seeing a fertility specialist and undergoing initial

exams at the fertility clinic we'd been referred to, however, we found that wouldn't be a problem, since there were several options available under the circumstances. We were so excited! The first step involved going off the birth control pills I'd been taking since I was seventeen, then waiting a few months for my cycle to go back to my original normal. For me, that was the hardest part, as those few months seemed to come to a slow crawl, and I wasn't sure I even had a normal after all the years I'd been on birth control. But a few months later, I was finally able to start charting my cycle and doing daily temperature readings to find the optimal time of the month to get pregnant. All that was left to do was watch for that optimal time, immediately call the clinic, and go in right away for the fertility procedure itself. I was beside myself when we were finally able to start the first procedure in July 1977.

We'd been told it might take more than a single procedure, so when August and September went by without getting pregnant, we were somewhat disappointed but not discouraged. However, when October went by without a pregnancy, the doctor decided to do a more extensive medical test on me before proceeding further. I started getting anxious and was even more so when they told me about the test they needed to perform and what it would entail. Yet we were determined. So, a few weeks later, I went in and had the test done. It was not only painful, but I started hyperventilating from the stress of having the test and the iodine drip they had to use. They tried to perform it quickly and keep me calm, but it was still daunting. The worst part, though, was the results of the test. It turned out I had endometriosis, an often painful disorder in which tissue like that which lines the inside of the uterus grows outside the uterus and on and around the ovaries and Fallopian tubes. Unfortunately, that was preventing me from getting pregnant, although they couldn't determine the extent of the damage and whether it could be removed. For that, I would need a laparoscopic procedure, which would have to be performed by a gynecologist. Sadly, that meant no more fertility procedures for a while.

Changing Directions for a While

While we were settling in with that news and deciding how to move forward from there, I applied for a part-time job as an educational assistant at an elementary school in the Edmonds School District and was hired starting in November. By then, James and Laurie were old enough to spend a few hours by themselves before I got home. Meanwhile, the hours allowed me to leave for work after Richard left for school and be home by the time he came home from school. It was a perfect compromise between being there for the kids and consistently making a little extra money for the household and future fertility procedures.

After that, time got away from us for the next ten months as I was learning my new job, adjusting the family to my new work schedule, celebrating the holidays, and finding a gynecologist in the area who was knowledgeable in endometriosis and taking new patients. Then, before we knew it, we were preparing for James to graduate from Lynnwood High School in June. In late July, Leo's parents sent us two nonrefundable, prepaid airline tickets to Alabama, and we started scrambling to go in August before school started. While I had the summer off, Leo put in for his one-week vacation. James was working, so he would stay at home. Gloria wasn't sure she'd be up to having both Laurie and Richard, so we decided to arrange for them to stay with my parents. It wasn't ideal, but it worked out in the end.

My First Time Visiting Alabama

In August, the height of heat and humidity season, we took our trip. Leo's parents really wanted us to come, as it had been seventeen years since Leo had been back to Alabama. They sent the two prepaid airline tickets just to ensure we both would come stay with them for a week. I always felt one of the reasons for the trip was a matter of personal pride for them. They wanted to show off Leo and his new wife to everyone, as they were so happy that Leo was in such a good place in his life. Plus, they'd taken to me and wanted people to meet me, see Leo again after such a long absence, and not just hear about us from them. Leo spent the week reconnecting and reminiscing with relatives and family friends. His parents wanted to show me where Leo grew up, all the other places they'd later moved to, and how life was for them back then. We had lots of fun, and the names, places, and time went by too fast for me to even comprehend it all. The only bad part for me was that I barely survived the heat and humidity. His folks had no air conditioning, only window fans, and there was only a small claw-foot tub, where I'd soak in cold water once or twice a day.

Disappointing News

Finally, after we returned from our trip and the kids started school, I had the laparoscopic procedure that would let us know what we were up against when it came to getting pregnant. Sadly, it turned out I had what my new gynecologist, one of the top experts in his field at the time, called the worst case of endometriosis he'd ever seen. It would require major surgery to remove all the endometrial tissue in and around my reproductive organs before I'd even be able to think about getting pregnant. It was disappointing. But since I was only twenty-six, we decided to wait a bit longer to have major surgery, and I continued working part-time for the remainder of the 1978-79 school year.

An Anniversary Surprise

It was Sunday, two days before our third wedding anniversary, in December 1978. Without my knowledge, Leo had invited my parents and grandparents to come to the house to join in on a big surprise for me. When they arrived, their ruse was that they'd been down to visit some relatives in Seattle and thought it would be okay to stop by on their way back to see us too. I was delighted, as we seldom got to see them, and I didn't think a thing about it. The house was small, but we managed to get all of us, including the kids, to sit around the table to visit.

Then came the surprise, which Grandpa almost gave away, as he wasn't aware that I didn't know about it yet. He said something to the effect of, "Let's get this party started," and I looked at him like, "What party?" Then Grandma elbowed him in the ribs, so then I knew something was up. Leo had me close my eyes, and when he said I could open them, I couldn't believe what sat before me. It was a beautiful two-layer wedding cake, complete with the bride and groom on top! I couldn't believe it and was totally surprised and overwhelmed with emotions! It seemed that everyone knew about it but me.

I'd occasionally kidded and teased Leo over the past three years about not having a wedding cake when we got married. Yet never in my wildest dreams did I ever think he'd do something like this. It was wonderful and only solidified my love for him once again. He was always thinking up and doing things to make me happy whenever he could. What did I ever do to deserve such a wonderful man?

Having No Control over the Situation

Just as we thought things had settled down between the two households with the kids, it once again came back on us.

One day in the late summer of 1979, Laurie (now sixteen) sat down at the kitchen table with us and asked Leo who he would save if both she and I were drowning. He and I were both taken aback by her question because it came out of nowhere. I also thought it was disrespectful that she would even ask Leo that kind of question, let alone with me sitting right there. Thankfully, Leo knew it wasn't a question Laurie would have thought to ask on her own. Gloria had most likely set it up and planted it in her mind. He told Laurie it was an unfair question and one that couldn't be answered, as he loved us both. I watched in shock, then, as she asked him the exact same question again. He told her that he'd already answered. She obviously wasn't very happy with his answer, but I could tell he'd decided he wasn't going to take the bait. She then told us that Gloria had said if she ever had to make that same choice between Laurie and her husband, Jim, she would pick Laurie over him. That part really didn't surprise me, as I'd always felt Jim was merely Gloria's way to not have to live or be alone, which I suspected she was more afraid of than anything else.

Laurie called Gloria, then informed us that she was going to go live with her and Jim. It sounded as if it had already been arranged and choreographed, which didn't surprise us at all. While Leo didn't think Laurie living with them was a very good idea and we still had full custody of her, we talked with our lawyer and found out the courts would say she was old enough to decide for herself which parent she wanted to live with. As a result, Laurie went to live with Gloria and Jim in Everett and started at Mariner High School that fall. She came to stay with us some weekends and a bit during the summers whenever she wanted, and that worked for us. In all reality, our household became way less chaotic with far less drama once Laurie went to live full-time with them and stayed with us only on occasion. Interestingly, however, Gloria never wanted to have the actual custody agreement changed once Laurie moved in with them. That way, she would still have the option of sending Laurie back to live with us if she wanted to.

From Renting to Owning

Our rental house was located on property that the landlord eventually sold to become part of Alderwood Mall. In early 1979, they were already digging out and putting in the utilities right up to the back door of our house, so we knew we'd have to move fairly soon. We decided that instead of renting, we should try to buy a house with my grandfather's financial help, since we didn't have that much money saved. By early summer, we finally found a three-bedroom fixer-upper in Edmonds that we could afford and had enough room for all of us. We took on a thirty-year mortgage along with a monthly payment to my grandfather and moved over Labor Day weekend. Richard was able to start the new school year at Westgate Elementary School, which was right at the end of our block. James continued to attend

Edmonds Community College with money he had borrowed from my grandpa after I vouched for him.

The only downside in moving to Edmonds was we were now seventeen miles away from Bob and Renee's place instead of three. We saw less of them as the kids got older and everyone's interests started going in different directions. We still got together with them and Ken and Dodie for dinner, and we went dancing on Saturday nights at the Eagles in Everett at least once a month. While we eventually got involved with friends and activities closer to home, we remained good friends.

Chapter Fourteen

PHYSICAL HELL INVADES MY BODY

Having a Baby, Maybe – Trying Again

Ever since the laparoscopic procedure in September 1978, life kept happening, and surgery to remove the endometriosis had been put on the back burner. Although I'd started having more cramping than normal during my periods and aching abdominal pain on my right side after the laparoscopy, it wasn't enough to affect my work or daily activities. Once we'd settled into our fixer-upper, however, the abdominal pain went from simply cramping and aching to an excruciating pain. It felt like I was constantly being stabbed with a sharp, serrated knife all the time. The doctor originally had me take ibuprofen to help ease the pain, but considering this recent development, I was scheduled for surgery in February 1980.

During the surgery, they were able to remove the endometriosis as well as a section from each of my ovaries that the endometriosis had attached itself to (a partial hysterectomy). Since I was only twenty-nine, the doctors wanted to make sure I could still get pregnant and were very careful to salvage as much of my reproductive organs as possible. Afterward, it was exciting to think that after I healed, we could try again to get pregnant.

It was late summer, and we were set to schedule a new set of fertility procedures when I started experiencing abdominal pain again, this time worse than before. The doctors weren't sure what was causing the pain, since the endometriosis had been removed. They ran a variety of blood tests and X-rays, experimented on me with different kinds of medications, and then finally sent me to an assortment of specialty doctors to rule out any major disorder or illness.

It was so frustrating not only because it was taking way too much time to find out what was causing the pain, but it was beginning to feel like the clock was running out for Leo and me to get pregnant. It also felt like the doctors were weary of dealing with me as they continued to be baffled about a diagnosis. As the months kept passing by with no answers, my abdominal pain worsened even more. Once again, it felt like I was constantly being stabbed. A heavy depression settled inside me, as there was no end in sight to finding out what was wrong.

Finally, after a year and a half of different doctors, potential diagnoses, and medications that didn't help, I was scheduled for exploratory surgery in March 1982. As I was preparing for surgery, I was scared and sad to think that what Leo and I had hoped for would never come true. Yet the pain had become so excruciating and unrelenting that all I wanted was to get this surgery over with and hopefully be rid of the pain, no matter the consequences. When I finally woke up after surgery, it was to the news that the endometriosis had come back so pervasively in my abdomen that it required a total hysterectomy to get it all out, saving me from the potential of developing ovarian/uterine cancer. It took several days for the news to completely sink in, and then came the realization that there would never again be any chance of getting pregnant.

On one hand, I was devastated about no longer being able to have a child, and I felt numb most of the time. On the other hand, the relief of no longer being in pain made me feel guilty, and I eventually got to a point where I no longer cared about having a baby. My emotions were all over the place. I was sad, angry, happy, mad, and relieved all at the same time. I just didn't know what to think anymore. Although I knew Leo felt sad about the situation and was worried about me, he already had three kids. What about me? What about us? Self-pity was trying very hard to take control of my mind and how I felt.

The one reprieve from all of this was the estrogen shot they gave me shortly after surgery. As the days went by, I began to feel much better and more rational. According to the doctor, my body hadn't been making estrogen for years, most likely since my teens. When I got the estrogen shot, it jump-started my system into what it should have felt like all along. I also started on estrogen pills, and my body felt better than it had in years.

As for my emotional and mental state, it took a while before I could accept the situation. Essentially, it meant coming face-to-face with the fact that I was the end of my family bloodlines. That may not have made a difference for some people. But, for some inexplicable reason, it did for me, at least at that point. I supposed it to be a fitting end to a childhood dominated by the feeling that neither Dad nor Mom should have had kids to begin with since they didn't like them. They didn't like even being around kids. Perhaps it was even God's destiny for me to end the cycle of feeling unloved by biological parents by being unable to become a biological parent myself. At least that was how I rationalized it.

Again with the Pain!

Unbelievably, pain returned in my abdomen within a few months of recovering from the hysterectomy. This time, it was a different kind of pain though, something I hadn't experienced before. I would be fine for about four or five days, then I would get physically sick from the pain, throw up several times over the course of a day or so, be fine again for four or five days, then start throwing up all over again. After it happened twice, I went to see my regular doctor, who told me if it happened again, I was to go to the ER as soon as I started throwing up. The next time it happened, Leo took me to the ER, where they immediately gave me a shot of Demerol (strong pain medication) until I could relax enough for them to take a series of X-rays of my abdomen and run an array of diagnostic blood tests. The results: they couldn't find a thing wrong with me. My regular doctor then referred me to a gastroenterologist.

As I saw the gastroenterologist over the next six weeks, I continued experiencing these episodes of pain and vomiting. Each time, I was told to go to the ER, where they would immediately give me a shot of Demerol, take X-rays, and run blood tests. And each time, the results were the same. There was nothing they could find wrong. One time I was even admitted into the hospital, fed only liquids, and had tubes sucking out my stomach for a few days in hopes they would find something to explain what was happening. It was extremely frustrating, as the gastroenterologist started treating me for IBS and depression, yet it was obvious to me that nothing he had me do or try was helping. By then, I'd pretty well stopped eating, which at least made the episodes happen less frequently. But the result was I started losing weight at an alarming rate. Finally, the gastroenterologist suggested that perhaps it was an emotional/mental issue and I should consider seeing a psychiatrist as soon as possible. All I could think of at the time he suggested was, *What the hell? You think I'm not physically sick, and it's all in my head?* After I left his office that day, I was so angry that I seriously debated whether I ever wanted to go back to him again.

A few days later, I started having a more severe episode. I was beside myself with pain and had vomited so much that the only thing coming up was green bile. Even though it was after midnight and I no longer wanted to deal with him, I felt I had no choice and called the gastroenterologist's service. He called within minutes, but I could tell he was annoyed with me. Yet I felt I needed his input since the pain and vomiting had never been this bad. He had me go to the ER again, but this time, because of the urgency of the situation, he wanted the X-rays taken immediately. Then I was given a shot of Demerol to relieve the pain. Lo and behold, they found something. Before I knew it, I was scheduled for a laparoscopic procedure the following day.

It was early August 1982, and my gynecologist (assisted by the gastroenterologist) performed a very simple surgical procedure to fix a problem that had kept me in its grip for the past three months. It turned out there was a narrow loop of scar tissue completely wrapped around my colon that, once I ate something and my colon expanded, would tighten like a slipknot, stopping almost all the food from going through. Thus all the vomiting. Once the scar tissue was clipped and there was no longer a loop, the problem solved itself. Apparently, every time I'd gone to the ER and received Demerol first, it relaxed me enough that the loop of scar tissue wasn't visible in the X-rays. However, when they took the X-rays before the Demerol, they were able to see the problem.

After I woke up from the laparoscopic procedure, my gynecologist came to check on me and explain what the problem had been, including how he'd fixed it. I was relieved to know that there was a very clear physical reason for all the pain and sickness and that it wasn't all in my head. A while later, the gastroenterologist also stopped by to check on me, surprisingly with an apology. He said it wasn't that he didn't believe me. But in his area of expertise, he'd never come across a case such as mine and was sorry he hadn't discovered it earlier. Although I could tell he was sincere and accepted his apology, I never did go back for the follow-up appointments that had been set up for me to see him.

Will a Third Surgery Be the Charm?

For over a year, the pain in my abdomen subsided, and my physical health (as well as my emotional and mental health) improved. Then the unthinkable began all over again. My old nemesis, abdominal pain! Only this time, it was a bit higher, where I'd never had pain before. The pain gradually increased over the next year, though I was able to tolerate it with over-the-counter medications most of the time. By the next year, however, I was once again in excruciating pain all the time. So I was back to the blood tests, X-rays, and potential treatments and medications just like before with my regular doctor and an internist. Just as last time, they were perplexed as to the cause. And since I'd already had a total hysterectomy, they ruled out endometriosis. Finally, I was referred to a surgeon for an exploratory laparotomy surgery. I was told that the difference between my first two surgeries and this one would be the direction and length of the surgical cut. The first two surgeries had lower-abdominal bikini cuts, and this one would be from the lower-abdominal bikini cut up to my belly button.

It was a terrifying prospect, but I knew this continual cycle of pain I'd been experiencing on and off for the past five or six years was dragging me down into a spiral of constant depression. I needed answers, and I needed the pain to GO AWAY! After an initial intake with the surgeon, I was scheduled for surgery in March 1985. And afterward, I finally had a diagnosis. It turned out that in my previous surgeries, they'd taken out all the endometriosis they could see. Unfortunately, while the invasive endometriosis around my reproductive organs had been removed, the bikini cut didn't allow them to check farther up into other parts of my abdomen. This time, with the diagonal cut, they were able to see and remove some endometriosis that was still in the tissues surrounding my other organs, which rarely ever happens. Apparently, endometrial tissue in your body can still grow if you take estrogen after a hysterectomy. Lucky me. That's what happened in my case.

After this surgery and eight sessions at the Everett Pain Clinic—where I learned how to cope with the residual pain assumed to be caused by scar tissue—my body was able to heal. It felt great to finally be free of the physical pain that had held my body hostage for over five years.

Chapter Fifteen

LIFE'S EVENTS MOVE FORWARD AROUND MY SURGERIES

From late 1979 through early 1985, even as I was battling all the pain and disruptions of surgeries, life continued moving forward for all of us. As difficult as it was, we attempted to maintain as much of a normal routine as possible.

Will You Marry Me?

December 12, 1980—our fifth wedding anniversary—was memorable.

Leo took me to a restaurant that we'd been to a couple times before. It wasn't that fancy, but it was upstairs and had a lounge decorated in 1920s style, with couches, chairs, end and coffee tables, and low lighting that created an ambiance that drew people in. Unfortunately, that night, the upstairs was closed for remodeling. Leo seemed a bit agitated about this. I thought it would be no problem, because their dinners were always good anyway. When the greeter tried to seat us at a center table, Leo requested a table up against the wall instead. I couldn't figure out what was going on but went along with whatever was making him antsy so we could just enjoy the evening. Then, after they'd brought the drinks and breadsticks and taken our order, Leo stood up as if he was going to leave. All I could think was, *What now?* Then, to my surprise, he turned around to face me, got down on one knee, and pulled a small jewelry box out of his jacket pocket. He opened the box, which held a beautiful single diamond on a gold band, and asked, "Will you marry me?"

I was thoroughly taken by surprise. Tears welled in my eyes, and my emotions were bouncing out of control. When we'd decided to get married, it was a joint decision that never included a formal Will you marry me?" moment. When we got married, we exchanged ten-dollar K-Mart special gold wedding bands. He'd never bought me an engagement ring, as money was tight at the time. Now, on our fifth anniversary, he felt it was time I finally had an engagement ring.

There was just one slight problem. I had a hard time being the center of attention, and at that moment, we both were. Everyone was staring at us after realizing what was going on, and it felt like they were all awaiting my answer with bated breath. I was so anxious, flustered, and unprepared for what was happening that the first thing out of my mouth was, "I can't. I'm already a married woman."

I don't know who was more shocked by what had come out of my mouth—me, Leo, or all the onlookers. There was this hushed silence all around us, but thankfully, within seconds, I realized what I'd said and started laughing, telling him, "Yes, of course I'll marry you." After that, everyone started laughing and clapping, so the night turned out very well in the end.

Leo's Parents: Losing Their Home to Fire Again

In April 1981, Leo's parents' house in Silas, Alabama, burned down, and they lost (almost) everything once again. This time, it was suspected arson by a neighbor who was in a property line dispute with Leo's dad. But instead of resettling there, his parents (he was seventy-two, she was sixty-eight) decided to move to Washington to be closer to us and their grandchildren, even though they'd been in Alabama all their lives. They packed up a small U-Haul trailer with what few items they were able to salvage, plus items that the community had donated to them, hooked the trailer up to their car, and drove across the country to move in with us until they could find a place of their own. It was cozy with the six of us (sometimes seven) in our small three-bedroom, one-bathroom home. Yet it was exciting to think about them eventually living closer so we could see them more often and help them out when we could.

It was great that we got to celebrate some memorable milestones once they arrived. We celebrated their forty-sixth wedding anniversary with them on May 1. They attended Laurie's (GED) graduation ceremony at Mariner High School in early June and a family party for James's twenty-first birthday on June 22.

Unfortunately, their expectations didn't coincide with the reality of our day-to-day lives. Leo and I both worked, Richard and James attended school, and Laurie no longer lived with us, although she often stayed with us on the weekends. While we were home most evenings, it was getting into the time of year when Leo and I spent Saturdays in the woods, gathering, cutting, and bringing home firewood for the winter. We had a real estate lady working with us to help his parents find a place of their own, but they didn't like anything they were shown. They hated the weather, as it was always too cold for them. We'd come home from work on a 75-degree day, and they'd be bundled in jackets with a fire going in the fireplace. Leo's mom was chronically depressed and spent most of the time sick in bed, so it was hard to take them anywhere or do anything with them when we did have time. By the end of July, they decided they didn't want to live in Washington after all. They packed their belongings into a small U-Haul trailer, hooked the trailer up to their car, and drove back across the country, this time settling in Butler, Alabama, closer to several of their cousins.

The Two Older Kids End up in Las Vegas

In the fall of 1980, James transferred to Washington State University and moved to Pullman in Eastern Washington to continue his education. During the summer, he lived at home, and that's when his drinking started to show. We talked to him about it, but he was twenty-one. We couldn't tell him what to do anymore. Ultimately, when it came time for him to go back to WSU for his last year of college, we sent what few belongings he left at home since we didn't know what he planned on doing.

In early 1982, Gloria, Jim, and Laurie moved to Las Vegas so Gloria could be close to her cousin Midge. Shortly after, James dropped out of college one quarter shy of graduating and moved to Las Vegas to be near where Gloria, Jim, and Laurie were now living. Sadly, he'd quit writing to Leo and me, and he was too embarrassed to let us know himself. We had to find out through the family grapevine. We were surprised and a bit disappointed that he chose not to finish. He'd struggled the last year, as he couldn't decide what he really wanted to do, having changed majors several times. Also, I'm sure his drinking didn't help. At the same time, I was upset and angry that, as time went on, James never mentioned or ever attempted to pay back the loan from Grandpa that I'd vouched for him on. In the end, Leo and I paid off the loan without Grandpa knowing it was coming from us, not James. I wasn't about to let Grandpa down in his belief and faith in people to always repay a loan, no matter how small or large the amount was.

Transferring Jobs within the School District

At the end of the 1981-82 school year, the school I worked at was permanently closed. Everyone (students, district employees, assistants, etc.) had to be placed in an existing open school. By then, I was second in seniority within our union, so I pretty well had my choice of open job positions I could transfer to. The job I'd originally wanted—elementary school math assistant at the school within walking distance of home—was chosen by the only person above me in seniority. Instead, I took my second-choice job, and in September 1982, I transferred to a middle school as a math/computer lab assistant for five hours a day.

I was assigned to one of the seventh-grade math teachers to assist/tutor students a few hours per day. The remainder of the time, I sat in an empty room to teach myself how to use the new educational computers the school was contemplating purchasing—first a VIC-20, then a Commodore 64. It also became my job to test on those computers the educational math software administrators were interested in using so they could decide what direction they wanted to go.

Finally, the school bought six Commodore 64s, and it became my job to show the teachers how to use them so they could work with their students on them. When the school bought a few more computers, I oversaw setting up and running a computer lab both during the school day and two days a week after school for students who wanted to use them.

In the beginning, I instructed the students while the teachers observed. Eventually, once the teachers learned enough, they took over instructing the students. In the five years I worked in that job, we went from six computers to thirty-two, and I was also hired to teach adult night classes on computer education twice a week for four weeks each quarter at our community college. While I enjoyed working with the computers themselves, in all those five years, I was always self-conscious and uncomfortable about being in front of and teaching large groups of people. Yet I found myself interested in working with computers, so I made the decision to pursue a master's degree in computer education.

Master's Degree

I enrolled in night classes for fall quarter 1983 at Seattle Pacific University and started working toward my master's degree. I attended classes three nights a week (Monday, Tuesday, Thursday) during fall, winter, and spring quarters from fall 1983 until I graduated in spring 1986. Bless his heart, Leo was 100 percent behind my return to college. He was my rock and always encouraged me when I started feeling overwhelmed, even though it meant he and Richard were on their own much of that time. Plus, we were dealing with my health issues. Leo would cook dinner three nights a week for himself and Richard. He'd also sometimes cook, clean, and do laundry on the weekends when I had an over-abundance of homework. Yet he knew how important it was to me to complete my degree as a path to a higher-paying job. So we all sacrificed some, but it was well worth it in the end.

Leo's Job Crisis

During this same time frame, we were also dealing with Leo's work crisis. He'd worked for Olympic Foundry Inc., a family-owned business in south Seattle, since January 1975. During that time, he'd worked himself from shipping and receiving clerk to shipping and receiving supervisor, and ultimately to purchasing agent. After nine years, he had full medical insurance benefits, a 401(k) with company-matched contributions, and three weeks' vacation a year. Then, in December 1983, the owner filed for bankruptcy. The company was sold to a Canadian firm in early 1984 and renamed Olympic Foundry (1984) Inc.

Two major events happened right after the company sold. The original owner moved to Mexico, taking all the 401(k) money and leaving all the employees with no job guarantees. And when the Canadians took over the foundry, they transferred their Canadian employees to the main jobs at the foundry. All the previous employees (including Leo) were laid off and had to reapply for the remaining jobs. Leo was only one of three employees rehired by the company, but he had to start out working manual labor outside in the parts yard. It broke my heart because he'd worked so hard to get where he was before being demoted, and now he was moving heavy iron castings around and keeping inventory of product. He was totally exhausted at the end of every workday and dropped twenty pounds within two months. I was worried about his health, both mentally and physically, but he was bound and determined to do the best job he could. Leo was always a loyal employee, and it felt to me like he didn't want to change employers, especially at forty-seven.

Thankfully, he was promoted about four months later to his previous job as purchasing agent and eventually to inside sales. He once again had full medical insurance, though no vacation until after he'd worked there a year (then it was one week), and his retirement was in the form of profit-sharing. However, after three years of profit-sharing with no profits, the company finally switched to mutual fund investments as a retirement option. Finally, at the age of fifty, he had a retirement plan in place twelve years into his employment at the foundry.

Richard Gets to Experience Alabama

It had been almost three and a half years since we'd seen Leo's parents, so Leo, Richard, and I decided to spend Christmas and New Year's 1984 with them in Alabama. The foundry was closed during that week, and both Richard and I had it off, so the timing was perfect. It was, however, an extremely emotional trip for me, as it was the first time I'd ever missed Christmas at my grandparents' house. Yet I was glad that Richard was finally able to see where his dad had grown up, be with his paternal grandparents at Christmas, and maybe experience a bit of Southern culture while we were there. We'd always hoped all three kids would have that experience, but finances and circumstances hadn't made a trip like this even possible before. And now the older two kids were already living their own lives and doing their own things in Las Vegas.

Lingering Anxiety and Hypervigilance

Although the honeymoon phase was over, Leo and I were still deeply in love. I also really enjoyed my part-time job with the school district, which gave me holidays and summers off. Yet even then, I was constantly dealing with all the medical issues that had invaded my mind and body during those five to six years, and it took all my time, energy, and sheer willpower to maintain some semblance of normality.

While my self-esteem and self-confidence had improved, I continued to feel anxious and hypervigilant, with an elusive sense of unease and anger under the surface of my being that had nothing to do with the present situation. I felt uncompromising and rigid in certain situations, and overly sensitive and defensive in others. I refused to consciously think about my past and instead stayed focused on moving forward in my life with Leo. It wasn't always easy, but I was bound and determined to keep my past bottled up tightly and deeply inside.

Chapter Sixteen

THE REVOLVING DOOR OF FAMILY

The Family

Family meant a lot to Leo and me. While all the kids still lived with us, it felt like a family, albeit a dysfunctional one most of the time. When the two older kids graduated and moved on with their lives and Richard remained with us, we became a small family of three.

James and Laurie remained in Las Vegas close to or with Gloria, who'd divorced Jim in 1983. We had addresses for both kids, yet they moved often. It was hard to keep up with where they were living. Since we had very little communication with them unless they needed something, we were always in the dark about what was going on in their lives.

Laurie

Mid-year 1984, Laurie called to tell us she was pregnant and the father wasn't in the picture. On New Year's Eve that year (when Leo, Richard, and I were in Alabama), Laurie had a baby girl she named Shelly, our first grandchild.

Then, in August 1985, when Shelly was about eight months old, Laurie called and wanted to know if she could "temporarily" stay with us until she could save enough money to get a place of her own in the area. We weren't sure why all of the sudden she wanted to move away from Las Vegas, but we agreed to let her and Shelly move in with us. After all, Leo pointed out, she was family, and getting away from Las Vegas to make a new start was probably a good thing. And with only Richard living at home, we had the extra bedroom to spare at the time.

Laurie had an airline ticket to get here, but when we picked her up at the airport, she only had a few diapers and no baby food with her. So I took her to the store to get some of both after we got home. It wasn't until we went through checkout that she looked at me, shrugged, and said she had no money, so I ended up buying everything for her. She'd been back with us a mere few hours, and it already felt like the start of the same manipulative and disrespectful behavior she'd exhibited since Leo and I first got together.

She had no driver's license, which was a slight road-block when it came to finding work. She was eventually able to land a job at Skipper's, mainly working swing shift. One of us usually took her to work, she'd get a ride home from a coworker or friend, and we'd babysit at night while she worked. We weren't charging her anything for staying with us, for the meals she ate with us, for using the wash-er/dryer, for driving her when she needed rides, or for babysitting (which was a wonderful opportunity to get to know our grandchild). That was our way of helping her out financially, and we assumed she was saving up whatever money she was making to eventually move into a place of her own.

Over time, she started coming home later and later on the nights she worked. It was very frustrating and stressful, since, in the beginning, she always came home right after work and was there for Shelly's middle-of-the-night feeding and diaper change. Now I was getting up in the middle of the night to take care of Shelly, who was a really good baby. But that wasn't the point. I simply wasn't getting the sleep I needed in order to be up on time in the mornings and function well at work the next day. We talked to Laurie about it, and things got better for a while. But she soon slipped back into her old ways.

After the first year, we finally talked to her about moving into a place of her own. However, she always either had a reason for not having quite enough money or claimed there wasn't anything available that she could afford. Then, as her "temporary" stay passed the seventeenth month, we found out she was pregnant. She didn't tell us. We found out when we noticed a slight baby bump and asked her about it outright. In hindsight, it made sense that something like that would happen after we discovered her and her boyfriend sleeping together in the living room hide-a-bed one morning when we got up. She hadn't asked us if he could stay over (she knew we would have said no), and we didn't know if that was even the first time he'd stayed over. It simply felt like the same old Laurie, doing exactly what she wanted to do regardless.

Then, in August 1988—when Shelly was almost four and Cynthia, Laurie's second daughter, was almost one—Laurie decided to move back to Las Vegas to be close to her mother again. And, with little communication from her after she moved back, it seemed once more like we were left in the dark about what was really going on with her and our granddaughters. The next thing we heard from Laurie was that she'd had another baby, born in March 1990. This time, she had a boy she named Phillip. And again, there was no father in the picture.

Brother Bob

I knew Leo had a brother, Bob. I'd heard stories and seen a few pictures of him early on in our marriage. But apparently, they weren't very close. In 1984, while I was at night class, Bob (who was a pilot) flew into Vancouver, BC, with a twenty-four-hour layover. He rented a car and drove down to see Leo. And that was the first time Leo had heard from or seen his brother in twenty years.

In the months to come, I finally got to meet him as he came to see us a few more times when he had layovers. Then, in August 1985, just after Laurie and Shelly arrived to stay with us, Bob asked if he could temporarily stay with us too. He was divorced by then and had no children—only his two outdoor (trained search-and-rescue) German shepherds. Having just quit his job at the cargo carrier company he'd been a pilot for, he needed a place to stay on and off every week or so (and someone to take care of the dogs while he was gone) as he flew different places around the country, looking for another pilot's job. Leo and I talked it over, and since he was also family, our household grew even more.

Once he moved in with us, I immediately sensed an underlying, unspoken friction between Leo and Bob that apparently had been there since childhood. In the beginning, I didn't know him personally or anything about him, so he and I seemed to get along fairly well. Yet it wasn't long before reality set in and things got a bit more complicated. He was always extremely secretive about his past and what it was that he'd done after his stint in the army as a helicopter pilot in Vietnam. If anybody called looking for him, we were told to say we hadn't seen him and that the last we'd heard, he was somewhere in South America. I never knew if it was a joke or not, but he was somewhat quirky. So we didn't want to rattle his cage any.

Since we didn't have any more extra bedrooms, the living room became his bedroom. Even though we had a nice hide-a-bed in there, he preferred sleeping in a sleeping bag on the floor. He used our closet to hang his clothes and store his one small suitcase. He never ate with us, instead buying his own food and coffee beans to grind because our food and coffee weren't up to his standards. He was always trying to educate us on a healthier and more intellectual lifestyle. And he definitely had a way of trying to make us all feel inferior, with his need to be right no matter what was said or discussed.

Bob didn't get along with Laurie and wasn't fond of babies. When he was home, he would tell us about every little thing she did or didn't do when we weren't there. During this same time frame, we also started noticing a change in Richard's behavior. It seemed there was more friction between him and Leo, which Bob would inevitably point out. At times, it felt like I was living in a house full of tattling and misbehaving children. I know it was hard on Leo to have all this going on in our home, but it was literally driving ME nuts!

Bob always walked everywhere or depended on us to take him to the airport any time he needed to fly somewhere. As time went on, it became apparent that he needed a car of his own. He found a used car, and I cosigned the loan. He said he'd give me the money to make the payments for him. At first, he made several payments. Then it was hit or miss when it came to him getting all the money to me, let alone on time. So I ended up making the payments out of our budget.

Leo's Mom and Dad's Ultimate Decline

Leo's mom had been sick for a long time. It was something to do with her heart, although none of her doctors could pinpoint the exact problem. For several years, his dad had patiently taken care of her—doing all the shopping, cooking, cleaning, and gardening and taking her to all her doctor's appointments. Then, on February 20, 1987, she went to lie down for a nap after dinner. And when Leo's dad went to check on her a short time later, he found that she'd passed away. Although there was no autopsy, the doctors concluded from her age and medical history that she'd died of a massive stroke.

Bob, Leo, and I flew back to Alabama to attend her funeral, help Dad with the insurance paperwork, go through her things for donation, and make some minor repairs on their mobile home. Everything went smoothly for the first few days. But then Bob got into an argument with his dad about (of all things) the correct way to fix a broken showerhead. Instead of staying to help, Bob immediately packed up his things and left to go back to our house, leaving the remaining tasks for us. It was very sad, especially for Leo's dad, that Bob couldn't set aside his need to always be right. I learned, however, that's what usually happened when he came to visit. He and his dad never did see eye to eye.

Later that year, Bob got a full-time pilot's job and was

gone for quite a while. During that same time frame, Leo's dad decided to sell everything he owned—with the exception of his car, which he left with his niece Margaret and her husband, Carl—and came to live with us.

By this time, he'd been diagnosed with prostate cancer. He had been undetected until it had already spread to his back, hip, and leg bones. While still in Alabama, he had both chemo and radiation. Once he moved in with us, though, he was having only palliative radiation to help ease the pain. I would take him to radiation when I got off work, but it was excruciatingly painful for him, as he couldn't sit comfortably in a car anymore and often had to have the seat totally reclined the whole time. It was heartbreaking to watch as nothing helped. Since we were both working full time, he had no one to keep him company during the weekdays except for an occasional visit from Richard or our neighbor lady. Eventually, in early 1988, he decided to move back to Butler, Alabama, into an assisted living facility that was located within a block of where Margaret and Carl lived. Carl absolutely loved him and had just retired, so he walked to the facility to spend time with him every day. Although we missed having Leo's dad with us, at least we knew he was well cared for at the assisted living facility and had a daily visitor.

Right after Leo's dad returned to Alabama, Bob briefly came back to stay with us. He'd decided to buy a house in Montana and asked Leo for a $5,000 loan to help with the down payment. Although he still owed us money for his missed car payments plus a few years left of car payments themselves, he assured us that as soon as he got settled and returned to work, he would start paying us back. Leo and I trusted him (at that point), so we lent him the money, and he bought a house in Kalispell.

Bob flew back to see his dad a few days before his eightieth birthday and called to give us a heads-up that he wasn't going to make it much longer. We tried talking to him on the phone for a little bit, but it was apparent that he was no longer fully aware of things. He died September 29, 1988, the day after his eightieth birthday. Since Bob was already there, he cleaned out his dad's room, donated his usable belongings, and signed his car over to Carl, who had faithfully visited him every day in the assisted living facility. Leo flew back immediately so he and Bob could take care of all the funeral arrangements and remaining bills. I flew back two days later, just in time to attend the funeral, support Leo through this very difficult time, and pay my last respects. Afterward, Bob immediately wanted to go close out his dad's bank account. Once he got a check for his half of the money, he said his goodbyes and went back to Montana. We stayed with Margaret and Carl for a few more days to visit, tie up loose ends, and drive down memory lane before we returned home.

Richard

After Richard graduated from Edmonds High School in 1987, he continued to live with us on and off for a couple of years while he worked at a movie theater, attended the Art Institute in Seattle, and tried out sharing an apartment with a few different roommates. When he finally moved out for the last time, he ended up working and living a short distance from us, so we always remained close with him over the years.

Chapter Seventeen

MEANWHILE, A NEW JOB IN THE
SCHOOL DISTRICT

In August 1987, I was hired full-time for an administrative job as the special education data processing/records specialist for the Edmonds School District. I wasn't sure when I first applied for the job if I'd be able to handle working seven and half hours a day and having only three weeks off during the summer versus the five hours a day and three months off I'd had with my previous job. However, the kids were now all grown and out on their own, and the pay and benefits were good. Plus, it was another one-of-a-kind job entering data for state and federal funding reports for special education students in the district, as well as organizing and filing all the individual paper record folders for each special education student. I was happy to finally have an office to myself, with a door that closed, which worked great for me since it gave me peace and quiet to do my work without anyone watching over my shoulder.

When I took the job, I didn't realize that, while it was a much more challenging job that I enjoyed, it was also a very intense and stressful job—especially the week the reports came due on the first of every month. It was a work cycle that started out busy but calmed down after the first of every month. Then it continually built to a crescendo, with a frantic flurry of paperwork and phone calls by the third week of the month to get the information I needed from all the psychologists, audiologists, physical therapists, and occupational therapists in the district—approximately seventy-five staff members total.

My work evaluations were always great because of my attention to detail, organizational skills, and computer knowledge, which was essential for this job. Even though I had sick leave, I couldn't afford to miss work the last week or first day of each month. Since it was a one-of-a-kind job, no one else knew how to enter the data or run the funding reports. My attention and commitment to performing these tasks translated to my supervisor as dedication. I sometimes felt it was taking a huge toll on my health, as my workload became heavier due to an increasing number of students and staff. Yet I continued doing my job, and doing it well.

Chapter Eighteen

OUR TIME FINALLY CAME

I n the fall of 1987, Leo and I decided once again to take up square dancing. We took lessons to refresh our memories, then joined the Checkerboard Squares in Edmonds. Through the square dance club, we originally met a group of six to eight couples we would become close friends with over the years. In addition to the caravans, holiday dances, and activities with the club, as friends, we would plan additional activities. We'd have five-course progressive dinners, where each course was served at a different person's house, birthday/anniversary/no occasion parties, camping trips, and overnight destination trips. We officially named this group Tacky Tours, and the only requirement was you had to wear an outfit where nothing matched for as long as you were literally traveling on the road. We'd go on day trips to local places and weekend destination spots to places like Victoria, BC, and Whistlin' Jack's Outpost & Lodge in Naches, Washington. Eventually, the number of people changed from the original eight couples, fluctuating both up and down as new people joined in and other people either dropped out, moved out of the area, or passed away. Throughout it all, we maintained life-long friendships, especially with DJ and Sheri, and Andy and Lydia.

Even with the kids out on their own and both of us working full-time, we would go camping on weekends, sometimes with friends, sometimes with my grandparents, and sometimes just the two of us. Now, though, it didn't always involve blue tarp camping. We were finally able to afford a tent trailer, later sold that for an older motorhome, and eventually sold that for a used fifth wheel. Beyond camping, we also started taking vacations to places we'd dreamed of going.

When Richard graduated from high school, as a graduation present to himself, he and a friend decided to go on a vacation to Disneyland. Not long after he took his trip, Leo and I decided it was time that we finally take an actual vacation of our own to somewhere we'd never been. I'd always wanted to go to Hawaii, and it just happened that Olympic Foundry owned a condo in Honolulu that management could use for free. All we had to do was reserve our week, then pay for our own airfare and save up spending money. In July 1987, Leo and I spent a romantic week on Oahu, relaxing on the beach, taking in the island sights, and making memories of a lifetime together. To this day, it remains my absolute favorite vacation we've ever taken, perhaps because it felt like the honeymoon we would have liked to have taken but couldn't afford when we got married almost twelve years earlier.

Two years later, we went to Oahu again for a week with friends DJ and Sheri to celebrate their twenty-fifth wedding anniversary. Then Leo and I went on to Maui for another week. That was followed by a week-long West Caribbean cruise in 1990, a week-long Mexican cruise in 1991 with Bob and Renee to celebrate our sixteenth wedding anniversary, and a two-week Alaskan cruise/land tour in 1993. Plus, for several years, we started making yearly two-to-three-day trips to Reno with Bob and Renee.

There would also be many shorter weekend trips (Winthrop, Leavenworth, Ocean Shores, Long Beach, Cannon Beach, Vancouver, Victoria) in between longer trips (Yellowstone, Grand Tetons, Crater Lake, Glacier Park, San Francisco, Las Vegas, Missouri, Alabama, Tennessee, and Washington, D.C.) over the years, but they would come later.

We even took two long driving trips with our friends Andy and Lydia in their motorhome. For the first trip, we headed for Cabo San Lucas via the Southwest states but turned around partway down the Baja. It was too hot, we had a hard time finding gas stations, and the motorhome broke down in the middle of nowhere. (Thankfully, Andy and Leo fixed it.) But I think the main reason we turned around was my panic attack and emotional breakdown, which included me screaming, "Take me to the nearest airport!" Instead, we all voted to head back to Ensenada and spend a few extra days before meandering back up the West Coast.

On the second trip, we drove into Canada-Yukon-Alaska across the Top of the World Highway and back. Aside from a blown tire, a broken windshield, long drives on deserted "off the beaten path" dirt roads, giant mosquitoes, and coasting into gas stations on fumes, we did great.

We enjoyed each of our trips and wouldn't have done them any different, as they were all fun, exciting, and unique. I was especially thankful that we decided early on in our marriage, especially with our age difference, that once we could afford to, we would travel as much as we could while we were both financially able and healthy enough to travel.

Chapter Nineteen

SHARING A LAST DAY WITH MY LOVING GRANDPA

I loved my grandpa as much as any person can love someone. He was a quiet man, spoke very little, but had a heart of gold, at least when it came to me. He was also one you'd never want to cross, as it seemed he could hold a grudge for eternity. But I never had to worry about that. I always felt he loved me as much as I loved him.

It was a Tuesday night when I got the call from Mom that Grandpa had been moved from home to the hospital. He had been in a hospital bed in their living room at home for several months, but now his time was near. As a lifetime smoker of Lucky Strikes unfiltered cigarettes, he'd developed emphysema and lung cancer in his later years. Once the cancer developed, doctors convinced him he needed to quit smoking. That lasted a very short time, however, as his body couldn't withstand the addiction withdrawal at his age. The doctors gave up, and he continued to smoke for the remainder of his days when he wasn't hooked up to oxygen.

Mom said she was just giving me a heads-up about the inevitable, but I took off work Wednesday to go see him, sixty miles away, in United General Hospital. He seemed in good spirits, so I sat with him most of the day, just holding his hand and quietly watching TV with him. When I left that night, we both knew I would never see him again.

I got the call the next afternoon that Grandpa had passed away that morning, Thursday, March 28, 1991, at the age of eighty-three. I was so glad I'd taken the time to be with him, say goodbye in our own special way, and find closure by being at his side the day before he crossed over.

Chapter Twenty

BROTHER BOB RETURNS

Things for Bob had not gone well since their dad died. He had totaled the car on one of his trips to and from Montana. Apparently, it was extremely foggy, so he'd slowed down to match the weather conditions. However, others didn't, and he became the first car in a multi-car pileup. When the tow truck came, it caused a secondary slowdown, and there was another multi-car pileup in the same location in which someone standing on the side of the road was hit and killed. Although I never understood it, Bob was being sued for a wrongful death. In the meantime, he had quit working as a pilot to take care of his aging German shepherds (to him, they were immediate family). Without any income, his house went into foreclosure in 1991, and he was forced to move.

At that point, he asked if he could come live "temporarily" with us again until he got back on his feet. He never got back on his feet, though, as his focus became a lawsuit against several airline companies (age discrimination and forced retirement at a certain age) and the lawsuit against him as a result of the car accident. For me, it was nerve-wracking dealing with his constant coming and goings and never knowing exactly when he'd be there or not, as he was so secretive about what all he was doing. And as before, I felt his condemnation of our lifestyle and intelligence. While all this was taking place, he lived with us on and off through mid-1994, until we ultimately had to ask him to find another place to live, giving him a month's notice. After he'd lived with us on and off since 1985, we finally had enough. I felt he was taking advantage of our hospitality and basically mooching off us.

Being the person he was, however, he simply moved into our son Richard's shed (Richard was renting the house across the street from us at the time). Then he told our neighbors we'd kicked him out. He claimed he was broke with nowhere to go, so he was forced to live in the shed. He forgot to mention to the neighbors, though, that he was also breaking into our house after we went to work to do his laundry, use the bathroom, take showers, and make himself something to eat/drink. While he had met several people he probably could have stayed with, that most likely would have cost him money. And he must have had some of that tucked away, as he was always able to travel a lot and buy his own food, toiletries, and clothes.

A few weeks after he moved out, Leo went out the back door to go to work and heard a weak whisper-like voice calling out, "Help me, help me!" coming from inside our motorhome. It had been broken into, and when he opened the door, there was Bob lying on the floor, all bloody and beaten to crap. Leo helped him into the house. I was up by then, so we got him settled on the recliner to assess what his injuries were. Of course, he absolutely refused to go to the hospital, so the first thing was getting him patched up the best we could. He was barely able to breathe, and it was apparent he had several broken bones. But all he wanted was to have his torso wrapped tight. He also had several head wounds that needed stitches, but he just wanted them pulled together and bandaged. He had massive bruises on his calves, which we could do nothing about. At least we had enough supplies to do his ribs and bandage up his face. Then came the "What the hell happened to you?" out of my mouth, along with "You better not die on us!" I was so upset, torn between sympathy for all his pain and anger that we'd been pulled back into his screwed-up life because of his actions.

When we moved into our area in 1979, it was a safe array of family homes and affordable apartments between an elementary school and the high school. Unfortunately, in the last few years, the area had become infiltrated with gang and drug activity. Bob, now in his early fifties and extremely fit, said he was walking down the main street a few blocks over in the middle of the night (why then?) when a car with three young guys drove by and yelled something at him, so he yelled something back at them. Before he knew it, the car turned around and drove up next to him, and out came three guys with a baseball bat. A fight ensued, and, according to Bob, who shared no other info, once he got the baseball bat away from them, the three guys looked worse than he did before it was over. They crawled into their car and left quickly before the police arrived, while Bob limped back to our place and broke into the motorhome, where we found him that morning.

For the next week, Bob lived in the recliner as we continued to change the wraps and bandages, feed him, and make him as comfortable as possible. When it came time for him to leave, as usual, he didn't know where he was going or what he was going to do. Although, he didn't go back to living in Richard's shed.

After that, Bob would occasionally stop by to talk with me when Leo wasn't around. One day, he called me to come meet him at a small coffee shop in Edmonds. When I got there, he wanted to know if I thought Leo might lend him an additional $5,000, as he was trying to do some investing to recoup all the money he'd already gone through. I was so tired of being the go-between with him and Leo that I told him he'd have to ask Leo directly and leave me out of it. Eventually, he set a time to meet Leo at the coffee shop, and, though I never knew exactly what was said, Leo told him NO. Then, apparently, somewhere in the conversation, Bob told him that unless he lent him the money, we'd never get any of the money back that he already owed us. Leo ultimately refused to lend him any more money at all. And, as Bob had indicated would happen, he never did pay back the original $5,000 he owed us from the down payment on his house in Montana or the money for the car loan I'd had to pay off after I'd cosigned for it in the beginning. Consequentially, by May 1995, we were no longer of any use to him and would never see or hear from him again.

Chapter Twenty-One

THE EFFECT OF THE NARCISSIST'S ACTIONS IN MY LATE YEARS

Dad's Health

Dad had never taken very good care of himself. He had a food addiction, especially sugar, and he'd always worked with his mind, not his body, so he never exercised. He was overweight and pre-diabetic, had high blood pressure, and experienced his first heart attack when he was in his early fifties. He had several more over the next several years before finally having double bypass surgery in April 1983 at the age of fifty-nine. After eight days in the hospital and recovery at home, he went right back to the same lifestyle he'd had before. He told me around that same time, "When I was young, a fortune teller told me that I'd be dead at fifty-nine." Now that he'd reached that age and was still alive after heart surgery, he proclaimed he was on borrowed time, so he could do whatever he wanted. I never knew whether it was true or not, but he believed it and acted accordingly. (As if that wasn't what he'd been doing all along.)

After that, he developed abdominal hernias, which the

doctors meshed the first time but couldn't thereafter because of his weight. There was no longer anything to attach the mesh to. He was in a lot of pain from the hernias, but there was nothing more they could do for him except tell him to lose weight. A few years later, he was diagnosed with prostate cancer. They did a radical prostatectomy to remove his prostate before the cancer spread, but not without the side effect of partial loss of bladder control. Most of the time, he lived in a bathrobe or long dashiki, and he wore abdominal belly belts for the hernias, although he refused to wear pads or Depends for bladder control. He hated that he wasn't in control of his own body functions, and it seemed to fuel his narcissistic behaviors even worse. Mom ended up taking care of him and cleaning up after him, which only increased her anger, so they argued more often as the years went by.

On one hand, I felt guilty that I couldn't be there more for Mom, but I was working full-time. Plus, they would still go to Quartzite every winter and set up for business for three to four months. On the other hand, I'd gotten to the point where it was difficult to be around Dad. If we did go see them or spend a weekend with them, I would avoid him as much as possible. Instead, I'd try to spend more time with Mom and especially my loving grandparents, who lived just a few houses down the road.

Dad's Retirement

Back in 1973, Dad retired from his state job to go full-time into the bead business. He closed down the Native American handicraft and bead shop and decided to deal strictly in the bead business. They bought from my grandma my great-grandparents' old property east of Sedro-Woolley, had a mobile home brought in, and moved everything over from Anacortes to begin that journey. After that, Mom quit her job as a receptionist for the doctor in Anacortes and joined Dad full-time in the bead business.

From that point on, Dad always took care of all the accounting, the checkbook, correspondences, and ordering and pricing the merchandise. He also did most of the sales and helped pull orders. It was Mom who had to make sure the counting, weighing, packaging, and labeling of all the merchandise got done. She also pulled the orders and helped with sales. That, of course, was in addition to all the cooking, cleaning, laundry, and taking care of the garden, yard, acreage, and Dad.

Then, in 1989, at the age of sixty-five, Dad decided, because of his health, to retire from the business and draw his Social Security as well as his state retirement pension.

If that wasn't a heavy enough burden on Mom, it turned out that Dad had paid into his Social Security all those years but hadn't paid anything into Mom's from 1977 forward. As a result, she was short credits to even draw Social Security. So Dad had the business put in her name and showed her the basics of what else she needed to do (the tasks he'd always done), although he unofficially continued to oversee it all whenever he wasn't doing whatever he wanted to do. Unfortunately, Mom had to work another five years, until she turned sixty-five, to earn enough credits to draw her own Social Security. At least her check was more than half of Dad's would have been, so that worked in her favor. The only halfway decent thing that came out of this was that Dad had opted for his state retirement income to be less so that Mom would receive a survivor's benefit for the remainder of her life if he predeceased her. It wouldn't be much, but it would be something.

Dad's Move to Korea

Dad had always had an affinity for Korea. As early as 1972, he'd started importing beads from Korea for their business. In 1976, he (and Mom) took a two-week trip to Korea, the first of many he would take over the next two decades. Most times, Mom accompanied him on these trips. But sometimes, he'd travel there on his own for several weeks at a time, like the time he decided to try his hand at sumo wrestling (apparently, he was pretty good at it). He seemed totally enamored with the people, the food, the culture, and the scenery.

A few years after he retired but before Mom was eligible for retirement, Dad decided out of the blue that he was going to temporarily move to Korea in hopes of a cure for the side effects of his radical prostatectomy, which were worsening over time. (He'd read about new miracle techniques being done there.) He cashed in his IRA, booked his airline ticket, packed up his things, and left Mom to deal with everything at home (including the business) with no indication of where he would be staying or when he was coming back.

My sister and I knew nothing about any of this until Mom told us quite a while after he'd already been gone. Apparently, he'd written her a few letters to say he was doing okay, so at least she knew where he was staying. However, he didn't know yet when he was coming back, claiming he needed more time. Although Mom tried to keep up a good face, it was extremely hard on her not knowing where things stood between them.

My sister and I tried to convince her that she should divorce him on the grounds of abandonment, which, of course, fell on deaf ears. She was bound to see it all through no matter what happened. I'm not sure exactly how many months that went by, but when Dad finally blew through all his IRA money and decided to come home. And as I thought, Mom took him back in, and nothing was ever said again about his time in Korea.

On the night his flight came in from Korea, his first stop before going home was our house in Edmonds. He was all excited and wanted to show us pictures of "his girls," who'd been working to improve his health and help with the side effects of his prostatectomy. As was typical with Dad, not only was the topic inappropriate for a father-daughter conversation, but the pictures of scantily clad "girls" with their arms draped over a shirtless Dad were outright disgusting. Even Leo had a hard time trying to figure out what the hell was going on or why Dad felt the need to show us the pictures in the first place. Thankfully, his visit was very short, but the images were burned into my brain for a very long time.

After Dad returned home, he and Mom lived off his Social Security, his small pension, and what little income the business was bringing in. Even though Mom wasn't sixty-five and couldn't yet draw Social Security, Dad put the business up for sale, hoping it would sell quickly so they'd have more disposable income. He even asked us if we were interested in buying it, as he had several times over the years. Once again, our answer was no, as we both had full-time jobs and our life and friends were in the Edmonds area. Unable to sell the business itself, they eventually started bulking out the merchandise with plans to have it all sold by the time Mom retired.

Chapter Twenty-Two

THE VOLCANO WITHIN ERUPTS

Through all my years with Leo, beneath the overall happiness and contentment of my life, there was always an undercurrent of anger that I'd managed to control and stuff down inside, as it really had nothing to do with my present life. I wasn't sure exactly what all it was about, but when I started finding myself getting into angry, often irrational arguments with Leo (like the one about the correct way to clean a stove burner), I knew it was time to find out. I talked with Leo about my going to counseling, and he supported my search for answers. I warned him that I didn't know what kinds of things counseling would unleash, but it was something I needed to do regardless of the outcome.

I started first with the six free counseling sessions offered through the school district, only to realize that we were just barely scratching the surface of my anger. It turned out that this anger came from all the trauma and emotional, mental, and psychological abuse I struggled with at Dad's hands. After the six sessions, it was suggested that I continue on with counseling, and I was referred to a private counselor.

At first, it wasn't too difficult to talk with the counselor about some of the less traumatic issues. As time went on, however, the issues got more difficult to express out loud, let alone process, and I became SO angry with Dad. Yet, instead of taking it out on him, I got angrier with Leo, myself, and seemingly everyone around me. I began to hate my life, just wanting to hit a restart button and begin it all over again with a different father and a happier childhood. I could hardly eat and lost a lot of weight, and coworkers asked me if I was okay. I wasn't ready yet to explain anything, so I'd just say I was going through a difficult time. In reality, all I wanted was for people to stop asking me questions and leave me alone!

At one point, I even contemplated moving out and finding a place of my own where I could figure things out without interruptions or anyone around. In the end, I decided not to because, underneath it all, this wasn't a problem between Leo and me. It was between Dad and me. Consequently, my only true reprieves from all the emotional crap running through my head came from delving into work, then taking a lot of time for myself, alone and away from the house, to work things through. That meant staying after hours at work, parking down by the beach, mindlessly driving around, or wandering through stores or the mall.

I knew this was my battle to fight, and I really needed to see it through for the sake of my own sanity. But it was taking way too long, longer than I'd expected. It felt like one step forward, two steps back, one step back, two steps forward. At the same time, I felt the need to maintain as much normalcy as possible between Leo and me, which was getting extremely difficult. We still square danced twice a month, went on our two-week cruise/land tour of Alaska, and took a weekend trip with friends to Seaside, Oregon. They were all enjoyable events, yet I could feel the strain of it all and the distance between Leo and me widening. I knew our marriage was on the line if I couldn't get past all the trauma regarding Dad and deal with the anger once and for all.

As I continued with counseling, I kept reaching deeper and deeper into my psyche to rid myself of the immense anger I felt toward Dad. After dredging up various issues with my counselor for over a year, I was finally able to make a major breakthrough inside my mind regarding my anger— a breakthrough that set me free to truly begin the healing process. There was also a very strange incident around that same time that convinced me I was on the right track after decades of hanging on to some deep anger that I really should have dealt with years before.

Leo and I were at a curio shop in Cannon Beach when I happened to look up at Leo as he was checking out something in the next section over. As I stood there focusing on his face, I felt a pulsating energy of pure love enveloping my whole body, reminding me how very much I loved Leo and confirming that everything I'd always felt about him was true. While I continued to focus on his face, that feeling vanished. As my eyes closed, I started feeling a sensation of water flowing down my body, starting at the top of my head and going right down to the bottom of my feet, like I was standing under a waterfall. Then, as suddenly as it had appeared, this sensation disappeared. I realized Leo was now standing by my side. Of course, I knew this had happened only in my mind, yet there was no denying it felt very real, as if all my anger was being washed away.

All I knew was that immediately after this incident, I knew for sure that Leo was my forever love and would always support and stand by me as I dealt with all my issues. I also no longer felt the anger toward Dad. I still didn't like him, wouldn't forget what he'd done, and wasn't into forgiving him yet, but at least I no longer felt the anger that had been with me since childhood.

I continued seeing the counselor for quite a while after my breakthrough, and we started to concentrate more on building up my self-confidence, self-esteem, and self-image, as well as identifying what appropriate behaviors and boundaries looked like, especially when I had to deal with Dad. As my frame of mind improved, the tension between Leo and me faded away, and our lives seemed to be back on track. Love was once again in the air for us!

Chapter Twenty-Three

A LEAP OF FAITH: STARTING ALL OVER AGAIN

A Major Accident

It was May 23, 1994, and Leo had just left work in South Seattle for home. He'd gotten on the freeway and was the last vehicle in his lane in the normal backup going through Seattle at four in the afternoon. As he later told it, he looked into his rearview mirror and saw this white van coming toward him in his lane, going full speed. As the van kept getting closer, Leo realized it wasn't going to stop, and he tried to brace himself for the hit. Without even braking, the van hit him going 60 mph, smashing into the back of Leo's Toyota truck and sending him careening into the car in front of him. Leo's neck whipped back, hitting the back window, then the roof of the cab. He claimed he wasn't unconscious but perhaps blacked out for only a nanosecond.

The next thing he remembered, the driver of the van was standing in front of him, screaming expletives because he thought the accident was Leo's fault. That was, until he saw the pileup behind the truck. Leo was able to get out of the truck, but both the front and back were smashed in. When the police got to the scene, the guy admitted that he'd been distracted looking at the construction of the new stadium. By the time he looked ahead, he'd had no time to brake and crashed into the truck at full speed.

Leo refused to go to the hospital, instead opting to ride in the tow truck as they took what was left of the truck to a collision clinic not far from where we lived in Edmonds.

The first I knew of any of this was when Leo called me from the collision clinic, wanting me to come pick him up. I don't know if I was more upset that he hadn't called me earlier to let me know what was going on or that he didn't go directly to the hospital from the scene of the accident to be checked out! At that point, it didn't matter, since I immediately took him to the emergency room at our local hospital when I picked him up, with Leo protesting all the way. As it turned out, there were no major injuries (whiplash and a possible concussion), and I was able to take him home to recuperate.

Unfortunately, Leo started having daily headaches after that. Because he'd never had headaches prior to the accident, we hired a lawyer. The doctor and chiropractic visits, plus X-rays and other assorted medical tests, were taking a toll on Leo's health, and the medical bills were quickly mounting up. After a few years, he found a chiropractor who worked with him specifically on the damage from the accident. Over time, he ultimately got relief from the headaches. At that point, we were finally able to settle the lawsuit, although Leo received little more than what we owed for his medical care.

A Major Decision

A few days after the accident, we found ourselves car shopping, since the truck had been totaled. It was very sad and emotional to say goodbye to the only brand-new vehicle either of us had ever bought, but the reality was we both needed a reliable vehicle to drive to and from work. We eventually settled for a used rental car with low mileage, and life went on.

While life went on, though, we found ourselves questioning whether we were still content working where we'd been working, living where we'd been since 1979, and what we wanted our future to look like. The kids had all moved out by then and were busy with their own lives. Leo had always wanted a business of his own, and the same thought had crossed my mind over the years. Both of us were getting tired of our jobs, as they were increasingly stressful. Leo had been born and raised in the country, while I'd always been a small-town girl at heart. And for sure, at ages forty-two and fifty-seven, we weren't getting any younger.

Suddenly, my parents' previous offer to sell us their business in Sedro-Woolley was sounding a whole lot better in spite of having to deal with Dad. When we talked to them about it, though, it turned out that now it wasn't only the business they wanted to sell but their mobile home/property too (my great-grandparents' homestead). To say the least, we were overjoyed! It was as if God was giving us an opportunity to fulfill our dreams. All we had to do was agree to it all and somehow make it happen. Without giving it another thought or coming up with reasons we couldn't possibly do it, we agreed to buy both the remaining business stock and the mobile home/property. It was for sure a leap of faith, especially since Leo didn't know anything about the bead business and it had been over twenty years since I'd worked in the business. Yet we were determined to see it through and make it work!

Moving to the Country: Starting a New Business

From there on, things happened quickly. We put our house up for sale in July, it sold in late August, and Leo retired from the foundry on September 15. Since I was still working, he pulled our fifth wheel up to the property and started packing up our house. We spent the weekends on the property, bringing a load of our belongings each time. We were finally able to move the last of everything to Sedro-Woolley on October 15, 1994. It took help from several of our friends, their cars packed full of boxes and clothes, plus the large Olympic Foundry delivery truck filled to the brim, but we did it! Then the fun began!

We had two legal contracts drawn up by a lawyer—one for the mobile home/property and a separate one for the remaining stock from the business. Since Dad and Mom needed our down payments on both contracts to purchase the motorhome they wanted to travel and live full-time in, we temporarily stayed with them as the process was being completed. In the mobile home, our boxes were stacked up and down the hallway, in the living and dining rooms, and in the extra bedroom. Mom fixed meals for all of us, we spent the evenings relaxing/watching TV with them, and we slept in our fifth wheel at night. Dad, Mom, and Leo did a thorough inventory of our stock, then Dad ordered what stock we still needed to add back in. When I wasn't working, I spent a lot of time learning the actual workings of the business and started data entry of all the stock, inputting information from handwritten inventory sheets into a new computer program to keep daily track of the inventory. We also applied for our own business license under a new name, Beadman Enterprises; had business cards printed; and set up a business bank account. It was a huge transition that felt like an insurmountable task, especially for me, as I was still working full-time for the Edmonds School District. And since we weren't sure how long it would take to rebuild the bead business from the bottom up, we decided I would keep working full-time until we'd put a few years into it.

My Job Transitions

When we first put our house up for sale in July, I gave a heads-up to my supervisor as to what our plans were. But I didn't give any kind of notice at that time, as I needed to find a job in the Skagit Valley area first. For sure, I didn't want to make the daily hundred-and-thirty-mile round-trip drive from Sedro-Woolley to Edmonds for too long after we moved in October. However, the district REALLY didn't want me to leave my one-of-a-kind job. So once we made the actual move, they made an exception for me to work four ten-hour days per week (vs. five eight-hour days). I would continue looking for a job closer to home, but in the meantime, I worked Monday and Tuesday, had Wednesday off, and worked Thursday and Friday. To make it less stress-ful, I drove to work Monday, spent that night with good friends DJ and Sheri, then drove home Tuesday night. Wednesday I spent at home, drove to work on Thursday, spent that night with good friends Andy and Lydia, then drove home Friday for the weekend. It was exhausting but at least gave us one stable income during this transition. It also gave me an extra day and part of a weekend to continue doing the data entry on the inventory and help Leo learn more about the beads (and refresh my mind) as we set our new business to officially open on January 1, 1995.

From mid-October 1994 through mid-May 1995, I continued commuting my four-day work week and applying for jobs in our local area. I was finally hired by Job Corps as a records technician, which was a mere ten-mile round-trip commute, and started work on May 23. Of course, it meant going back to a five-day workweek at much less pay and a less challenging (boring) job. The offset was it was close enough for me to come home for lunch every day and be home every night to sleep in our own bed.

On my last day of work for Edmonds School District, May 19, 1995, the department I worked in had a big going-away party for me, which Leo and Richard also attended. It was a very happy, endearing, exciting yet sad day for me. Although I'd prearranged at my new job to make a three-day return to Edmonds to train my replacement, the realization finally set in that I was finally leaving this chapter of my life behind and starting all anew without the friends, activities, and places we'd become familiar with over the last twenty years. I was extremely anxious and had a lot of self-doubt. I was unsure and uncertain of exactly what we'd gotten ourselves into. But we'd made our decision, for better or for worse, and there was no going back now.

After four months as a records technician, I applied for and accepted another position at Job Corps as the group life secretary for the Counseling/Residential Living program starting September 25, 1995. Not only was it much more responsibility, it was quite challenging to work with and schedule all the shifts for the residential advisors in the multiple dorms. I also had my own office in one of the dorms and was basically told what needed to be done, then left alone to do it. I loved the job, the hours, and my supervisor, who was the head of the Residential Living program.

Questioning Our Leap of Faith

With work at Job Corps, home life (dealing with Dad), and trying to run a business we weren't exactly prepared for, Leo and I started to question whether we'd done the right thing. Without telling me about it, Leo had started praying to God for a sign, any kind of sign, to indicate we were on the right path, although it didn't feel like it at the time. Then, on August 8, came the first sign. For me, it was a scary, eerie, yet reassuring sign!

Years before, Leo had bought me a beautiful red heart pillow that played three different love songs by Elvis. The batteries in it had long since died, and it hadn't played in years, no matter how many times or ways we pushed the button. It was still cute, though, and we had it hanging on our bedroom closet's outside doorknob.

On the night of August 8, 1995, Leo and I were both sound asleep. All of a sudden, I bolted upright in bed with my heart pounding out of control, as the Elvis heart had started playing "Love Me Tender," "I Can't Help Falling in Love with You," and "I Want You, I Need You, I Love You."

I was totally freaked out while Leo appeared calm as it played through all three songs, then stopped. I finally crept out of bed, walked over to the pillow, and made several attempts to push the button. But nothing happened. It simply didn't work, and I was both terrified and mystified by what had just happened. It took hours for me to fall back asleep, and the next morning, nothing was said except, "Wasn't that strange?"

Then the same thing happened a few nights later when

we were sound asleep in bed. Although it didn't scare me quite as much as the first time, it was still unnerving. Once again, after it finished playing, I made several attempts to push the button on the pillow, but nothing happened. And once again, Leo remained calm about it.

The next morning, he told me he'd been praying for a sign that we'd taken the right path with our leap of faith in buying the property and the business, and basically starting our lives over in an area where we knew no one except family. Leo said the heart pillow playing on its own was the sign he'd been waiting for that meant we were exactly where we were meant to be. While the red heart pillow has remained hanging on the bedroom closet door, it has never played again.

Transitioning to Working Full-Time in the Business

On November 19, 1997, I quit my job at Cascade Job Corps and took a job as office manager at my brother-in-law's machine shop (Ward Machine). I worked there until he closed down mid-July 1999. Leo turned sixty-two less than three months later, in October, so he took early Social Security. This gave us one source of consistent monthly income, as the business income fluctuated month to month, season to season. That allowed me to finally stay home and work full-time in the business, which was a great step forward in continuing to establish the business the way we envisioned it.

In the beginning, we were a mail-order catalog company backed up by advertising in four or five publications. We also did several local and greater Seattle bead shows, as my parents had done for years. That business, along with previous repeat customers we'd inherited from my parents' time, held us over the first five years that Leo spent at home with the business full-time while I worked full-time outside the home and part-time at home. Now it was time for some big changes as we decided to turn the business in another direction. We turned the business from an on-the-road one to a full-time at-home business that was open year-round. Since we'd computerized the inventory and print catalog already, it didn't take much to start an initial website, which served mainly as advertising. From there, we built a new website, adding pictures, prices, discounts, etc. And from there, things just took off.

Chapter Twenty-Four

THE DEATH OF THE GUITAR MAN

As the years went by, I heard various things about my first husband, Dave, through the valley grapevine. My aunt saw him once when he was a cook at a restaurant in Sedro-Woolley. Later, I heard he was driving a taxi cab in Mount Vernon. After that, I saw him when Dad, Mom, Leo, Richard, and I were dining at a restaurant in Burlington, where it turned out he was head chef. He came out to our table to chit-chat for a bit and eventually flashed a cross he had hanging on a chain around his neck, saying he'd found God. Next thing I heard, he'd been drunk, walking down the centerline of a Mount Vernon city street in the middle of the night, and got hit by a car. He still played music, but his alcohol and drug habit had made him so unreliable that he was offered few gigs.

Early in 1995, word was that he was working a twelve-step program. Around that same time, he tried to contact me twice by calling my parents' old phone number, which we hadn't changed after we bought their place. The first time, he ended up talking to Dad. The second time, he talked to Leo. Unfortunately, I was at work both times and was never able to connect with him. I waited for a third phone call from him, but it never came.

In May 1995, I saw an obituary for his mother, who passed away after a lengthy illness. In November 1995, I saw an obituary for his dad, who was killed by a hit-and-run driver at his mailbox, which Dave witnessed from his dad's kitchen window.

Then, about six months later, I saw an obituary for Dave. He died on May 16, 1996, at the age of forty-nine. Between the obituary and his sister, whom I had contact with shortly afterward, I was able to piece together what had happened in the twenty-one years since we'd last been together.

He had a longtime companion yet lived by himself and never remarried. He had a son I'd met when we were together. He also had a daughter I never knew about, even though she was born around the time we started going together. He apparently quit drinking and taking drugs for a while but suffered a severe back injury, for which he'd taken pain medications. As his parents got older, he helped them out quite a bit, cooking their meals, mowing their lawn, and staying with his mom during her illness to give his dad some respite. But after both his parents died, he fell into a deep depression and started up with the alcohol and drugs again. While his passion was still playing music, gigs became almost nonexistent. However, a few weeks before his death, he'd lined up some with a new band. Ultimately, however, he died alone at home in the middle of the night from a drug and alcohol overdose. He choked on his own vomit, resulting in asphyxiation. Even after all that time and everything that had transpired, I couldn't help but feel sad and sorry that he'd never been able to rid himself of his demons.

Around midnight a few nights later, I woke up to the

intense pain of being stabbed deep in my heart. I bolted straight up in the bed. It felt so real that I thought I'd been stabbed, and my chest hurt for hours afterward. The episode terrified me. I didn't know why I felt that way or what it meant. After researching dream interpretation, the concept of being stabbed in the heart means that someone had deeply hurt you, and you couldn't get over the fact that this person had done this to you. That exactly fit what Dave had done to me. While I acknowledged that, I continued to keep the awful memories and details of our time together a secret (except for the minimum details I'd shared with Leo) and buried them down even deeper inside my heart.

Chapter Twenty-Five

SAYING GOODBYE TO MY LOVING GRANDMA

For the last several years of her life, Grandma had required twenty-four-seven live-in caretaking, as she'd become weak and was confined to a wheel-chair, even though her mind stayed strong. She went through several caretakers before my mother took it upon herself in the summer of 1998 to move both herself and Dad in with Grandma, who agreed to it even though she didn't care for Dad. I always felt it made things harder for Mom, what with all the problems she already had dealing with Dad. But she insisted on doing it. Unfortunately, it didn't last long, as Dad's health was deteriorating. He still wanted to go south for the winter, so mid-fall, they left for Desert Gold (near Brenda, Arizona), where they'd stayed every winter since 1994. So Grandma was back to having live-in caretakers.

One Wednesday night, a group of ladies from our family had gathered at Grandma's house to do some acrylic tole painting, which she also seemed to enjoy doing. We'd been getting together to paint about twice a month for several years, but that night, everything changed. About halfway through the evening, Grandma put down her paint-brush, announced to everyone, "I can't do this anymore," and had her caretaker put her to bed. When she did that, I got an eerie feeling that she wasn't just saying she was tired. She was ready to let go and move on.

After everyone had left and she was settled in bed, I went to sit with her. We held hands for a while, then she looked at me and told me she loved me. I told her I loved her, and she fell asleep for the night. And in those precious moments, I knew she was telling me goodbye.

Early Saturday morning, I got a call from my aunt that Grandma had just passed away. It was November 21, 1998, a mere nine days before her eighty-ninth birthday. Although I'd known her time was short since Wednesday night, it still hit me hard. My saving grace for making it through the grief of her death, however, was knowing we'd always had a loving relationship and that I had a lifetime's worth of wonderful memories I would forever cherish.

Since Dad's health had continued to decline fairly rapidly in Arizona and it would most likely be my parents' last winter there, Mom and my aunt decided to hold off on a celebration of life for Grandma (she didn't want a funeral) until my parents returned in the spring. In the meantime, I helped my aunt take care of the arrangements for Grandma's burial and anything else that came up regarding Grandma until my parents returned.

Chapter Twenty-Six

THE DEATH OF THE AUTOCRATIC NARCISSIST

A mere six weeks after Grandma passed away, Dad passed away while he and Mom were still down south. He had a massive heart attack early on a Saturday morning while they were staying at a resort hotel to attend a jazz festival in Laughlin, Nevada. They were walking from breakfast to the first venue, and, as Mom put it, his body dropped instantly to the ground. In her mind, she knew he was already gone.

However, there was an ambulance right on the premises that got to him within a minute or so. Although Mom requested no CPR because he had a DNR in writing, it wasn't on his or her person, so the EMTs wouldn't honor her request. They immediately started CPR, got him to the hospital across the state line in Bullhead City, Arizona, and hooked him up to life support. Later that morning, she drove their pickup back to Desert Gold RV Resort, packed up, secured the motorhome, hitched the pickup to tow behind (with the help of some neighbors), and headed back to the hospital in Bullhead City, arriving right at dusk. That way, she had everything she needed with her, including Dad's DNR paperwork.

She called me Sunday morning. All she would tell me was Dad was in the hospital and it didn't look good. Knowing she was alone, I flew down late that night to assess the situation. Like Mom, as soon as I saw Dad, I knew he was already gone. I called my sister, and she flew down the next day, since Mom wanted both of us with her when they finally disconnected the life support. She thought that would give us all the opportunity to say our final goodbyes to him. Plus, we were her only support system, since she knew no one there. Not long after my sister arrived, we were at the hospital, where final preparations were being made. It wasn't long before his life support was disconnected. Within minutes, Dad's body ceased to function. By then, it was Tuesday, January 19, 1999.

Since Dad was Bahai, we were on a timeline in accordance with his religious beliefs. Things needed to happen quickly. Due to his beliefs, Dad needed to be buried within two or three days and without embalming. He had to be laid to rest in a plain pine box no more than a one-hour drive or thirty-mile radius from where he passed away. By late that afternoon, all the arrangements were finalized for him to be buried the following day.

Leo flew down early the following morning. I picked him up at the airport right before we left for the mortuary in Laughlin. Then it was on to the cemetery where he was being buried in Needles, California. The four of us had a small graveside ceremony for Dad, after which we left for the nearest campground, where we spent the night. The following morning, my sister and I flew home, and Leo stayed behind with Mom. Although she was the one who always drove the motorhome (Dad hadn't driven in years), she let Leo drive it the three days it took to get back home. She spent the time processing everything that had just happened and the decisions she had ahead of her.

When I finally got home and had a few days to myself before Leo and Mom made it back, I had a chance to think about all things Dad. Over the past few years, I'd learned to tolerate and set boundaries when it came to interacting or being around him. I'd even overcome my anger at him and the way he treated Mom, my sister, and me. I realized, however, that I still wasn't prepared to forgive him, even after his death. And as terrible as it was to admit, while I was a bit in shock at his sudden death, I felt no sadness or grief. All I felt was relief for Mom, my sister, and myself.

About two weeks later, I had a very vivid dream about Dad. I saw him in the grocery store and followed him through the frozen food aisle. He was reading a book and turned abruptly. Then he looked directly up at me and said, "It's okay. I've come to find peace here with myself." He hesitated a moment, then, with a wide grin, said, "And there's great massages."

It was typical Dad, and I couldn't help but think it was actually him sending me a final goodbye message.

Chapter Twenty-Seven

MOM RETURNS HOME

The first thing on Mom's mind when she returned home was to have a celebration of life for Grandma, which was wonderful and brought back all kinds of great memories for me. After that, it was another several weeks of Mom and my aunt dividing out Grandma's estate and finally cleaning out her house. Then it was time to plan a celebration of life for Dad. It was an exhausting and emotional time for Mom. But somehow, she made it through on sheer strength and determination. She seemed definitely ready to move on with her life.

Since returning home in January, Mom lived on the property in the motorhome. Now that things with Grandma and Dad were taken care of, she decided she really didn't enjoy living in the motorhome or traveling anymore. She wanted to move into a house or apartment of her own. Knowing she loved living on the place, Leo and I applied for a special use permit so we could put a manufactured home right next to ours.

On Mother's Day, we surprised her with the approved permit, and she was so excited that she and I went home shopping that afternoon. She found a smaller manufactured home she liked right away, so everything got put into motion immediately. It was a four-to-five-month process, but she sold her motorhome and was settled into her new place by the time fall rolled around. She couldn't have been happier, and we were glad to have her nearby, especially now that she was seventy.

By then, we were living where we'd always wanted to be, working flexible hours as dictated by the amount of business at hand, and were able to spend more time with family. The most important aspect, however, was that we were able to help Mom out when she needed it now that she lived on the property with us.

Although living right next door and seeing Mom every day was nice, she was still a very private and guarded person. We did lots of things together—shopping, lunches, day trips to the scenic areas around the state, trips to the Tucson Gem & Bead Show in February every few years, and even a trip with my aunt down the Oregon Coast, then inland to Crater Lake. As we hadn't been close when I was growing up, I'd hoped the years to come would bring us closer together. But in spite of always enjoying our times together, I never felt like I'd gotten to know the person she really was. I knew her favorite foods, colors, and clothes. I knew how artistic she was, and we often painted and beaded together. Yet I was never able to get her to tell me how she felt about things. And she refused to talk about what I most wanted to know about her. That's just who she was, and I eventually had to let go of my desire to get to know her the way I would have liked to.

Chapter Twenty-Eight

MOM'S TRAGIC DEATH

Early in 2005, Leo and I noticed Mom was becoming forgetful. It was more than normal age-related forgetfulness. She also seemed to be having health issues, although when she went to have it checked out with the doctor, she'd tell us he'd told her there was nothing wrong with her and it was all in her head. She was very good at bluffing her way through conversations, so no one else noticed it at the time.

It was extremely frustrating for Leo and me as we watched her health appear to ever so slowly deteriorate, but she was as stubborn as they come and refused to push her doctor for further testing. By that fall, it was becoming quite noticeable, so I called her doctor and explained what we were seeing. Knowing she wouldn't let anyone go to the doctor with her (he'd already suggested that), he finally convinced her to let me accompany her so I could take notes for her so she could just concentrate on what he was saying at the time and read my notes later to refresh her memory if needed. Once we started doing that, it finally became obvious to him there was something wrong! After running several tests, they discovered there was something unusual going on with her gall bladder, so surgery to remove it was scheduled for January 2006.

The surgery was successful. Unfortunately, it also led them to find that she had stomach cancer and immediately refer her to an oncologist. My sister and I went with Mom to her first appointment, and we were told the cancer was right where the esophagus goes into the stomach. As soon as she healed from her gall bladder surgery, they went in and removed as much of the cancer as possible so she could still eat. Tragically, since the cancer was already at Stage 4, neither radiation nor chemotherapy was an option. Mom immediately went into hospice care for comfort care, and, as her only remaining wish was to remain in her home and not be placed in a facility, I agreed to become her primary caretaker.

Leo continued to fill the business orders, then he'd take over with Mom so I could do the paperwork, process invoices, and get the shipping labels ready for the orders. My sister helped when she could, but she already had her hands full taking care of her husband, who also had severe health problems.

The first few months, Mom was still pretty strong and often worked out in her garden, so I checked on her during the day and fixed meals for the three of us at her place. She was able to stay by herself at night with the use of baby monitors between the houses. Over the next several months, as her dementia worsened and she became weaker, Leo and I traded staying with her during the day. Eventually, it got to the point where I was also spending the nights with her so she was never alone in her house. By her seventy-sixth birthday on May 24, she no longer recognized anyone and slept most of the time. She passed away comfortably in her own home on June 24, 2006.

Even at her sickest before she totally lost her memory, I continued to ask her about things, and she'd say, "I have my own thoughts (or beliefs) about that." It was as if she was never able to shake the notion Dad had ingrained in her that she wasn't allowed to speak or think for herself. And she was obviously still angry with my dad at the end, as she told the hospice nurse that it took her fifty-two years to get rid of her mistake. Even though she'd disavowed being Bahai just a few months prior to her death ("That was your Dad's religion!"), we went ahead with her pre-dementia wishes and had her buried in a plain pine coffin, without embalming, and laid her to rest one plot over from her parents at Union Cemetery in Sedro-Woolley.

Although I knew she was now at peace, it was sad on so many levels. I couldn't help but feel sorry for the life she felt she could never escape. However, her death gave me time to think about both her and Dad's lives, the era they were raised in, how they were raised, and their lives together. None of it was easy, considering their backgrounds, the circumstances and expectations of their times, and their respective personalities. I realized I was no longer angry at either of them and had even forgiven Dad for all the trauma and abuse I felt I'd experienced because of his words and actions. I knew I would never forget the trauma and abuse, but I was now able to recall it through a slightly different lens.

A few weeks later, we had a celebration of life for Mom at her house. Leo, my sister, and I cleaned up the house, arranged things to highlight her hobbies (beading, crafting, playing accordion, etc.), and made the walls in her bedroom a picture gallery of all the amazing places she'd visited and the variety of different things she'd done over the years.

After that, my sister and I slowly started clearing out her house and dividing up what we each wanted to keep, what we were going to donate, and what needed to be tossed. At the same time, Leo and I had a major decision to make regarding Mom's mobile home itself.

Chapter Twenty-Nine

AN EXHAUSTING DOUBLE MOVE

om had wanted us to move into her newer (2006) manufactured home and get rid of the older one (1977) we were living in. The problem was that even though they were both three-bedroom two-bathroom homes, hers was only 900 square feet while ours was around 1,600 square feet. There was no way we would have enough room for us, our big dog, two cats, and an office for the business without being too cramped. And there was also the matter of having to buy out my sister's half of Mom's home.

Ultimately, my sister gifted her share of the home to us for taking care of Mom, especially during the last six months of her life. But that still left the dilemma of space, or rather the lack of space, if we kept Mom's and had our old one removed.

In the end, Leo and I decided to look at new manufactured homes until we found one with a layout and size we liked that was perfect for our lifestyle. It also turned out that the place where we found it was willing to take both existing manufactured homes as a down payment on the

2006 model we chose. The only stipulation was that we would have to move out of our home into Mom's home to get the process started. The seller would let us live in Mom's house until our new one was move-in ready, as long as we let them bring people in to show the home (while we lived there) so it could be sold on-site. That way, when we moved into our new house, they only had to move Mom's from our property to wherever it was going, saving them the hassle of moving it twice. A win-win situation all the way around.

However, that meant we would have to move not just once but twice. Also, we would have to get rid of a large amount of our furniture, since our new house would be smaller AND we'd have to live minimally and out of boxes in Mom's house for four to five months while our new house was constructed. Not an easy task, but we signed the papers to make it happen, and the fun began!

We downsized as much as we could, switched out some of our old furniture with Mom's newer furniture, packed up boxes of all the things we didn't need for the next three to four months, and used our utility trailer to load up and move items back and forth between Mom's place and ours. When only the extra furniture, things we wouldn't have space for in our new place, and odds-and-ends household items from both Mom's place and ours were left, we had an indoor estate sale. Both moves and the sale were exhausting endeavors, but we managed to do it ourselves with the help of only one of our friends. It was a great feeling to finally be able to sleep in our new home and ring in the new year of 2007.

Chapter Thirty

FIBROMYALGIA HITS WITH A VENGEANCE

A Possible Heart Attack

Leo had gone over to Andy's to help pour cement, and I went off on my morning walk. About halfway through, I started having chest pains. I finished my walk with my chest still hurting, then called the doctor. He got me in right away. After a quick exam, he told me to immediately go to the Skagit Valley Hospital ER because they were best equipped for this type of emergency. Driving to the ER in Mount Vernon seemed to be most efficient, though maybe not the wisest, decision. I called Leo and explained what was going on, but he couldn't come right away, as they'd just poured the cement and needed to spread it. So I told Leo to go home when they finished and that I would call when I had some news. I called my aunt, and she was able to meet me at the ER, so at least I wasn't by myself.

At the hospital, they ran their heart attack procedure, with wires and tubes coming out all over. I was there for two hours, given dozens of different types of pills, and had their reactions—all to be told it wasn't a heart attack. Perhaps, they said, it was pleurisy or costochondritis. The bottom line was I was released. I left my car there, and my aunt drove me home (where Leo was anxiously waiting). I still had the chest pains, only now I had a new prescription for pain meds. After that episode, I went back to my family doctor, who started treating me with low-level antidepressants and muscle relaxers in an effort to lessen my anxiety and depression over what had happened and the pain that would continue despite all his efforts.

Fibromyalgia "Diagnosis"

Over the next couple of years, I was shuffled between an internist, neurologist, and oncologist, with all their different tests, to figure out the cause of all the pain as well as my new inability to sleep, inability to concentrate, constant exhaustion, and even greater anxiety and depression. Although I felt like the doctors mainly dismissed my symptoms as being all in my head (a leftover notion from when I was a child), the word *fibromyalgia* was mentioned as a possibility. But since it wasn't within their medical specialty or expertise, it wasn't considered a diagnosis.

Fibromyalgia "Treatment"

My official diagnosis of fibromyalgia came in 2008 during my very first appointment with the rheumatologist. My health had regressed to the point where I was having a difficult time functioning, along with an overabundance of brain fog. So Leo accompanied me to the appointment. The doctor looked over my last two years of medical records, and we went over the questionnaire I'd filled out. Then, just for good measure, he pressed on all eighteen fibromyalgia tender points. If eleven are painful, it helps determine the diagnosis. (All eighteen were painful for me.)

Finally, based on all the information he'd collected, the doctor told me I did have fibromyalgia and followed up by saying, "I have good news, and I have bad news. The good news is that you won't die from it. The bad news is that you happen to have a brain that misfires pain signals."

Although I didn't understand the ramifications that diagnosis would have in the long run, at the time, it verified that what I'd been feeling and experiencing was real and had a name.

Then I was totally stunned when the next thing he asked me was, "So, when did the abuse start?"

So there I was. I couldn't even finish a sentence when I was speaking, so Leo already had to translate most of the answers to this doctor's questions. And then he asked me that? I was angry because I wasn't there to be psychoanalyzed. I was there to find help for the pain, inability to concentrate, lack of sleep, and extreme fatigue I'd been dealing with for the past two years and were getting worse by the day.

I didn't know it then, but, as I would learn along the way, there's a high correlation between abuse and fibromyalgia in terms of how much or how well one has dealt with the abuse and the intensity of fibromyalgia symptoms, especially the pain. And even though my initial impression of this rheumatologist wasn't the best, he helped me understand my condition and make it through some of the roughest times early on, when I was learning to manage my fibromyalgia. In the long term, my body would be assaulted by many other autoinflammatory and/or autoimmune conditions that were often related to fibromyalgia:

costochondritis (inflammation of the cartilage of the rib cage), IBS (irritable bowel syndrome), IC (interstitial cystitis/painful bladder syndrome), RLS (restless leg syndrome), RAS (restless arm syndrome), and CRPS (chronic inflammation and pain due to improper healing of an injury) of my left foot.

For eight years, along with medication that helped with the pain, I took all the advice my rheumatologist gave me, including changing my diet, getting more exercise, taking yoga and tai chi classes, getting cognitive behavioral therapy, and having EMDR therapy. Although they weren't cures, they did help me manage the fibromyalgia.

Chapter Thirty-One

LEO'S CANCER DIAGNOSIS

Leo's dad had died of prostate cancer that was undetected until it had spread to his bones, so Leo was always proactive in having a yearly prostate checkup starting when he was in his early fifties. In his 2004 checkup, they discovered a benign tumor in his prostate, which was immediately removed without any repercussions. Then, during his 2009 checkup in late December, they discovered a fast-growing cancer, and Leo was told it needed to be dealt with in no more than four to six weeks. The choices were between having radiation seeds planted in his prostate to kill the cancer or having his prostate taken out totally intact, which gave him a better chance of complete removal of the cancer.

Both came with a different set of potential long-term side effects that potentially could be life-changing. As Leo and I talked about it, we found ourselves preparing mentally, emotionally, and physically for the consequences of whatever decision was made. It was so stressful, and there was no right or wrong choice, just a personal choice that needed to be made quickly. In the end, Leo opted for the prostate removal surgery, which finally took place on January 31, 2010, just within the window of time the doctor had given him.

The surgery was successful, and though it was still quite stressful for a while, especially as I was trying to deal with fibromyalgia, Leo experienced only a few side effects, so it wasn't the worst-case scenario we'd anticipated. As the next ten checkups gave him a cancer-free diagnosis, we knew that no matter what, we'd made the right choice.

Chapter Thirty-Two

MY RHEUMATOLOGIST AND I
PART WAYS

As the years went by and my body started aging, the condition felt like it was progressively getting worse on its own despite all I did. I kept having to adjust medication, along with doing what I physically and mentally was able to do.

Then, in early 2016, my rheumatologist went from being a private practitioner to one of four rheumatologists in a medical group. As a group, they voted to stop treating fibromyalgia patients with any kind of medication. Instead, they decided to treat confirmed fibromyalgia with recommended lifestyle changes. If you didn't agree with their choice of treatment, you were more than welcome to find another practice. Although my doctor told me he didn't agree with the changes, he had to go along with their decision to continue his practice in the medical group.

I felt totally abandoned by the rheumatologist and the medical group, which made it much harder for me to manage the condition. It also put me in limbo as far as being able to find another doctor in the area who would treat fibromyalgia as a legitimate and serious condition. Eventually, I ended up going back to my family doctor, who told me to take ONE of the medications I'd been taking—a pain medication—in a mere half dose of what the rheumatologist had been prescribing. It was the only choice I could make, however, since I needed the pain to ease at night to help me sleep. It didn't help much, but at this point, there was no other alternative.

Sadly, the research and studies on fibromyalgia still hadn't come anywhere close to the reality of living with it, and the information out there rapidly continued to change and evolve over time. I knew progress was being made. But most of my progress came simply from listening to my body and dealing with the pain as best I could. I became a fibromyalgia warrior and continued working to remain strong and vigilant by keeping up with the most current research, potential cases, and new treatments, plus advocating for awareness and education around fibromyalgia.

Chapter Thirty-Three

BALANCING WORK, PLAY, AND OUR HEALTH

Over the years, one of the biggest challenges of being self-employed and working from home was making sure Leo and I took time for ourselves to keep the excitement alive in our marriage, especially as we navigated our health issues. We made sure we had mini vacations to destinations around the state, day-trip picnics, and date days/nights.

On a trip in 2000, we flew to Nashville, then rented a car and drove to Memphis, Pigeon Forge, and Dollywood. Then we went through the Smokey Mountains to Alabama and back to Nashville. In 2002, we drove through Yellowstone, the Grand Canyon, and the Tetons. We picked up some friends in Leroy, Kansas, went to Branson for two days, dropped them off in Leroy, and meandered home. We were in Washington, D.C., in 2005 for the opening of the Native American museum. And in 2012, we went to Crazy Horse and the Custer Buffalo Roundup, then went on through the Badlands, seeing Mount Rushmore, Devils Tower, and Little Bighorn on the way home. Finally, we kicked back, rented a condo for a week in 2014 on the Big Island in Hawaii, and relaxed. Those were exciting times, and we treasured them, as they were respites from the business and gave us the downtime we needed.

Business had started to take a toll on us. When we started in 1995, we still had a corner on the Japanese market. By 2000, trade with Japan opened, and companies had wholesalers in the States that undercut our prices sharply. To stay competitive, we had to buy larger quantities with fewer options. Yet we managed for several years. Since we had an abundance of old stock, we eventually changed it to new AND vintage stock. That kept us busy for a while, until the old guard started selling their businesses. New, trendier, smaller stores took their place, and the whole bead business changed. So, by 2015, we'd started to put feelers out that we wanted to sell the business and were keeping up with the changes as much as possible.

In March 2016, I started seeing a psychotherapist whose specialty was talk therapy. It wasn't that there was any one thing that was bothering me. It was more all the things that seemed to be simmering under the surface of my being. What started as a recap of all my issues surrounding Dad ended up an unleashing of anger and hostility over being stalked, being raped, and suffering all the chaotic circumstances surrounding my life with Dave. It was the first time I'd ever opened up and talked to anyone about it. There was no holding back anymore, and it all came out, whether I meant it to or not. I talked about what had happened to me, how it affected me over the years, why I felt the way I did, and why I acted the way I did. There was a rush of anger and hostility, then shame and self-blame. It was such a relief to have it all out in the open at last. We talked it all out, and what had never made sense finally made sense. Now, I thought that if I could just hang on to these things, life would be okay.

Chapter Thirty-Four

NO PARENT SHOULD HAVE TO BURY
THEIR CHILD

I 've always had a soft spot in my heart for James. He probably had the most difficult life out of all three of the kids, although it was a difficulty that was often of his own making.

Leo never developed as close a relationship with James as he would have liked to since he was stationed on board ship right after James was born. Later, he worked one full-time and often one or two other part-time jobs to make ends meet. Consequently, he was working a good portion of the time while Gloria stayed at home with the kids. And of the three kids, she had an unusually close relationship with and attachment to James. They were so close when he was younger that she overlooked or excused his obviously defiant and bad behavior as him "just being a kid." Apparently, that behavior had been rampant since he was a very small child, and it had been evident from day one, when I met Leo when James was fourteen. Leo and Gloria took him to counseling several times, and he even stayed a short while at a Boys Ranch shortly after Leo and I got together. Nothing, though, seemed to make a big difference or change his behavior.

As the relationship between Gloria and Leo disintegrated, they tried marriage counseling. But anytime the idea was presented that perhaps Gloria might be part of, or share responsibility for, their problems, she would pull out of counseling and cling even more to James, turning him against Leo. It got to the point where, for a while before their divorce, Leo was afraid James would do him physical harm if that was what Gloria wanted to see happen. That never happened, but consequently, even when he lived with us, James never formed a close relationship with either of us.

There is much that can be said about James—the lying, the stealing, the malicious behavior. There was SO much anger below the surface. On the other hand, I always thought he was an extremely smart kid whose anger was a reaction to his constant struggle with his sexual orientation. He had few friends in high school, although for a while he seemed to enjoy square dancing and was a teen caller for their square dance group. He even had a girlfriend for quite a while. Although it was clear to me that he was gay, when I mentioned it to Leo, he didn't think that was the case. So essentially, that was the end of the subject. Nothing was said until sometime later in the mid-1990s when Gloria called to tell us James was in the hospital and not doing well. He'd been admitted with pneumonia-like symptoms, and it turned out he was HIV positive. That's when he finally announced to everyone (who didn't already know) that he was gay.

During his college years, while he was still living with us, he started drinking. He eventually dropped out of college his last year and moved to Las Vegas to be closer to

Gloria despite their love-hate relationship. He also started gambling heavily and lived a wild lifestyle for several years, essentially until he was diagnosed as HIV positive. It was somewhere around that time that he met Harold and settled down. After that, he eventually managed to quit gambling, but he never quit drinking.

For years after he dropped out of college and moved to Las Vegas, we rarely heard from James. There were no cards or letters, just a few phone calls here and there. The first time we saw him after college was at Laurie's wedding in October 1994. After that, he came to visit us on one of his trips to Seattle, but we didn't know he was coming and weren't home. The next time we had contact with him beyond just the occasional phone call or Christmas card was in 2008, when we started making the occasional trip to Las Vegas to see Laurie, the grandkids, and the new great-granddaughter. He'd been with Harold since about 1995 and had a steady job working as head waiter at the Market Street Cafe at the California Hotel, and we would get together with him and Harold each time we made the trip down there.

James, along with Harold, came up here for Richard and Hannah's wedding in 2014, and we started hearing from him more than we had at any time before. The conversations were always general and mostly nothing personal, but it was nice to stay in touch with him more often. He seemed to have mellowed over the years, and everything on the surface appeared fine. James was still working at the same place he'd been for twenty years, they were buying a house and a car, and there were no gigantic red flags except for Harold's strange and often offensive Facebook posts. The only seemingly odd thing was that James always communicated on Facebook and email through Harold, although he did have his own phone number we could reach him at in an emergency.

Then the calls changed, and James started sharing more personal information. He was in several car accidents and experienced lots of falls that ended with him in the hospital. He lost his job in 2015 for being drunk on the job, and it apparently wasn't the first time he'd been drunk at work. The real story started coming out about all his years of drinking, gambling, and prescription drug use and abuse. He said they were problems of his own creation and insisted that he wanted to fix things on his own. He'd applied for but been denied unemployment, and Harold had never worked. They decided to both go to school to do medical transcription so they could get jobs, and James took out loans to cover the tuition.

Then the calls became more desperate. "I'm broken and can't be fixed." "I'm depressed." "I have no job." "I have no friends left here." "I can't get unemployment because I was fired." "I've broken my shoulder and have been in the hospital." "We're financially broke." "We've gone through all the money in my retirement account." "We're filing for bankruptcy." "We're being sued by the last person I rear-ended." And it went on and on. Plus, from what Leo and I learned about Harold, he'd been no help because of all the baggage of his own. That just made matters worse and created drama above and beyond what was going on with James.

Each time James called, we talked about his wanting help, needing help, and getting help. We'd encourage him in every conversation to go for it. He agreed he needed help and said he was even seeing a psychiatrist and a counselor. Then, the next time we talked with him, it was the same story. He just wanted things to be the way they used to be before his world fell apart, and it was apparent he was having a difficult time adjusting to the new reality he was living in.

The next time James called, we talked for only a short while. But at the end of the conversation, he whispered that he would call us the next day. I asked if Harold was right there, and James indicated yes and that he couldn't talk freely. When he called the next day, we talked for about forty-five minutes. It was the best conversation we'd ever had with him. Just before he hung up, he told us that he felt so much better about everything. He thanked us for being there for him and talking things through with him. It sounded like he was genuine about wanting to get his life straightened out.

Then, a week later, on Sunday, June 26, 2016, all hell broke loose. James called and immediately put Harold on the phone. Then it went back and forth between them through the course of several phone calls. They were both crying and carrying on, so it was hard to figure out exactly what was happening. We had a conversation with James again about reaching out and getting help, which he agreed he needed. The one thing that perked up our ears, however, was that he'd said the night before that he'd just wanted to die, so he'd taken a bunch of pills and drank a whole bunch. He put Harold on again. According to Harold, James had already been drinking and taking pills that evening, but Harold didn't think it was as much as the night before. When we pressed Harold more, he said he really didn't know what was going on. The only thing he said about the night before was that, "Well, he did look a bit more relaxed lying on the floor than usual. But I just thought he was being extra quiet." Then Harold started crying and carrying on, talking about how much he missed his dad, who'd died fifteen years earlier.

It was frightening and felt like there was something more going on than Leo and I were comfortable with. So after hanging up, we called the crisis center hotline and described the situation at hand, telling them what had transpired and been said in the past week. They suggested we have a welfare check done on James and Harold, so they transferred us to the Las Vegas Police Department. After a conversation with dispatch, they sent two officers to check on the situation. They couldn't get them to answer the door, so they called for a phone number and were finally able to get ahold of Harold to open the door. A while later, an officer called and said they'd separated James and Harold but had some questions about the situation, so we repeated what had transpired in the past week and been said that evening. We were relieved that at least someone could get a reality check on the situation and felt it was under control.

Then, a while later, the phone rang again, and it was James. He was yelling that all he wanted was for Harold to SHUT UP. When I asked where Harold was, he said he was sitting on the bed next to him. Then he said he really didn't want to go to the hospital, so I asked him what he did want. He said all he wanted was for Harold to SHUT UP! I asked him to put the officer on the phone, and the officer indicated that James had given his consent earlier to go to the hospital, and they were just waiting for Social Services to get there to take him. I got the impression from the information he was able to share with us that they thought it was a good idea for him to be checked out.

Later, we called dispatch to see what the final outcome had been. They said James had been taken to Sunrise Hospital under a code that meant he was being placed under a seventy-two-hour psych hold, but he was able to take his phone and could come and go as he pleased until they actually started the evaluation. At last, James was getting some direction and help. Or so we thought.

After that, we didn't hear from James and assumed he'd gone under the seventy-two-hour psych hold and was now home working things through. Since it was normal for him not to call us except every three to four weeks, we weren't worried. Plus, this had happened before when a friend of his called for a welfare check from the police. James wouldn't talk to him for a couple of months.

On July 4, 2016, I received three different text messages from Harold. The first was at 1:25 p.m.: "Haven't heard from james." The second text was at 1:30 p.m.: "I havent found james. Im concerned. He doesnt answer his fone." And the third was at 6:17 p.m.: "Im in sunrise hospital." Thinking this all to be a bit strange, I called Harold to find out what exactly was going on. Harold said he'd gone to Sunrise Hospital early Sunday morning, June 27, before James's psych evaluation, and he and James checked James out. According to Harold, James didn't want to stay in the hospital and have the evaluation. After that, the story got a little sketchy. Depending on which version I got—there were two—Harold had heatstroke either later Sunday or Tuesday and had to be in the hospital either three days or two weeks because he couldn't walk without a walker and had to have physical therapy. It was obvious he was a little out of it.

I tried calling James, but it went straight to voicemail. When I talked with Harold a second time, I asked when he'd last seen or heard from James. He told me it was either Sunday or Tuesday. He couldn't remember which. I asked him if there was anyone who could check on James, and he said he'd already sent a text to the neighbor, who replied that they'd seen him around the house in the past few days.

So we assumed he really hadn't disappeared. Apparently, he just didn't want to see or talk to Harold. Still, Harold wanted me to keep trying to call James. Then the next day, July 5, Harold sent another text message at 10:54 a.m.: " Hes bit reticent to talk to you because you had him in the spych ward."

At this point, Leo and I wondered where we should go from there. We talked about the entire situation, and as much as we loved James and wanted him to get the help he claimed to want and so desperately needed, the stress had become too much for us, and we couldn't keep going around in circles with him. We could no longer handle the drunken phone calls and drama that ensued with each conversation.

After the last text from Harold, I called James again, and it went directly to voicemail. I told him that we wanted to help and that he might not be ready yet. But I said we loved him and told him to call whenever he got the chance so we'd know he was okay. Realistically, though, we knew James might choose not to speak to us again for a while.

We realized that James, and only James, had to be the one to decide when the time was right to get some help. The sad thing with him, though, was realizing that time might never come. And that was the hardest reality we had to face. It's terrible to see someone you care about self-destruct and know there's nothing you can do to stop it from happening. At that point, all we could do was pray for him and hope for the best.

I sent him a text on June 28, asking how it was going. With no reply, I tried calling a few more times in July. The first time, his voicemail box was full. The second time, it wasn't taking messages at all. That's when we started to really get worried. As time went on, we realized that the reality was worse than what we could ever imagine.

Over the first few days in August, we got texts from Richard, Laurie, and one of James's friends from Washington, asking if we'd heard from James lately. We tried calling Harold but got nothing—no answer. Even their home phone just rang and rang when we tried to call and leave a message. We talked to Laurie and had her call the police again to have them do another welfare check. According to the police, the place was all locked up. After talking with neighbors, the concluded that no one had seen anyone there for about three weeks. No garbage cans had been put out, and their car was gone. At that point, no one was hearing from them. But there was no missing person's report on either of them, so the police had no legal reason to enter the premises. As far as the police were concerned, they simply could have gone on vacation and not told anyone.

In the interim, Laurie said she was going over to their house the next day to look around and see if she could find out anything more than what the police told her. Leo told her to make sure to call the police first and have them meet her there. Under no circumstances should she break in, he said. He insisted that she just wait until the police got there before trying to enter.

It was August 6 when we got a hysterical call from Laurie! She and her daughter Shelly's boyfriend had gone over to check on James. And instead of calling Metro first, they went in through the unlocked garage and into the house. They found a body in the bedroom, and it was obvious from decomposition that it had been there a long time. She thought it was most likely James, since there was a cast on one arm. It was only then that she called the police, and they came out to deal with the situation.

The coroner, a crime scene investigator, and a homicide detective were all called. An autopsy was scheduled the next morning, but based on the amount of decomposition, they weren't sure how much information they could extract from the body. We were told body identification and cause of death could take up to two weeks and that we needed to be patient. Beyond that, because they didn't know for certain who it was, James or Harold, that's all the information they could legally tell us. That was the beginning of a terrible nightmare that would bizarrely unfold over the next several months.

The next day, we received a call from the homicide detective, who had questions about when we had last been in touch with James and Harold. The coroner was unable to do an autopsy due to the advanced decomposition, and they were sending fluid and tissue samples to a different lab in order to help determine cause of death and verify that the body was indeed James. As it tentatively stood, however, it appeared that Harold had something to do with James's death and had left thereafter. The police were still trying to locate him, and a search warrant had been issued on both their house and the car. In fact, they were on their way to the house with the search warrant as we spoke.

Waiting for any word, any kind of information, was excruciating. Leo and I were both nervous wrecks, needing to know one way or the other whose body that was and holding out all hope that it was truly not James.

Three days later, the coroner's office called to inform us that they had a 100 percent positive ID that the body was James. I know that, on one level, we'd taken the last few days and prepared ourselves for the worst. But now, somehow, hearing it definitively out loud made it a shocking and numbing reality. At the same time, the coroner also informed Leo that he was now the designated next of kin for James. (Gloria had died in March 2001 of lung cancer.)

That's when we realized that meant Harold was also dead. It was strange, as there was nothing said to us about Harold. Again, we were frustrated by what we weren't being told and were told only what they were allowed to tell us.

We needed to go to Las Vegas to sort out his house and claim his body. What happened with Harold was still being worked on. It was getting bizarre, and we still didn't have the whole story. We decided, along with Richard and Hannah, to go that weekend. The detective said they would go over to the house, remove the carpet where James's body was found, and air the house with fans to dilute the smell. The plan was to meet us at the house, and we'd be able to retrieve any of James's personal items we wanted.

We stayed at our granddaughter Cynthia's, and early Monday morning, we arranged to meet at James's house at 10 a.m. It was decided that only Leo and Rich would go into the house to retrieve personal items. When they got there, they realized the house had been broken into. When the detectives pulled up immediately thereafter, they cleared the scene and found the house had been ransacked. All the valuables had been stolen, and everything had been trashed or broken. Also, the air conditioner had been turned down, so it was very hot (air temps had been 105 to 117 degrees). It was heartbreaking. Leo and Rich were able to retrieve a few pictures, some photo albums, a few pieces of James's clown collection, and a stack of outdated personal papers. Aside from that, there wasn't anything in the rubble that was salvageable.

Cynthia had planned a special private family memorial dinner and ceremony for everyone in the evening. Everyone was there, and it was a wonderful evening of hugs, tears, laughter, and reminiscing. Cynthia, since she was home most of the time during our visit, had made Richard, Laurie, and us a beautiful framed memory collection of photos with a saying specific to each of us. What a wonderful gift for such a sad occasion.

We returned home the next day. We had no answers, but at least we'd taken care of James and the house, and it was good to see the family. We went through the two boxes, and l scanned the photos both we and Richard wanted, then I sent it all back to Laurie. All that was left of James's estate was some final paperwork. It was strange to think that all that was left of James was photos, a few mementos, and some memories.

Finally, on October 17, the detective called to say they were officially closing the case. They could never prove it, but the unofficial chain of events led them to believe that:

- June 29 – Harold checked James out of the hospital before the seventy-two-hour hold started on Monday.
- June 30 – Harold drove the car to his first day of work internship in Henderson but collapsed inside the door with heatstroke. He was taken to Rose Hospital, then checked himself out that evening and returned home, leaving their car at the complex in Henderson. Neighbors heard a loud fight coming from their house later that night. At some point late that night or early the next morning, Harold smothered and suffocated James with a pillow.
- July 1 – Harold left on foot and never returned to the house. From then on, he never called James's cell phone again. Timelines are unclear for several days, but Harold eventually ended

up at Sunrise Hospital because of his heatstroke.

- July 4 – Harold texted me two times from Sunrise Hospital. He talked with me twice about him not being able to find or get ahold of James. I attempted to get ahold of James with no luck, although I did leave a message for him to call us. I relayed that information to Harold, letting him know I would keep trying to reach James. Harold said he'd sent a text to a neighbor, and they'd seen James out and about over the weekend, so he must be okay. He just didn't want to talk with anyone now.

- July 5 – Harold texted me to let me know James was reluctant to talk with us after the June 26 welfare check we'd initiated. He felt the welfare check was probably why he wouldn't answer my calls. He told me that we should give him some time; James was sure to be in touch with us. According to the detective, these calls on July 4 and July 5 were lies. James was already dead at that point, and Harold most likely was trying to cover his tracks even though he had indeed suffered from some kind of major medical event himself by that point.

- August 1 – The owner of the complex in Henderson had their car towed to an impound yard, as it had been sitting in their parking lot since Tuesday, June 28.

- August 2 – Harold died at a health care facility (not Sunrise Hospital), and his body is sent to the coroner's office for an autopsy. No marriage or next of kin was listed on his paperwork from the facility. There was only a home address. Harold's death was ruled accidental, as he eventually died from sepsis as a result of hyperthermia caused by heatstroke.

- August 6 – A body was discovered in James's home, and a homicide investigation ensued. It was assumed the body was James's because of the cast on his arm, but we had to wait for a positive ID from the coroner's office.
- August 9 – The police finally made all the connections between Harold and James.
- October 17 – James's death was ruled undetermined, as nothing could be proven. Both parties were dead, and the body was too decomposed to rule otherwise.

What started off on June 26 ended on October 17. It was heartbreaking for so many reasons. It was especially so because Harold's death, on paper, showed up before James's death, which made it impossible to prove Harold killed him. In essence, it gave us no closure other than that James was gone.

Chapter Thirty-Five

LEO'S OPEN-HEART SURGERY

Our family doctor had been monitoring a very slight arrhythmia he'd discovered in Leo's heart several years earlier. A few months after James's death, Leo went in for his yearly checkup, and the doctor was quite concerned about the change in Leo's arrhythmia. The doctor set up an appointment for him with a cardiologist. In December 2016, he had a heart catheter and trans-esophageal echocardiogram procedure to determine the extent of the problem. Ultimately needing aortic valve replacement, he had open-heart surgery on January 30, 2017. Although the surgery was a success, it required two electro-cardioversion procedures to get his heart back in rhythm.

A few months after the surgery, he went through an eight-week session of physical therapy for recovering heart surgery patients three times a week in Mount Vernon. For the first six weeks, he wasn't cleared for driving, so I took him. While he was doing therapy, I would read or write. He was finally cleared to drive in the last two weeks, which made it easier on me. I was so proud of him for sticking it out and making it through the entire session, as it wasn't easy for him. His recovery was slower than he thought it would be, and his energy level would never return to his pre-surgery level. As time went on, however, he was able to do most everything he'd done before—just at a slower pace.

Chapter Thirty-Six

A FRIGHTENING EMOTIONAL
BREAKDOWN

Although I was seeing the talk therapist for help dealing with James's death, Leo's heart surgery, and the ongoing chronic effects of the fibromyalgia, I realized I was still battling a frightening emotional breakdown that was taking place inside my mind. When I found myself wandering mindlessly around the house in my housecoat, having not gotten dressed, combed my hair, brushed my teeth, taken a shower, or slept more than a few hours at night for three days straight, I knew it was time to seek further help.

My family doctor originally referred me to a particular psychiatrist he wanted me to see. However, when I called to make the appointment, I was put on a three-month waiting list. When I saw my family doctor again a few days later and told him about the situation, he made a phone call, and I was seen by another medication-only psychiatrist in the same medical group the following day.

It was June 2017. He did an initial intake, including a lengthy medical and psychological history, as well as an assessment of my current mental state, which turned out to be the best thing that could have happened to me at that point. His approach was to start me off with a different class of antidepressants to deal with both the depression from James's death as well as the chronic pain from the fibromyalgia. Meanwhile, we experimented with other medications to help me with the insomnia. He also encouraged me to continue with my talk therapy, which I did for several months, until I felt like things had turned a corner and I no longer needed therapy. Over the next year or so, the psychiatrist and I experimented with several different types of medications until we found what I felt was the optimum combination that has worked as effectively as possible ever since.

Chapter Thirty-Seven

RETIREMENT BECKONS

O ur goal had always been to work the bead business full-time until I turned sixty-six and could draw my full Social Security. For the first fifteen years, the business was mainly smooth sailing. Unfortunately, starting in the early 2000s, there was a tremendous shift in where beads were manufactured and the competition between the main countries we were importing from. Then, the lowering of purchase quantities became the norm for retail bead stores. That basically eliminated small wholesalers like us from being able to compete with direct sales from the manufacturers. We were mom-and-pop wholesalers and had lots of other types of stock to offer. Most, however, was becoming vintage stock. And as our supplies dwindled, so did our business income. To supplement our income a bit more, we made the financial decision for me to take early Social Security in 2014, at age sixty-two.

From there, life kept happening, and not in a good way. Between my fibromyalgia, James's death, and Leo's open-heart surgery, it felt like it was just too much for us to handle. The time had come to put our health first. We'd put the word out in 2015 that we were selling. And even though we had two prospective buyers, neither were able to secure loans.

We started bulking out sections of stock at a time, which worked well. When it became more difficult to sell the remaining stock, we decided to auction off the rest. We found a local company willing to do the auctioning on the condition that we pack it all up into the containers they supplied for us and haul it to their location.

We started in June 2017. At first, it seemed insurmountable, as we needed to do a final inventory as it was being packed. It took seventeen loads in our small trailer, amounting to three hundred and fifty-four tote bins. We packed, labeled, and transported eight tons of beads and jewelry findings when it was all said and done! Leo began growing a beard when we started and said he wasn't shaving until the last load was dropped off. That meant working daily on packing until two days before Thanksgiving. At last, it was done, and Leo shaved for Thanksgiving. Except for some year-end paperwork, we officially closed the business on December 31, 2018, with a huge sigh of relief.

Retirement has been wonderful! Our days became less hectic with no pressure to make a living anymore. We ended up with more play and downtime, our schedule and routine became more flexible, and we had more time to enjoy each other's company without the business duties hanging over our heads. We continued driving Meals on Wheels for our local senior center, which we'd done since 2016. We got three therapy goats for me and pampered our cat more than ever. It felt like I could relax for the first time in my life.

That's when I started delving deep into my psyche to

continue healing myself and work on my physical health more than I ever had. I finally had the time to take all the information I had found out about myself over the years and process it in sequence to make sense of all the things I'd always felt but never quite understood.

Chapter Thirty-Eight

MY HEART GRIEVES FOR MY
FIRST LOVE

It started the morning of May 5, 2020, with a feeling of something wrenching me from deep down in my heart. It felt like some kind of unfinished business from my past, but I couldn't put my finger on it right away. Suddenly, I had this nauseating feeling. Frantically, I did an online obituary search for my first love, Brad. It took a while, but eventually, a picture of a handsomely aged Brad scrolled down the monitor. He still had that kind, fun-loving, full-of-life look on his face. Sadly, he'd died ten years earlier at the young age of sixty-three.

His obituary was short, sweet, and filled with loving memories from family and friends. He'd married seven months after he moved to California, had two sons, and divorced when the boys were tweens. After that, he met and eventually married the love of his life, who had two daughters. Together, they continued raising their blended family. All the comments showed how genuinely happy he'd been right up to the very end, which made me genuinely happy for him. The accompanying pictures showed he'd had a wonderful and full life, still doing all the things he loved doing when I knew him, plus so much more. Through those pictures, I was able to see just how extroverted and family-oriented he truly was. I'd always felt it would never have worked out between us in the long run, and seeing his life through those pictures showed me why this truly introverted homebody wouldn't have fit into his lifestyle over the long haul.

That's when I totally lost it.

I found myself crying uncontrollably as memories of the past rapidly fired through my head. I read all the memorial comments, browsed through all the pictures, and even brought out the old photo album I'd kept from the time we were together. I looked through all those pictures repeatedly. I just couldn't get Brad off my mind. For days, I went through crying jags and was unable to eat or concentrate. For several nights, I struggled with flashback dreams and vivid memories of things I hadn't even remembered until then. I couldn't process the fact that Brad was dead. Even worse, I didn't understand why it was affecting me so much and so intensely. After all, I hadn't seen or talked to him in forty-nine years.

I spent almost two weeks trying to process what was going on. I was getting worried and embarrassed about what I considered to be an overreaction. I told Leo early on I was going through an emotional crisis of sorts revolving around Brad and that as soon as I could figure out what was going on, we would talk. Bless his heart in knowing and trusting me. He left me to work it out on my own and didn't make me feel guilty about the time it was taking to do so.

Eventually, I realized a lot of the emotions I was experiencing weren't necessarily about Brad, but about me. I'd never forgiven myself for the hurt and pain I'd inflicted on him when I broke up with him right before he was sent to

Vietnam. I'd also never forgiven myself for not being able to say a final goodbye to him. The truth is that a part of me still felt like I needed to apologize for all that had happened. There was a leftover message in my head that had been drilled into my psyche by my parents: I was a screwup. I did bad things to other people. And it was always my fault, like when I broke up with Brad.

In all reality, my breakup with Brad should have been a normal part of growing up, maturing, learning life lessons, and being able to move on. Not for me though. I'd unconsciously been carrying the emotional burden of the eighteen-year-old within me, who was still being held hostage by her parents' belief in who they thought she was. While I should have been able to put closure on it years ago, I just didn't know how to at the time. Instead, I'd buried things deep down inside my heart for forty-nine years, and they'd never been brought to the surface.

Now that it had all resurfaced, I thought I'd figured out where my emotional upset stemmed from. Using a technique my therapist had recommended, I wrote Brad a very personal and detailed letter. Not only did I tell him everything I'd wanted to say to him forty-nine years before, but I also told him what I would like to have said to him and asked him in person today if he were still alive. It felt cathartic and like I might finally be at peace. Yet not quite.

For the next several months, I still couldn't shake my sense of unfinished business. I couldn't explain it, but my mind wouldn't release whatever was continuing to rumble around inside it. For days on end, I wracked my brain for answers as to what was keeping me from moving on. I prayed to God, even to Brad, to please help me figure out what I was missing and what lesson I hadn't yet learned. I asked for some kind of sign so I could find peace of mind.

Several more weeks passed. Then, when I was working at the senior center one day, a friend told me she had something she wanted me to have. She handed me a small black bag. Inside was an amethyst palm stone and a key chain with a carved-wood symbol. The amethyst palm stone was both striking and beautiful. But it was the key chain that truly touched my soul. As soon as I saw it, I immediately burst into tears, as I realized then that my prayers had finally been answered.

Unbeknownst to anyone, the carved-wood symbol attached to the key chain was the symbol for Brad's last name, which no one knew. He'd told me about how he interpreted its meaning—the sound of the universe that helps align the body, mind, and soul—though he never displayed it anywhere at the time. Along with that, he always told me something Einstein had said: "Energy can't be created or destroyed. It can only be changed from one form to another". However, in the pictures posted on his obituary notice, I could see that in his later years, he had the symbol on his shirts, his son had a tattoo of it on his arm, and it was beautifully engraved on his headstone. That symbol and its meaning had always been a part of him. A part of his soul.

I felt then as if Brad had read my letter, and the key chain was his way of answering it. He was letting me know that despite the pain he'd experienced when we broke up, he'd always understood. There was nothing for me to be sorry for, and he had nothing to forgive me for. Then there was the dream that followed, a dream that was so vivid it was like I was living it in real time:

Leo and I had gone to pay our respects to Brad's wife at their house. She invited us in, then went outside for a minute, leaving their grandson playing on the floor beside us. As I looked at their grandson, I saw Brad standing a few feet behind, watching over him. Not the aged Brad but the young Brad, wearing a striped T-shirt and old blue jeans, just like I remembered. He looked up, saw me, and walked over to stand beside me. I reached up to touch his face, but I couldn't feel it. I asked him if I could take his picture, and he said, "You know you can't." Shortly after that, Leo and I left. As we were walking away from the house, I glanced back and saw Brad staring at me from the window. Then, instantly, he was standing directly in front of me. Suddenly, time literally stopped, and I could feel our souls meld together as his energy wrapped around me as if he were giving me a big hug. He said, "I truly loved you," and I said, "I truly loved you." Then there was an unspoken meeting of our minds. He was now watching over the love of his life and his family from his dimension, and I was with the love of my life in this dimension, exactly where each of us was meant to be. Then, just as suddenly as time had stopped, time started again, and Brad was gone.

I woke up crying with the realization that, in his mind, I'd been worthy of his love all along. We'd loved each other in a way that made both of us very happy back then. There was never anything to be forgiven for since our love for each other had been real for both of us. It's just that we weren't meant to be the love of each other's lives, and being together long term wasn't our ultimate path in this lifetime. I found that processing this was easier said than done, yet it felt like a tremendous load had been lifted off my shoulders. I was certain that all my memories of Brad had finally been resolved.

Except for one thing.

As the next six months passed by, the uncontrollable crying jags, vivid memories, and intense emotions periodically continued to erupt from deep within my heart. I just didn't understand what was going on! One day, God finally whispered to me, "It's time to grieve." I realized then what was happening. Brad had been my first love, an experience that only happens once in a lifetime. But it was a very happy first love with amazing memories—and a very sad breakup, making it one of the most intensely wonderful and deeply painful memories of my entire life. I'd been holding all of that inside my heart, ignoring its existence, for over fifty years at this point. It was only when I learned of Brad's death that I no longer had any control over those memories. I could no longer hold them back, and they'd continued to come crashing out on their own, flooding my mind, body, and soul with all these heavy emotions.

With a gentle hint and nudge from God, it dawned on me that I was never allowed to grieve. I'd never given myself permission or taken the time to grieve the loss of Brad, the loss of our love for each other, the loss of the future we'd dreamed of together, or the deep and intense pain I'd felt over that loss—including the pain it caused him. While I'd spent the first few days after it happened fifty years ago crying and trying to process it all, I was totally alone in my grief. I had no family support, none of my friends had even met Brad, and the wife of the one married couple we did things with had moved back in with her parents as soon as the squadron shipped out. Essentially, it had been one of my happiest times, with some of the most wonderful memories of my life and one of the most painful and traumatic times of my life. And I'd never spoken to anyone about it—not even any of my therapists over the years. It was something that I alone had been unconsciously carrying for way too long until it all came gushing out when I learned of Brad's death. Now it was time to release and deal with the depth and intensity of these emotions. I finally gave myself permission and as much time as I needed to grieve the loss of Brad.

It took quite a while. And even now, I still break down occasionally. But I was ultimately able to honor those wonderful memories I had of our time together, along with the love and happiness he'd given me at a time when I truly needed it. As even more time passed, I noticed those memories gradually started to blend in with all the rest of my life's wonderful memories that I consciously hold on to tightly in my heart. After half a century, I was genuinely able to come to terms with all that had been swirling in my head regarding Brad. I could finally close out that very long-ago chapter of my life that had held itself deep within the crevices of my heart all that time.

Peace of heart, peace of mind at last.

Chapter Thirty-Nine

MAKING SENSE OF IT ALL

Coming Full Circle

My memories of Brad had never come out from where I'd buried them deep down inside my heart fifty years ago because the time had never been right. In truth, his was the only past memory I'd never dealt with. In my mind, in the short nine months I was with and engaged to Brad, he'd been the only one who'd given me enough confidence to get a tiny glimpse of the person I could become and was ultimately meant to be. Unfortunately, I hadn't learned enough about myself and wasn't strong enough mentally or emotionally at the time we broke up, so my self-image got sucked back into who my parents defined me as. These final memories of Brad were the last pieces I needed to remember in order to finally put all my memories in sequence, understand it all, and make sense of it all. It was a trigger for bringing together a lifetime of memories into full circle, from the beginning of what has been a remarkable and eye-opening journey of my life to date.

Understanding the Feelings in My Life

"Feelings are real, but not reality."

"You may think feelings are real, they may feel very real, you may believe they are real, but they're just feelings."

"Feelings aren't facts."

Try telling that to a child who was told children are to be seen but not heard, who wasn't allowed to voice her own views or opinions, and who felt emotionally void of love from those she sought it from most. My reality was that growing up with an autocratic narcissist as a father in a family that didn't understand or know how to deal with me —a highly sensitive introvert—was deeply painful and traumatic. I was raised to be dependent, as opposed to independent, and not think for myself. My feelings were of anxiety, stress, and low self-esteem due to high and often unreasonable expectations. My facts were I was deemed the troublemaker and the screwup. Things were always my fault, and I was the one who constantly overdramatized when it came to pain. My reality, feelings, and facts were that I was not as smart as I could be, as I didn't apply myself to my highest potential, which meant I would never amount to much. At that point in time, my feelings, facts, and reality were one and the same.

Outside home, those same feelings followed me and, in my mind, defined me, which is why I felt I often had trouble making friends and navigating social situations. I would sometimes say or do things that seemed to surprise or offend others, though I never quite knew why. I was told it was normal childhood, teenage, college, or young adult growing pains, but I never felt that was the answer. I only felt like I didn't fit in. I was naive in so many ways, yet grown-up way beyond my years in so many other ways. Perhaps it was part of normal growing pains, but it was also because of unresolved trauma and abuse, as well as not knowing at the time that I was a highly sensitive introvert. Several decades later and after years of different therapies, I didn't even know what "normal" looked like for a person like me, whose brain functions differently from most and who always felt different but had no one who truly understood them.

When it came to relationships, I could not figure out at the time why my relationships didn't go well. Now I realize that first with Brad and then Bob, when they left, though not by choice, it brought up intense and irrational feelings of my being abandoned—echoes of the feelings I had as a child. Even though neither was gone for that long, my fragile being just couldn't handle those deep feelings of abandonment. I think it was also because I was so young that I hadn't yet learned anything about being independent and was so dependent on Brad, and later Bob, for my happiness and well-being. It wasn't anything they did or didn't do. It was what I wasn't doing for myself. I had no idea how to be happy and independent from within myself.

Then there was Dave. No one could understand what drew me to him in the first place. It felt at times as if I was the only one who could see through all the chaos to the beautiful soul he expressed through his music. I never thought of him as a bad person. In my mind, he was a good person who, like me, was simply lost and trying to find his way through his own pain. Because of that, I refused to see or accept the reality of what was happening with him, between us, and with me. Instead, his emotional and mental abuse gradually sucked out what little remained of my self-confidence and self-esteem. At some level, I even felt I deserved it. It sent more leftover messages from childhood, akin to "You've made your bed, now lie in it." Only when it became physical abuse did it go beyond anything I'd ever experienced before. After that, I just feared him as I finally accepted the reality of the situation. That's when I knew I needed to leave him before something worse happened to me.

With Leo—though it wasn't in the usual way a relationship starts—I've had a wonderful and lasting relationship. Yet, until I sought out help the first time, I was still living under a veil of what I thought was expected of me. I looked at life as black and white, glass half empty, always waiting for the other shoe to drop, and walking on eggshells. Leo always assured me that wasn't the case, but I wasn't sure and never wanted to take a chance for fear of losing him. It was a throwback to the belief that I had to be dependent on a man, that I wasn't good enough or smart enough to think for myself. It wasn't until I confronted these feelings and events that I was able to see myself through the reality of what they really were.

Now, as a late-in-life adult, I know and feel differently about myself. It has taken most of my life, even with Leo by my side, to truly believe—through all my life lessons, therapies, classes, seminars, and research—that I'm smart and able to think for myself. I'm not a screwup, and not everything is my fault. I'm a kind, caring, considerate, thoughtful, and loving person worthy of being loved. I happen to also have the extremely deep and intense sensitivities and emotions of a highly sensitive introvert, which I wasn't allowed to be as a child. Nor did I even understand at that time what it meant. I only knew that I never felt like I could be my true self.

Understanding the Loves of My Life

One of the most prominent traits that I've possessed deeply and intensely since my mid-teens has been the desire for a long-term close companion and love relationship in my life. The loves I've experienced all happened very quickly with so much emotion, depth, and intensity that they even took me by surprise at times. To those looking in from the outside, they always appeared like hastily formed and fast-moving relationships that I couldn't explain except to know it's what I truly felt. With all my loves, there was a deep and intense desire for a close emotional and spiritual connection as well as a physical connection—a touch of affection, holding hands, hugging, cuddling, kissing, and the feeling of being made love to when being intimate as opposed to just having sex. This didn't always happen, but it's the kind of love that I always dreamed of having.

A while back, I found this great article called "We Only Fall in Love with 3 People in Our Lifetime—Each One for a Specific Reason" by Kate Rose. As soon as I read it, I realized how much it related to the loves in my highly sensitive, introverted life. This was an important insight for someone who, for many years, felt unloved and undeserving of love yet still craved the feeling of deep love with the right person. The article gave me a much better understanding and appreciation of just how much love I've already experienced in my life, even when I didn't realize it. In summary:

Falling in Love the First Time: The Love That Looks Right

"It's the idealistic love—the one that seems like the fairy tales we read as children."

Life with Brad was about going to new places, doing things I'd never done before, and spending a lot of time in the great outdoors. It was all about feeling incredibly happy, being in love, making love, and loving my life. It was a care-free time with no responsibilities, just dreams about a Pollyanna future. I was too young to understand my inherent traits at the time, but I was at least aware enough once Brad left for sea duty to know something wasn't quite right for me with our relationship. After his leave two months into his deployment, I called off our engagement, as painful as it was at the time. I instinctively knew I'd made the right decision and never regretted leaving this magical and loving but unsustainable relationship. They say that your first love often becomes the model for the type of person you really want and need in your life. You may even end up with someone—the love that lasts—who has many of the same traits and interests. Ironically, that's exactly what happened to me, and for that, I'm forever grateful to Brad, the wonderful person he was, for being my first love.

Falling in Love the Second Time: The Hard Love

"... the one that teaches us lessons about who we are and how we often want or need to be loved. This is the kind of love that hurts, whether through lies, pain, or manip-ulation."

Falling in love the second time is more of a cycle and can include more than one person, which it did for me. Bob was more of a calm, safe love. Yet during his absence and when I saw him in Pullman, it felt like the wrong kind of love for me—one of less depth than his love for me—and I knew I couldn't continue with it. Even though they weren't necessarily loves, Dale and Gary were intense connections that provided me lessons and insights about my own needs. Then there was Dave, the charming guitarist, who I fell deeply in love with the very first time we went out together. I thought I could change him, help him heal himself from his own demons, and perhaps heal parts of myself as well. I just didn't realize at the time that this kind of love never works and would eventually turn into the abusive relationship it became. I also didn't realize how much my fear of constantly living in survival mode before escaping this relationship would affect my emotional, mental, and physical health in all the years to come. There was never any question that I made the right decision, nor did I ever regret leaving this highly dysfunctional, abusive relationship and marriage.

Falling in Love the Third Time: The Love That Lasts

"This is the love that comes so easy it doesn't seem possible. It's the kind where the connection can't be explained and knocks us off our feet because we never planned for it."

As my friend and guardian angel, Leo was so easy to talk to. He had all the values I was wanting in the disarray of my life at that time, as well as connections to those things that meant the most to me. We never planned for what happened to happen. It just did. Even though I initially had self-doubts because I felt so broken inside, I always knew on a deeper soul level that I'd made the right decision to stick around and marry this remarkable man. I've never regretted staying in this forever marriage. In the last forty-eight years of Leo's unconditional love and nonjudgmental attitude toward me, he has made me realize that true love and self-love can exist, and he showed me that I can be the true me. Consequently, I've gradually been able to discover all I was meant to be. Without him by my side, helping and supporting me even when I didn't realize or recognize that I needed his help or support, I don't know if I would have made it this far in my journey. For that, I'm forever grateful to my friend, guardian angel, lover, husband, and soulmate.

Understanding the Emotional, Mental, and Psychological Pain in My Life

When it comes to emotional, mental, and psychological pain, it's taken me almost my entire life to heal from the long-term effects of trauma and abuse in my early years. The feelings of abandonment and betrayal, and the absence of someone who really saw or understood me, seemed to haunt me the most during those early years and kept me from learning how to live as who I was truly meant to be. In order to change that, I had to stop buying into the deep, lasting image that family and people around me had molded me into and had me believing about myself from as far back as I could remember. I also needed help from professionals to acknowledge, identify, and help heal the damage from the wounds of the trauma and abuse I'd experienced and never dealt with.

The important thing I was ultimately able to understand and come to terms with was that I really did experience traumatic and abusive episodes in my life. When I was young, everything was downplayed. I always felt that no matter what happened to me, it wasn't as bad as what other people experienced. I simply needed to ignore how it made me feel about myself at the time—messages ingrained in me from my parents, my experiences, and life with Dave. The truth is, I never really ignored it and always felt bad inside, all the while wearing an "I'm okay" face. If things surfaced, I'd stuff them deep down inside until it became too much to handle. It would eventually spew out, like an erupting volcano, from the depths of my heart. It wasn't until these eruptions were happening that I sought professional help and finally confirmed what I'd always felt underneath it all. I really had experienced trauma and abuse, and it wasn't my fault.

The other important thing was that it was mine, and mine alone to release. I had to release all the anger, hate, and silent victim attitude that I carried around underneath in order to find peace. I didn't have to forget, but I did have to forgive both myself and others.

As for physical pain, I have zero tolerance for it (imagine a 10+ on a scale of 1-10). It has been a struggle from birth to get those around me to understand that trait. For many years, I tried to tell my parents, my doctors, my friends, and anyone who would listen what physical pain felt like to me, but it mostly fell on deaf ears. Even as an adult, it continues to be one of the most difficult things to explain or talk to health care professionals about, as the study of pain thresholds and tolerance is still in its infancy.

It wasn't until the physical pain of fibromyalgia collided with the emotional, mental, and psychological pain of fibromyalgia that I was finally able to start piecing it all together and understand all the different kinds of pain in my life, along with how they'd affected me. I continue to research and learn as much as I can about fibromyalgia and the effects of the pain so I can better cope with it and live the best life I possibly can.

Chapter Forty

MOVING FORWARD AS THE TRUE ME

Occasionally, I regret the decades of time it has taken for me to understand my past and accept the true me. However, I wouldn't change anything I've experienced along the way because each step of my journey has eventually provided a lesson or insight, a stepping stone, pointing me in the direction I needed to move toward. I am still able to keep on peeling back the layers of my past in order to reveal my center core, the true me.

Due to the help I received over the years, I am able to understand and overcome the issues I have been dealing with all my life. My panic and anxiety attacks are at an all-time low, while my self-confidence and self-esteem are at an all-time high. I know the issues that affect me the most, understand what triggers them, and am learning how to effectively deal with them in a positive manner.

The older I've gotten, along with my increased knowledge about the traits of being an HSP, an introvert, and a traumatized abuse survivor, the more self-aware I am about my strengths, unique abilities, and the contributions I can make to others. It feels so great to finally understand what makes me unique and not be embarrassed or ashamed to be my true self.

I know that as I move forward in the rest of my life's journey, there will still be lessons and insights that I need to learn along the way. I will have occasional setbacks that cause relapses to my old ways of thinking, reacting, and acting. Yet I'm prepared to tackle them head-on and keep moving forward, being the most authentic and true me I can possibly be.

More importantly, I've found that I really love the true me, the one I was meant to be. It has changed the way I think, act, and react. I know I don't have all the answers, but I'm at peace knowing that no matter where the remainder of my life's journey takes me, I'm ready to deal with it from my true perspective—through the eyes of a highly sensitive introvert.

Made in United States
Troutdale, OR
03/12/2024

18378735R00176